KAZANTZAKIS

AND GOD

SUNY Series in Constructive Postmodern Thought
David Ray Griffin, editor

KAZANTZAKIS

AND

GOD

Daniel A. Dombrowski

STATE UNIVERSITY OF NEW YORK PRESS

Published by
State University of New York Press, Albany

For information, address the State University of New York Press,
State University Plaza, Albany, NY 12246

Production design by David Ford
Marketing by Fran Keneston

Library of Congress Cataloging-in-Publication Data

Dombrowski, Daniel A.
    Kazantzakis and God / Daniel A. Dombrowski.
        p.   cm. — (SUNY series in constructive postmodern thought)
    Includes bibliographical references and index.
    ISBN 0-7914-3491-5 (hardcover : alk. paper). — ISBN 0-7914-3492-3
(pbk. : alk. paper)
    1. Kazantzakis, Nikos, 1883–1957—Religion.   2. God in literature.
I. Title.   II. Series.
PQ5610.K39Z487   1997
889'.83209—DC21   96-48025
                                                                    CIP

10 9 8 7 6 5 4 3 2 1

CONTENTS

SUNY SERIES IN

CONSTRUCTIVE

POSTMODERN THOUGHT

An Introduction

The rapid spread of the term *postmodern* in recent years witnesses to a growing dissatisfaction with modernity and to an increasing sense that the modern age not only had a beginning but can have an end as well. Whereas the word *modern* was almost always used until quite recently as a word of praise and as a synonym for *contemporary*, a growing sense is now evidenced that we can and should leave modernity behind—in fact, that we *must* if we are to avoid destroying ourselves and most of the life on our planet.

Modernity, rather than being regarded as the norm for human society toward which all history has been aiming and into which all societies should be ushered—forcibly if necessary—is instead increasingly seen as an aberration. A new respect for the wisdom of traditional societies is growing as we realize that they have endured for thousands of years and that, by contrast, the existence of modern society for even another century seems doubtful. Likewise, *modernism* as a worldview is less and less seen as The Final Truth, in comparison with which all divergent worldviews are automatically regarded as "superstitious." The modern worldview is increasingly relativized to the status of one among many, useful for some purposes, inadequate for others.

Although there have been antimodern movements before, beginning perhaps near the outset of the nineteenth century with the Romanticists and the Luddites, the rapidity with which the term *postmodern* has become widespread in our time suggests that the antimodern sentiment is more extensive and intense than before, and also that it includes the sense that modernity can

vii

be successfully overcome only by going beyond it, not by attempting to return to a premodern form of existence. Insofar as a common element is found in the various ways in which the term is used, *postmodernism* refers to a diffuse sentiment rather than to any common set of doctrines—the sentiment that humanity can and must go beyond the modern.

Beyond connoting this sentiment, the term *postmodern* is used in a confusing variety of ways, some of them contradictory to others. In artistic and literary circles, for example, postmodernism shares in this general sentiment but also involves a specific reaction against "modernism" in the narrow sense of a movement in artistic-literary circles in the late nineteenth and early twentieth centuries. Postmodern architecture is very different from postmodern literary criticism. In some circles, the term *postmodern* is used in reference to that potpourri of ideas and systems sometimes called *new age metaphysics*, although many of these ideas and systems are more premodern than postmodern. Even in philosophical and theological circles, the term *postmodern* refers to two quite different positions, one of which is reflected in this series. Each position seeks to transcend both *modernism* in the sense of the worldview that has developed out of the seventeenth-century Galilean-Cartesian-Baconian-Newtonian science, and *modernity* in the sense of the world order that both conditioned and was conditioned by this worldview. But the two positions seek to transcend the modern in different ways.

Closely related to literary-artistic postmodernism is a philosophical postmodernism inspired variously by pragmatism, physicalism, Ludwig Wittgenstein, Martin Heidegger, and Jacques Derrida and other recent French thinkers. By the use of terms that arise out of particular segments of this movement, it can be called *deconstructive* or *eliminative postmodernism*. It overcomes the modern worldview through an anti-worldview: it deconstructs or eliminates the ingredients necessary for a worldview, such as God, self, purpose, meaning, a real world, and truth as correspondence. While motivated in some cases by the ethical concern to forestall totalitarian systems, this type of postmodern thought issues in relativism, even nihilism. It could also be called *ultramodernism*, in that its eliminations result from carrying modern premises to their logical conclusions.

The postmodernism of this series can, by contrast, be called *constructive* or *revisionary*. It seeks to overcome the modern worldview not by eliminating the possibility of worldviews as such, but by constructing a postmodern worldview through a revision of modern premises and traditional concepts. This constructive or revisionary postmodernism involves a new unity of scientific, ethical, aesthetic, and religious intuitions. It rejects not science as such but only that scientism in which the data of the modern natural sciences are alone allowed to contribute to the construction of our worldview.

The constructive activity of this type of postmodern thought is not limited to a revised worldview; it is equally concerned with a postmodern world that will support and be supported by the new worldview. A postmodern world will involve postmodern persons, with a postmodern spirituality, on the one hand, and a postmodern society, ultimately a postmodern global order, on the other. Going beyond the modern world will involve transcending its individualism, anthropocentrism, patriarchy, mechanization, economism, consumerism, nationalism, and militarism. Constructive postmodern thought provides support for the ecology, peace, feminist and other emancipatory movements of our time, while stressing that the inclusive emancipation must be from modernity itself. The term *postmodern*, however, by contrast with *premodern*, emphasizes that the modern world has produced unparalleled advances that must not be lost in a general revulsion against its negative features.

From the point of view of deconstructive postmodernists, this constructive postmodernism is still hopelessly wedded to outdated concepts, because it wishes to salvage a positive meaning not only for the notions of the human self, historical meaning, and truth as correspondence, which were central to modernity, but also for premodern notions of a divine reality, cosmic meaning, and an enchanted nature. From the point of view of its advocates, however, this revisionary postmodernism is not only more adequate to our experience but also more genuinely postmodern. It does not simply carry the premises of modernity through to their logical conclusions, but criticizes and revises those premises. Through its return to organicism and its acceptance of nonsensory perception, it opens itself to the recovery of truths and values from various forms of premodern thought and practice that had been dogmatically rejected by modernity. This constructive, revisionary postmodernism involves a creative synthesis of modern and premodern truths and values.

This series does not seek to create a movement so much as to help shape and support an already existing movement convinced that modernity can and must be transcended. But those antimodern movements which arose in the past failed to deflect or even retard the onslaught of modernity. What reasons can we have to expect the current movement to be more successful? First, the previous antimodern movements were primarily calls to return to a premodern form of life and thought rather than calls to advance, and the human spirit does not rally to calls to turn back. Second, the previous antimodern movements either rejected modern science, reduced it to a description of mere appearances, or assumed its adequacy in principle; therefore, they could base their calls only on the negative social and spiritual effects of modernity. The current movement draws on natural science itself as a witness against the adequacy of the modern worldview. In the third place, the present movement has even more evidence than did previous movements of the ways in which modernity and its worldview *are* socially and spiritually destructive. The fourth and probably most decisive difference is that the present movement is based on the awareness that *the continuation of modernity threatens the very survival of life on our planet*. This awareness, combined with the growing knowledge of the interdependence of the modern worldview and the militarism, nuclearism, and ecological devastation of the modern world, is providing an unprecedented impetus for people to see the evidence for a postmodern worldview and to envisage postmodern ways of relating to each other, the rest of nature, and the cosmos as a whole. For these reasons, the failure of the previous antimodern movements says little about the possible success of the current movement.

Advocates of this movement do not hold the naively utopian belief that the success of this movement would bring about a global society of universal and lasting peace, harmony, and happiness, in which all spiritual problems, social conflicts, ecological destruction, and hard choices would vanish. There is, after all, surely a deep truth in the testimony of the world's religions to the presence of a transcultural proclivity to evil deep within the human heart, which no new paradigm, combined with a new economic order, new child-rearing practices, or any other social arrangements, will suddenly eliminate. Furthermore, it has correctly been said that "life is robbery": a strong element of competition is inherent within finite existence, which no social-political-economic-ecological order can overcome. These two truths, especially when contemplated together, should caution us against unrealistic hopes.

However, no such appeal to "universal constants" should reconcile us to the present order, as if this order were thereby uniquely legitimated. The human proclivity to evil in general, and to conflictual competition and ecological destruction in particular, can be greatly exacerbated or greatly mitigated by a world order and its worldview. Modernity exacerbates it about as much as imaginable. We can therefore envision, without being naively utopian, a far better world order, with a far less dangerous trajectory, than the one we now have.

This series, making no pretense of neutrality, is dedicated to the success of this movement toward a postmodern world.

David Ray Griffin
Series Editor

ACKNOWLEDGMENTS

I would like to thank several people for the help they have given to me in the writing of this book. First, David Ray Griffin's careful reading of an earlier version of this book has been most helpful in several respects. (The same could be said regarding the comments I received from an unnamed reader for State University of New York Press.)

Second, two Kazantzakis scholars who have also kept me honest are Peter Bien and Darren Middleton, the former because of his detailed knowledge of Kazantzakis's life and writings, and the latter because of his Zorbatic verve in the effort to speak accurately about Kazantzakis's process theism. As is customary in such circumstances, any defects in the book are my fault, but many of the better features of the book are due to the help I have received from Griffin, Bien, and Middleton.

I would also like to thank Dr. Patroclos Stavrou for permission to quote from Helen Kazantzakis's biography of Nikos Kazantzakis and from other works, and to use a photograph of her husband from this biography for the cover of the book.

Finally, Warren Drabek of Simon & Schuster should be thanked for his help in obtaining permission to quote from several works by Kazantzakis. Parts of the following works are reprinted with the permission of Simon & Schuster:

Report to Greco by Nikos Kazantzakis. Translated by P. A. Bien. © 1961 by Helen N. Kazantzakis, renewed 1993. English translation © 1965 by Simon & Schuster, Inc.

Saint Francis by Nikos Kazantzakis. Translated by P. A. Bien. © 1962 by Simon & Schuster, Inc.

The Last Temptation of Christ by Nikos Kazantzakis. © 1960 by Simon & Schuster, Inc.

The Odyssey: A Modern Sequel by Nikos Kazantzakis. Translated by Kimon Friar. © 1958 by Helen Kazantzakis and Kimon Friar. Copyright renewed 1986 by Simon & Schuster, Inc.

The Saviors of God by Nikos Kazantzakis. Translated by Kimon Friar. © 1960 by Simon & Schuster, Inc., renewed 1988.

Zorba the Greek by Nikos Kazantzakis. © 1953 by Simon & Schuster, Inc., renewed 1981.

I should also note that chapter 2 of this book appeared previously in *Encounter* 51 (1990): 81-96; chapter 3 in *Christianity and Literature* 34 (1983): 25–32; chapter 4 in *Religion & Literature* 26 (1994): 19–32; chapter 5 in *Sophia* 24 (1985): 4–17; and chapter 6 in *God's Struggler*, edited by Middleton and Bien (Macon, Ga.: Mercer University Press, 1996): 71–91. All of these chapters have been significantly reworked, however.

INTRODUCTION

At least since the seventeenth century with Spinoza's critique, the traditional conception of God in the Abrahamic religions (Judaism, Christianity, and Islam) has been in retreat. Despite the turbulent relations among Jews, Christians, and Muslims, religious believers in these traditions have generally had the same concept of God in mind when they declared their beliefs. God in the Abrahamic faiths has generally been seen as an immutable being outside of time who is omniscient, omnipotent, and omnibenevolent, and hence, as a consequence of these exalted attributes, was only with difficulty, if at all, amenable to accurate description by human beings. Further, it was held, God created the world through a free act of will: the world needs God but God could have done just as well without the world. (We will see that this view of God is not essential to the Abrahamic religions as such, but rather it comes to them under the influence of certain strands of Greek philosophy. It is ironic that Kazantzakis objects to the traditional view precisely because of its Greek side; or better, as we will see, Kazantzakis chooses one strand of Greek philosophy—Plato's view of God—rather than another—Aristotle's view of God.)

There are two problems in particular with this traditional concept of God, problems that have contributed to the attenuated place of spiritual concerns in modern life, in contrast, say, to the place of such concerns in the lives of people in the Middle Ages. It is significant that Nikos Kazantzakis (1883–1957) struggled with these problems throughout his life. The purpose of this book is to explore Kazantzakis's view of God, specifically his attempt to

1

develop a view of God superior to the traditional one, a view of God that, at the very least, deals with these two problems better than the traditional view of God deals with them.

The first problem concerns theodicy, the difficulty of reconciling belief in the existence of God with the obvious evil that exists in the world. Put simply, if God is all-powerful, God *could* eliminate all of the evil in the world; if God is all-good, God *would* eliminate all of the evil; and if God is all-knowing, God would *know how* to eliminate all of the evil. But evil exists, as Kazantzakis well knew, hence, to his way of thinking, either there is no God, or, if there is a God, this being is quite different from the being identified as God in the traditional view of the Abrahamic religions. In this book I will argue that Kazantzakis's antipathy to the traditional view of God in the Abrahamic religions often leads him to give the impression that he does not believe in God, but I will show that a more defensible view is that Kazantzakis *does* believe in God, but what he means by "God" is something that is very often heterodox from the traditional point of view.

However, as I will also show, the heterodox nature of Kazantzakis's theism can be, and often has been, exaggerated. His Christology is heterodox from the perspective of traditional Christianity, as the uproar created by the film version of *The Last Temptation of Christ* indicates. But his view of God is a peculiar combination of heterodox, or partially heterodox, views that grow out of solidly orthodox concerns and sources.

The second problem is that regarding human freedom. Specifically, the problem is the following: If God is omniscient, God knows everything that will occur in the future with absolute assurance and in minute detail; but if God has such knowledge, it is difficult, if not impossible, to see how human beings could be free, for if God has such knowledge, then human beings *must* do what God knows they will do, and hence they would not be free. Even if God does not physically compel human beings, if God is omniscient in the aforementioned strong sense, they are nonetheless logically compelled to do what God knows they will do. Even if a human being decides to fool God, the omniscient mind of God would know beforehand that the human being would try to do this. (Modern scientific determinism makes sense only to the extent that scientists can approximate the knowledge traditional theists attributed to God.)

But human freedom is a nonnegotiable item in Kazantzakis's *Weltanschauung*, hence God for him could not have the properties traditionally found in the Abrahamic religions. That is, Kazantzakis's God does not have all three attributes—omnipotence, omniscience, and omnibenevolence—because a God with all three of these attributes would be at odds with the presence of evil in the world and with the presence of human freedom. (We will see that it is omnipotence that is especially criticized by Kazantzakis.) And it should be noted that only a partial solution, at best, to these problems is offered if one accounts for the existence of suffering in terms of a misuse of human freedom in that only a fraction of suffering is due to moral evil; and to say that God *wants* us to suffer is to turn God into a sadist. (The fact that Kazantzakis's God is not a sadist perhaps indicates that in *some* sense his God is omnibenevolent.) If a being does not have all three of the aforementioned attributes, however, how can it be God, the greatest conceivable being?, it will be asked. It will be one of the aims of this book to respond adequately to this question.

The chapters of the book are arranged in what I hope is a logical order. The first chapter deals with the Bergsonian background to Kazantzakis's theism. Like Peter Bien, I see Henri Bergson as the key intellectual (or anti-intellectual) influence on Kazantzakis, especially as regards his theism. As is well known, Bergson was perhaps the most influential Western philosopher in the early part of the twentieth century, and Kazantzakis had the good fortune to attend his lectures in Paris. Bergson was a Jewish theist who converted to Catholicism, but who nonetheless confronted head-on the aforementioned problems associated with the traditional concept of God in the Abrahamic religions, and who was especially bothered by the view of God as immutable being. We will see that a careful analysis of Bergson's writings on God is the best possible introduction to what Kazantzakis has to say about this topic. Bien has done yeoman's work in this regard, but his magisterial book on Kazantzakis, *Kazantzakis: Politics of the Spirit*, the best written to date, does not deal primarily with Kazantzakis's view of God. The present book treats Kazantzakis's view of God as an end in itself.

I will be looking carefully at Bergson in chapter 1, but in chapters 2, 3, and 4 I will initiate a detailed treatment of Kazantzakis's texts themselves. These chapters deal in different ways with the topic of transubstantiation, a topic that has its roots in Eastern Orthodox and Catholic theology. However, Kazantzakis adopts transubstantiation for his own (Bergsonian) purposes in that he makes the transubstantiation of matter into spirit a *process*. Chapter 2 examines how Kazantzakis views the change of material substance into spiritual substance as the real presence of God; in fact, I will argue that transubstantiation is *the key to his writing*. That is, the sublimity of the transubstantiation that occurs in the Eucharist is spread across the whole of human life, indeed across the whole cosmos for Kazantzakis. There is no other modern writer concerning whom one could make this claim.

Chapter 3 continues the consideration of transubstantiation in Kazantzakis initiated in chapter 2. But here I focus on transubstantiation as it is exhibited in passages where eating is a prime concern, passages that indicate that for Kazantzakis the connection between eating and the spiritual life is a strong one. My thesis is that the ascetical treatment of eating given by St. Ignatius of Loyola in his *Spiritual Exercises* can, in many ways, be purified by the more insightful treatment of eating given by Kazantzakis in his own *Spiritual Exercises* and other writings.

In Chapter 4 we will see that transubstantiation has implications not only for the personal transformation of matter into spirit that is possible when eating, but also for human history. Specifically we will look at Kazantzakis's ambivalence regarding the Middle Ages, both the medieval period itself and the new Middle Ages that are upon us, a period that will perhaps last a very long time. The features of our civilization that Kazantzakis detested are treated here, features that tend to overpower the efforts of the few magnificent, fiery hearts left in the world. In the desert of contemporary culture, one's duty is to remain faithful to the flame. The purpose of this chapter is to explore why Kazantzakis sees modern Western civilization as spiritually barren, to determine what he means by the flame, and to ascertain how this flame illuminates Kazantzakis's religiosity, his concept of God, and his admiration for the Middle Ages, a peculiar admiration that as a liberal Catholic I nonetheless appreciate.

Whereas chapters 2, 3, and 4 deal in different ways with the common topic of transubstantiation, chapter 5 signals a transition to certain abstract, philosophical issues connected with Kazantzakis's theism. In this chapter I will argue that God, for Kazantzakis, is at least the transubstantiation of matter into spirit, but God is not merely this. My thesis in this chapter is that progress can be made in the understanding of his thought by looking at him as a dipolar theist. I will use the thought of Charles Hartshorne, a major twentieth-century philosopher of religion and (like Bergson) process philosopher, to explain what dipolar theism is, then I will use this explanation to examine Kazantzakis's texts. Further, I will try to show how it can be the case that God, for Kazantzakis, is both in constant becoming as well as eternal being.

In chapter 6 I explore the connection between Kazantzakis and mysticism, a connection that makes sense when it is realized that he uses the word "God" more frequently, perhaps, than any other twentieth-century writer. It makes sense to claim not only that Kazantzakis was a theist, albeit a heterodox one in some ways, but also to suggest that his writings are inspired with (literally, breathed into by) mystical concerns and experiences. In this chapter "mysticism" will be used to refer to two theoretically distinct realities: (1) the immediate experience of an immanent God in transubstantiating activity; and (2) the experience of a transcendent God as ineffable or paradoxical or awful precisely because of God's dematerialized condition. It will be the purpose of this chapter to argue that depictions of mysticism-1 and mysticism-2 play prominent parts in Kazantzakis's writings and that we can learn a great deal about both by taking Kazantzakis seriously. In this chapter I will also begin a consideration of the connections between Greek Orthodoxy and Kazantzakis's mysticism.

Implicit in much of what is said in the first six chapters of the book is a view of Kazantzakis's method and purpose in the development of his view of God, a method and purpose that obviously include a certain antipathy to method. In chapter 7 I make his method explicit, a method that consists in a systole and diastole tension between Western rationality and a harmonizing tendency, on the one hand, and an Eastern restlessness in the attempt to break this harmony, on the other.

Likewise, throughout the book evidence is cited in favor of the claim that Kazantzakis is a panpsychist, or better, a panexperientialist, but the evidence is scattered about in different chapters and used for purposes other than a defense of this claim. In chapter 8 I both defend this claim and argue for its significance. I end the book with a treatment of the relationship between Kazantzakis's panexperientialism and his view of time as asymmetrical, on the one hand, and his view of death, on the other. An appendix follows on the relationship between Friedrich Nietzsche and Kazantzakis.

In this book I will be more concerned with the different *facets* of Kazantzakis's view of God than with the *phases* of his religious career. Once again, it would be hard to improve upon Bien's detailed analysis of the different stages or phases of Kazantzakis's career, but at every stage it seems that certain tensions remain in his thought, especially in his thought about God, that deserve more attention. To take one example, Bien details how Kazantzakis's play *Buddha*, went through four versions from 1922 to 1941, but in each of these there is a fundamental tension between Kazantzakis's desire to take the world and its problems, including its religious problems, seriously, on the one hand, and his Buddhist desire to move beyond all desire to solve these problems, on the other. At least one fact is certain: Kazantzakis was interested in the issue of God from his very earliest works to his very latest, and it is with this issue that this book will be concerned. I will make remarks about the chronology of Kazantzakis's works in passing, especially in chapter 4, but these remarks will be subservient to my analysis of the structure of his thought on God, or better, to my analysis of the constant tensions at work in his thought on God.

I will examine all of Kazantzakis's works that have been translated into English, although I will also very often make reference to his original Greek when crucial words or phrases require this. Throughout, however, my goal is not literary criticism but defensible philosophy or theology; I am not a literary critic but a philosopher of religion. It should be noted that I will be commenting not only on the most famous works of Kazantzakis, most of which were translated into English in the 1960s: *Zorba the Greek*, *The Last Temptation of Christ*, *Saint Francis*, *The Odyssey*, *Report to Greco*, and others. In addition I will examine many of his works that have appeared in translation since around 1980, works that are still largely undigested by critics of Kazantzakis (in chronological order of translation): *The Suffering God: Selected Letters to Galatea and Papastephanou*, *Serpent and Lily*, "The Sickness of the Age," *Sodom and Gomorrah*, *Comedy*, *Japan/China*, *Alexander the Great*, *Buddha*, *Journeying*, *At the Palaces of Knossos*, and *Russia*.

I am well aware of the fact that Kazantzakis himself is not a theologian or a philosopher, but rather a novelist, a travel writer, and a spiritual seeker. Hence his writings are not meant to work primarily as "literary expression" to process theism. But he does offer what Darren Middleton refers to as a "poetics of faith," which, although not propositionally oriented like the works of most theologians and philosophers, nonetheless can be fruitfully viewed from the perspectives of theology and philosophy. To view Kazantzakis's works in these ways helps us to both understand Kazantzakis better than we would without a consideration of the theological and philosophical implications of his views and to understand some of the strengths and particularly the weaknesses of traditional theism.

There is a unique advantage in relying, as I will, on secondary studies of Kanzantzakis and primary sources in the philosophy of religion in the English language. Kazantzakis is widely seen as a process theist, and it is in twentieth-century America that process theism has been taken most seriously. The greatest living defender of process theism is Charles Hartshorne, an American, and Alfred North Whitehead, although English, published his most famous philosophical works that relate to process theism while at Harvard. In fact, Whitehead's works have found a more receptive audience in the United States than in Europe. In short, for scholars on the Continent and in Great Britain theism is usually equated by both theists and agnostics/atheists alike with traditional Abrahamic theism, whereas scholars in the North America have been less likely to make this equation. Even Bergson is taken more seriously these days in the United States than in France. For example, the journal *Process Studies* flourishes in the United States in its effort to think through a view of God that is perhaps best described as "neoclassical." The same designation, I will argue, fits Kazantzakis's theism. To the extent that his theism is neo*classical* he continues the tradition within Abrahamic religion. But the extent to which he is *neo*classical has provided a stumbling block for many readers. In this book I will use the tools of contemporary process philosophy of religion to do justice to both the "neo" and the "classical" dimensions of his view of God.

Two further matters need to be mentioned in this introduction before I move to the Bergsonian background to Kazantzakis's thought in chapter 1. The first concerns my transliterations of Greek words, which will involve the following procedures: (a) I will use the standard transliteration scheme employed by most scholars when transliterating ancient Greek words, a scheme that distinguishes eta from epsilon and omega from omicron by placing a macron over the first of each pair, indicating that it is a long vowel. (b) I will use the style sheet of the *Journal of Modern Greek Studies* when transliterating modern Greek words, a style sheet that transliterates for sound rather than for spelling. And (c), the ancient Greek transliteration will be used when a word exists in both ancient and modern Greek. Throughout my goal will be to show Kazantzakis using certain key terms rather than to do detailed literary analysis of his language.

I would also like to comment on the relationship between the present volume and the series of which it is a part, "Constructive Postmodern Thought."[1] As David Ray Griffin, the editor of this series, has successfully argued, there is a significant divide in modern thought between early and late, although the former stage leads to the latter. Early modern thought (exemplified by Boyle, Newton, Mersenne, Descartes, Galileo, the deists, and others) was characterized by both individual and cosmological dualism, that is, by both a ghost in individual human machines and a supernatural God largely or wholly external to the workings of nature. Eventually, as is well known, in late modernity the ghost was exorcised and a supernatural deity was seen as a fifth wheel that played little or no role in the drive of nature. Chapter 8 of the present book contributes to the effort within process thought, an effort initiated by Whitehead's classic *Science and the Modern World*, to escape from the hegemony the dualism-materialism debate has had over modern thought. And most of the remaining chapters of the book consist in an attempt to rethink along Kazantzakian lines the traditional view of God as supernatural, a view that reached extreme proportions in the early modern period, only to come to a crash in late modernity when materialism and mechanism held sway.

The spread of the term "postmodern" in recent years indicates both a dissatisfaction with the modern age and a hope that this age will come to an end. There are at least three different ways, however, in which this hope could be embodied. One is a sort of restorationism, where one would return to traditional theism, a stance that is more premodern than it is postmodern. We will see in chapter 4 that Kazantzakis was by no means premodern, even if he did try to recover the intensity of concern for spiritual matters found in the Middle Ages, a fiery intensity doused by modernity, where spirituality was (usually) commendably tolerated, but not so commendably ridiculed. A second sort of postmodernism is the deconstructionist variety, where an anti-worldview is offered rather than a postmodern one. Indeed, most deconstructive postmodernists deconstruct or eliminate the ingredients necessary for a worldview: self, God, purpose, meaning, *some* defensible sort of realism, and so on. These matters will be treated in detail in the appendix, which deals with the relationship between Kazantzakis's theism and Nietzsche.

From the perspective of *constructive* postmodernists or naturalistic theists like Bergson, Whitehead, Hartshorne, Griffin, and, I allege, Kazantzakis, these deconstructive postmodernists are actually *most*modernists because of their willingness to follow through on the relativistic and nihilistic tendencies latent in late modernity. That is, the present work consists in an attempt to understand the thought of a God-intoxicated writer who is neither premodern nor mostmodern, but is genuinely and consistently postmodern in his orientation.

THE BERGSONIAN

BACKGROUND

A good place to start an analysis of the Bergsonian background to Kazantzakis's theism is Bergson's 1903 essay, "An Introduction to Metaphysics."[1] This work incorporates his earlier triumphs, *Time and Free Will* (1889) and *Matter and Memory* (1896), and points the way toward his later works, *Creative Evolution* (1907) and *The Two Sources of Morality and Religion* (1932). It should be noted that Kazantzakis attended Bergson's lectures in 1908, just after the publication of "An Introduction to Metaphysics" and *Creative Evolution*, and in the very period when Bergson was working out the ideas that were eventually to appear in *The Two Sources of Morality and Religion*.

The early sections of this chapter will consist in an examination of Bergson's texts. However, in the last section of the chapter I will illustrate how the Bergsonian points made in the early sections are relevant to a reading of three of Kazantzakis's works: *Freedom or Death*, *Journeying*, and *Journey to the Morea*. In chapter 2 and later chapters, I will be concerned almost exclusively with Kazantzakis's works.

An Introduction to Metaphysics

In "An Introduction to Metaphysics" Bergson argues that there is a notable defect often found in the workings of the human intellect, a defect emphasized as well by Kazantzakis: The intellect deals with the world by means of discrete units, as though reality were fundamentally static and immobile. The intellect does this because it apprehends the world externally as a collection of things in space. Living beings, however, exist durationally, they become. Life's flow is asymmetrical and irreversible in that the past is settled, whereas at each moment one is always straining toward a future that is at least partially indeterminate, and often largely so.[2]

Both rationalism and empiricism are at fault in this regard. The former tries to interpret the world in light of some fixed structure of thought, whereas the latter assumes that experience is composed of static "elements" like impressions or sensations. Both schools of thought assume that the changing must be explained in terms of the permanent, and that there is more in the immutable than in the mutable. Bergson, like Kazantzakis, wavers between saying that the intellect, because of this defect, is helpful but needs to be supplemented by intuition or instinct, on the one hand, and suggesting that intellect is necessarily dissembling and should be thwarted, on the other. In this book I will argue that the former alternative is the more plausible interpretation to take regarding these two writers. In any event, Kazantzakis follows Bergson in the belief that reality, including divine reality, is better known intuitively or instinctively rather than discursively. For example, Aristotle's view of the gods as *unmoved* movers, a view that very much influenced traditional theism in the Abrahamic religions, is defective precisely because it is overly intellectual.[3]

Bergson is most famous for his view that there is an *élan vital* driving life, including divine life, to ever higher levels of organization. Intellect translates the *élan vital* into mechanical terms. Or better, to use an image from Bergson quoted by Kazantzakis: The vital impulse is like a jet of steam spurting continually into the air, condensing into myriad drops that fall back to the source. The drops represent the purely material aspect of the universe against which *élan vital* wages the continual warfare apotheosized by Kazantzakis. It is the summit of the jet with which Kazantzakis is often concerned and which he also divinizes. Matter, by way of contrast, is seen as devitalized life. That is, if God is not omnipotent—and this on the evidence of there being evil in the world—then there is no reason to believe that there was a creation of matter *ex nihilo*, nor is there reason to believe that there will be an apocalypse: continual struggle is the rule. (In this regard Kazantzakis *is* a bit like Aristotle, who saw the world as everlasting.) What is distinctive about Bergson and Kazantzakis is their concentrating on immediate experience within matter, the novelty ingredient in each fresh moment, a novelty missed or denied by mechanistic intellect.[4]

There are two quite different ways of knowing a thing, for Bergson, where the first implies that we move around the object and the second that we enter into it. The latter is what he means by "intuition." The waters are muddied a bit when he defines intuition as "intellectual sympathy," but his point quite clearly is that persons—divine or human—can only be understood adequately from within, with a simple act of entering—whether really or vicariously—into the temporal flow of the person in question. There is a succession of states in a person, with each state containing that which precedes it and announcing that which follows. But the states are not discrete in that they extend into each other; a moment is temporally "thick." Further, no two moments can be identical for a conscious being in that the later moment that is similar to the earlier one is different at the least because it can remember the former, as in Bergson's example that no two experiences of listening to the "same" piece of music can really be identical.[5]

In the present book, abstract ideas will be used in my analysis of Kazantzakis, but in order to be true to both Bergson and Kazantzakis it must be admitted that, finally, an understanding of Kazantzakis's view of God entails a simple intuition. Philosophy by its nature consists in a critique of abstractions, and for Bergson this consists in the effort to mold our abstractions and to make them as supple and mobile *as possible* so as to do as much justice *as possible* to the fleeting intuitions with which we are concerned, in this case with Kazantzakis's intuition regarding God, or more loosely, with his concept of God. The difficulty lies in the fact that Kazantzakis himself is very often trying to reconcile contrary tendencies that can, from one angle, appear to be antagonistic and, from another, appear to be mutual correlatives, as we will see in chapter 5, which deals with Kazantzakis as a dipolar theist. This makes our conceptual task all the more difficult. I will aim at developing concepts that will facilitate an intuitive grasp of how the contrary elements in Kazantzakis's view of God are at once opposed and reconciled.[6]

Both Bergson and Kazantzakis were exhaustively bothered by the immobility of the traditional God, a product of analysis, and they were both animated by divine mobility. Divine immobility is the extreme limit of slowing down the movement of God as one would a motion picture so as to be left with a single, static frame. Kazantzakis repeatedly attempts to speed up the frames such that the divine process be restored, a process that is best grasped through an active, indeed violent, intuition, says Bergson. What is called eternity is not the substratum for change so much as it is an abstraction away from living process. Eternity, for Bergson, is movement stripped precisely of its mobility; it is death. A life without end is perhaps better termed an everlasting or sempiternal life rather than an eternal one. Because there is a tendency in intellectual pursuits to deaden, to eternalize, to murder by dissection (to use Wordsworth's image), it is perhaps less dangerous to extol the virtues of philosophers philosophizing than the virtues of philosophy. My Bergsonian philosophical efforts to understand Kazantzakis's view of God in this book should be conceived on the model of various soundings, about which one feels that one has touched at greater or lesser depth the bottom of the "same" ocean, the thought of Kazantzakis on God.[7]

From Closed to Open Religion

According to Bergson, in *The Two Sources of Morality and Religion*, a book with which we will be concerned in this section of the chapter,[8] the first function of religion is to sustain and reinforce the claims of society. In this regard religion is an outgrowth of the two main lines of evolution in animal life, of the arthropods and the vertebrates. At the end of the former is found the instinct of insects, and at the end of the latter we find human intelligence. Whereas the former is laid down by nature in an immutable way, the latter is variable in form and open to progress. Or again, bees operate by *necessity*, whereas human beings have *obligations* that only make sense if they are free to disobey them. What is natural in human beings is overlaid with what is acquired. But this point, as Kazantzakis well knew, is likely to be over-emphasized. In time of war, for example, murder and pillage are actually praiseworthy, according to some, as when Captain Mihalis murders Eminé in *Freedom or Death*. Human beings still have need of that primitive instinct that they coat with so thick a varnish. If there is to be any progress beyond primitivism, beyond parochial allegiances, it is to occur in and through God, for Kazantzakis.[9]

The saints of Christianity, the sages of Greece, the prophets of Israel, the bodhisattvas of Buddhism are those who allow human beings to be carried beyond the mechanical workings of nature; they appeal to us precisely because of their perfect aspiration, if not their perfect morality and spirituality. Recommending the spirit of renunciation is not enough; it must be *embodied* in some hero or other for it to be efficacious. Whereas the closed soul rigidly adheres to societal mores and religious beliefs, the open soul extends its concerns to all of humanity, in fact to all of the cosmos, as Kazantzakis indicates in *Spiritual Exercises*. Kazantzakis's heroes (Zorba, Captain Mihalis, Jesus, St. Francis, Fr. Yanaros, etc.) have a Bergsonian effect on us like great music: they do not put feelings into us so much as they introduce us to the feelings already there. In chapter 6 we will have occasion to explore the role of mysticism in the transition from closed to open religion, but at present it is important to at least introduce the following possibility: that the familiar observation that mystics (including Zorba, as we will see) often express themselves in terms of passionate love may be due not so much to the mystics using passionate or romantic love as their model, as to romantic love (whose origin was in the Middle Ages) or passionate love using mystical experience as a model. That is, Kazantzakis's mysticism consists in open, mystical religion "resuming" possession of its own territory, much as Bergson emphasizes.[10]

Given the tension between instinct (or intuition or emotion) and intellect in Bergson and Kazantzakis, it is clear which of these two has the upper hand: emotion vivifies or vitalizes the intellect. For example, it is only after powerful emotions concerning God win people over that they then think it necessary to formulate a metaphysics. This point will have to be kept in mind as we discuss Kazantzakis's concept of God throughout the book. Those whose contagious emotions prepare the way for new concepts of God are truly religious heroes or "conquerors" for Bergson and Kazantzakis. "Progress" or "advance" for these conquerors, on Bergson's and Kazantzakis's interpretation, is indistinguishable from the spiritual enthusiasm itself, just as the struggle for political liberation is itself liberating for old Idomeneas in *Freedom or Death*. This spiritual enthusiasm allows a soul to break not only with nature (to the extent that this is possible), but also with the city's closed religion and with petty pleasures and pains. But there is nothing misanthropic about this transition from the closed to the open soul: all of the great mystics declare that they have the impression of a current passing from their souls to God and then *back again* from God to humankind.[11]

Nonetheless, the distance between the closed and open souls themselves is vast; it is the distance between repose and movement, respectively. The problem with closed religion, in general, and with the closed soul, in particular, is that they are too easy in that they only take snapshots of a complicated process. *Ataraxia* and *apatheia*, in the Stoic or Epicurean senses of these terms, are not the goals of Kazantzakian spirituality. Rather, his goal is to have no goal *in the sense that* one should continually try to spiritualize matter even if no one else seems to care about one's efforts. And both Bergson and Kazantzakis were well aware of the fact that most people are indifferent to the struggles of spiritual heroes, perhaps because, at least initially, the visions of these heroes seem impracticable. The closed society and its religion seem fresh from the hands of nature in the automatic equilibrium contained within its borders, but the open religion ushered in by religious heroes makes it clear that the "peace" and "naturalness" of closed religion are fraudulent. Even the thick humus of centuries of closed religion, reformed by progressive waves of open religion, barely covers the bedrock of original nature. A purely instinctual society of *human* beings is impossible, as is a purely open society or a purely mystic one. Pure aspiration is an ideal limit.[12]

Religious heroes, those who have open souls ready to receive divine influence, have the ability to stir up our souls. Yet the spectacle of what religions have been in the past and are today is humiliating for human intelligence to consider, and this despite the fact that the actions of human beings are at least partly indeterminate, hence they could make the situation better. Both instinct and intelligence are means whereby raw matter is turned into its finished, spiritual state, with instinct around the fringes of intelligence and gleams of intelligence in the depths of instinct. The two activities each retain something of the other in them. But those whose instinct or intelligence is used in such a way as to forge or receive some new view of God pose a danger to societal order and closed religion, hence they are often denigrated. The very function of a closed religion, according to Bergson, is to provide a defensive reaction against the apparently dissolvent power of mystic openness to God. I say "apparent" because it is the great religious heroes who ultimately save religion and, in a way, according to Kazantzakis, save God. Religion does not have to be mere custom.[13]

The intelligence of "primitive" peoples is not different in kind from our own; it has a tendency, like ours, to make the mistake of converting the dynamic into the static and to solidify actions into things. ("Primitive" peoples are different from us merely because they are ignorant of the things—many of which are not terribly significant—we have learned.) In stagnant societies and religions this solidification is an accomplished fact. Religion can either preserve this reification or strike individuals inwardly so as to transcend what is assumed to be final. In addition to being a defensive reaction against mystic openness, closed religion is, as Bergson notes, also a defensive reaction against the intellect's realization that death is inevitable. Unlike Bergson, however, Kazantzakis's theism does not include belief in an afterlife, hence in this regard Kazantzakis is thoroughly intellectual and not instinctual. One can well imagine, by way of contrast, according to Bergson, the primitive person looking into a pool of water and seeing "himself" detached from his tactile body and assuming that this separate self could go on living after the tactile body died. In any event, even if this is not an accurate account of the origin of the traditional view of the soul, it should be noted that this traditional view of the soul is rejected by Kazantzakis, a view that, as even Bergson admits, can lead to almost any imagined absurdity. The vital impulse itself knows very little of death; it may come into contact with the death of others, but it does not confront the inevitability of death. This is the work of intellect.[14] This is why the nonintellectual Zorba thinks he should live a thousand years.

Perhaps what is most significant about the connection between Bergson and Kazantzakis on the topic of God is that Bergson both reinforced Kazantzakis's belief that most of what existed, and had for some time existed, in organized religion was, for lack of a better word, bunk, *and* that the very topic of God was a significant one—the most significant one!—that needed contemporary rethinking. Organized religions are important, but only to the extent that they preserve the classics in the history of religious experience that make this rethinking possible. Re-form, after all, presupposes form. That is, Bergson helped Kazantzakis avoid positivism. The origin of belief in God does not lie in fear, as the positivists suggested; rather, belief in God is a reaction against fear. There are real presences in the world that we should fear, presences that our ancestors would have thought of as ghosts, as when the ghost of Kosmas's father in *Freedom or Death* haunts his new daughter-in-law, a Jew. Or as when Bergson felt some sort of mysterious personal force that took possession of the room when he read of the outbreak of World War I.[15]

Kazantzakis escapes positivism not only because he takes the issue of God seriously, but also because he is only a qualified defender of progress. Progress does occur, but along with it human beings drag with them the same basic human nature. We cannot puff ourselves up with the prejudice that suggests that we are *born* superior to our ancestors. Before anyone can theorize he or she must *live* first, as did our ancestors. Kazantzakis's constant desire simultaneously to praise the intellect as well as to put it in its place is thoroughly Bergsonian: closed religious belief is infra-intellectual and open religious belief is supra-intellectual. It is this supra-intellectual religion, present in the religious heroes of any age, that insures that God cannot be immutable. We will see in chapter 5 that the existence of divinity itself is necessary, but the actual, mutable experiences of God depend on creatures.[16]

At any moment there is a vast current of creative energy that is precipitated into matter, most of which comes to a stop. But the attachment to life enables some individuals to take advantage of this energy. Bergson puts the point in the following way, in words that summarize Kazantzakis's view as well:

> A soul strong enough, noble enough to make this effort
> would not stop to ask whether the principle with which it is
> now in touch is the transcendent cause of all things or
> merely its earthly delegate. It would be content to feel itself
> pervaded, though retaining its own personality, by a being
> immeasurably mightier than itself, just as an iron is pervaded
> by the fire which makes it glow.[17]

(The fire image here should be kept in mind when we consider Kazantzakis's view of God as a *consuming* flame.) This mysticism is usually found in diluted form in most of those who believe in God, but the true mystics experience God in such an undiluted form that they are transported, at least temporarily, to another plane. They experience the passage of a spiritual current through matter to a place that it could not quite reach without the intervention of humanity. But the fact that the diluted experience of God is prevalent should not escape our notice. Most who believe in God hear "the whisper of an echo," to use Bergson's words, of God. Belief in God does not have to be a futile effort of merely going through the motions. Yet it often is an exercise in futility, as if we were parts of some ceremony with an empty chair reserved for some high dignitary. As before, however, there is some value to organized religion in that its history can provide the spark for open religion when one of its members is touched by the inwardness of the tradition, just as an indifferent schoolmaster, mechanically teaching a science developed by previous geniuses, can nonetheless awaken in a pupil the scientific vocation. The contrast between the closed and the open in religion occurs when faint echoes of the tradition are heard, not of those "mysteries" concerning which there is nothing really mystical, but of those genuine experiences of the divine had by the saints.[18]

The mystics can grow on each other and improve not because of any enhanced faculties on their part, but because in each new epoch they can call up the peak experiences of previous mystics to guide them, as in the history of ancient Greek mysticism from the Orphics and Pythagoreans to Plato and to Plotinus. This effort of relying on previous mystics "is of God, if it is not God himself," according to Bergson. Each mystic catches a clearer glimpse of the promised land even if he or she does not touch its soil. Kazantzakis grows out of the *dynamism* of the Hebrew prophets and the *fervor* of the Christian mystics and proselytizers, even if he is not a proselytizer himself. This dynamism and fervor is produced by being attentive to that force or presence or voice that we call "God," an attentiveness that alternately produces repose and agitation. When God acts through the soul there is a superabundance of life, a boundless impetus, and an irresistible impulse to hurl oneself into vast enterprises, all of the vital phenomena that are commonplaces in Kazantzakis's writings. This Bergsonian-Kazantzakian vitalism directs the mystic to the wider and wider circles mentioned in *Spiritual Exercises*: beyond family and race and species to the whole cosmos.[19]

Mysticism or open religion means nothing whatsoever to the person who has no experience (diluted or undiluted) of it. But to the person who has had such experience, religion is the cooled, crystallized effect of what was once poured white hot into the human soul. Just as there is popularization of scientific truth (how many laypersons *really* understand Einstein's or Darwin's theories?), so also in religion there is popularization of the discoveries of Jesus, St. Francis, Buddha, and others. In between the agnostic or atheist, who claim to have no experience of God, on the one hand, and the active believer, on the other, is the philosopher who intellectualizes God. The latter is often chastened by Bergson and Kazantzakis because of the attempt that some intellectuals— philosophers and theologians, especially—make to supplant religious experience and action with abstractions. But neither philosophers nor theologians necessarily commit this error. In fact, Kazantzakis himself is at times a philosopher/theologian who attempts to develop descriptions of God and of the experience of God by human beings that are more accurate than those hitherto developed.[20]

Once again, the monumental mistake made by many philosophers and theologians is to take snapshots of change with their concepts. More precisely, this effort is not bothersome in its own right; the mistake lies in taking these snapshots for the real and the essential. Motion is then erroneously seen as agitation with a view to standing still. But duration is not a debasement of being, as I will argue in detail later, and time is not a deprivation of eternity. If there are those who see in the mystics' perception of God-in-process nothing but quackery and folly, it should also be noted that there are those for whom music is nothing but noise. The mystics experience what most of us could, with effort, experience: according to Bergson, they *unanimously* bear witness that

God needs us just as we need God. It will be one of the aims of this book to explain how this could be so, an especially important effort given Kazantzakis's often repeated claim that *we* save God.[21]

Suffering is a terrible reality, the existence of which disproves the existence of an *omnipotent* God, as Kazantzakis often illustrates, but does it disprove the existence of God? If God is omnipotent, then it appears that God willed, or at least permitted, innocent beings (humans or other animals) to suffer. It is actually, contra what one might expect, the atheists or agnostics who are not good empiricists. They have an *a priori* notion of God as omnipotent, from which they try to deduce the characteristics the world ought to show. When they notice that the world does not exhibit these characteristics, say when suffering crowds out joy, they conclude that there is no God. Their procedure, Bergson thinks, should be the reverse, as it was for Kazantzakis: Consult the experience of suffering in the world and then question what this might mean for belief in the greatest conceivable being-in-becoming. Is it necessarily the case that such a being would possess or delegate all power? Neither Bergson nor Kazantzakis would respond to this question in the affirmative. In effect, atheists and agnostics very often start with closed religion, where divine omnipotence is assumed without argument, and defeat it as a straw man.[22]

Despite the fact that the Middle Ages (which will be treated in more detail in chapter 4) were even more ensconced within closed religion than our own era, both Bergson and Kazantzakis have a peculiar admiration for this period. In some ways the modern desire to bring about easier material conditions is admirable, but this desire often degenerates into a hedonism that is detrimental to spiritual progress. By way of contrast, both Bergson and Kazantzakis as constructive postmodernists admire medieval asceticism and the simple life, a life of simplicity that acts as a helpful antidote to the overly complex lives of many people alive today. Asceticism evokes mysticism, as we will see, in that one must train oneself to use matter properly in order to get away from it. In Bergson's words, which are also similar to those of Kazantzakis, the material universe is a machine for the making of the divine.[23]

Laughter

One of the lesser read, yet nonetheless instructive, of Bergson's books is *Laughter*.[24] He defines laughter in general as a certain mechanical inelasticity where one would expect to find the wide-awake adaptability and the living pliableness of a personal being. For example, some human faces are humorous because they seem to be always engaged in weeping, laughing, whistling, or blowing an imaginary trumpet. Likewise, there is something comical about God *if* this being is supposed to be completely unmoved by both the Holocaust as well as by a group of teenage boys who proclaim their individuality while each wears a baseball hat on backwards. Exactly how can an intelligent being remain unmoved by tragedy and comedy? Or again, there is something comic about an eccentric individual who dresses in the fashion of former times (say the "roaring 20s"), just as there is something comic about a supposed divine being who bears all of the attributes of a Middle Eastern, nomadic tribe of 3,000 years ago, or of a feudal society from the thirteenth century.[25]

Not only is God often turned into something mechanical, and hence comical, in the Abrahamic religions, but also religious leaders within these religions are often comical. Many a religious leader exhibits the professional automatism of the customs official who rushed to the aid of those on a wrecked steamer, and began by asking them if they had any goods to declare. It is easy for orthodox religious believers to become impervious to novel forms of joy or pathos in that they have readymade phrases to deal with every contingency. Bergson's description of the comic applies equally to the traditional view of God in the Abrahamic religions:

> The rigid, the ready-made, the mechanical, in contrast with the supple, the ever-changing and the living, absentminded-ness in contrast with attention, in a word, automatism in contrast with free activity, such are the defects that laughter singles out and would fain correct.[26]

The chief cause of this rigidity, as we will see, is the neglect to look around to see alternative views of God. Kazantzakis was not neglectful in this regard.[27]

Peter Bien is correct in noting that Bergson and William James had a great deal in common and that they both influenced Kazantzakis.[28] But James's influence was not due merely to his criticism of idle abstractions, but also to the fact that he bathed in an atmosphere of great spiritual currents. James was interested in the varieties of religious experience, an interest that enabled him, like Kazantzakis, to benefit from the mystic soul as we would lean out the window to feel the caress of the breeze on our cheek on a spring day, a caress that nonetheless causes an immense unrest.[29]

In order to avoid a comic view of God one needs to realize that open religion is motivated by an attractive force rather than the impulsive one of closed religion. Further, it is crucial to notice that open religion or mysticism, as Kazantzakis well knew, is not to be identified with quietism, a preoccupation with idiosyncratic visions and voices. Rather, the mystics who interested Bergson (Saints Paul and Joan of Arc) are like those who interested Kazantzakis in the sense that they were persons whose religious experiences propelled them to act in the world in some nontrivial way.[30]

Some Kazantzakis Texts

Bien is alert in pointing out that the best place to look for instantiation of Bergsonian themes in Kazantzakis is *The Greek Passion*, but I will reserve treatment of the relevant passage(s) from this work until chapter 6.[31]

Freedom or Death

The point I wish to make here is that almost any work of Kazantzakis is a good place to look for Bergsonian themes, such that it does not much matter where one looks. Consider one of his best novels, *Freedom or Death*. Here we see that for Kazantzakis the whole of life involves struggle and trouble; only death or a statuelike existence brings repose. Captain Mihalis cast wild glances in agitation at a statue of the Archangel Michael because of the latter's inactive existence in the face of an unjust occupation of Crete by the Turks. The reified God of traditional theism could just as well have been the target of his indignation.[32]

The main character in this book, Captain Mihalis, prefers to think of God not only in process but, in Kazantzakian fashion, specifically in the process of fighting. If God is not present in the battle against the Turks it must be due to the fact that there is a war somewhere else that demands divine attention. (An omnipotent being could fight on two fronts, however.) The Cretans are tough, hence they can hold their own until God is available. For example, of the three sorts of human beings, the Cretans are in the most rugged category: some eat their eggs without the shells, some with the shells, and some (the Cretans) with the shells *and* the egg cups. Even God is afraid of those for whom death is not to be feared. Kazantzakis's suffering God is in one sense compatible with Christianity's incarnational theology, specifically with the crucifixion. But whether or not Kazantzakis violates the traditional condemnation of Patripassionism (the view that God the Father suffers) remains to be seen. In any event, Kazantzakis is comfortable with comparing the suffering of Crete with the trials of Jesus on the Cross.[33]

It is not only Christianity with which Kazantzakis's view of God is in dialogue. Consider the problem mentioned in the introduction, that of trying to reconcile human freedom with divine omniscience. It is well known that within Islam it is common to try to resolve the problem by emphasizing the latter at the expense of the former. To say "It is written by Allah" is to say that there is little, if anything, a human being can do to alter what will in any event happen. It is in this light that the exchange between the Metropolitan and Pasha Effendi in *Freedom or Death* is to be understood, especially when the Pasha tries to get himself off the hook when he is on the verge of shedding blood. It should be emphasized, however, that despite certain differences of emphasis, one finds the same problem in Judaism and Christianity as in Islam. After all, both the later St. Augustine and John Calvin (with their enormous influence on the Puritan tradition) also denigrate human freedom so as to accommodate divine omniscience.[34]

The characters in this novel in effect have a legitimate Bergsonian question: If God is omnipotent and omniscient, how can we also say that God is full of loving kindness while innocent people suffer? Unlike many thinkers who have asked a question like this, Bergson and Kazantzakis remain not only optimistic, but heroically so. Captain Mihalis, who in some sense represents Kazantzakis's own views, does not curse his fate at least in part because he does not assume that God is responsible for it. However, if the traditional theistic view is correct, God *is* responsible for it. The hard-nosed nature of Kazantzakis's theism can be seen in his identification of God with Charos, whose magical voice calls to us from beyond life, and not necessarily in a gentle tone.[35]

Journeying

Another book where Kazantzakis exhibits his Bergsonian tendencies is the recently translated *Journeying*, which details his trips to Italy, Egypt, the Sinai, Jerusalem, and Cyprus. He notes, like Bergson, the heroism of religious figures like Jesus, Mohammed, and Buddha, who, when confronted with the abyss (to be explained later), cast a bridge and cross over it. They are like shepherds who bring the human flock out of closed religion into an open one (and perhaps to a more advanced version of closed religion). Kazantzakis's own heroism, if there is such, consists in his ability to mobilize his letter-soldiers in the religious fight. It is not in victory but in the *struggle* for victory that his efforts to write well find meaning. In fact, like Captain Mihalis he believes that in the certainty that there is no reward, one's efforts obtain pride and valor.[36]

Kazantzakian freedom consists not merely in the license to choose, but in obedience to a hyperindividual rhythm that is not in the traditional theistic sense omniscient. Hence Kazantzakis recognized that the Russian peasant, when he or she came to believe the communist trope to the effect that there is nothing higher than humanity, would not really be free and would not be willing to make sacrifices. And the religious life *is* a sacrificial life, for Kazantzakis, especially in our current age, which is a new medieval period, a postmodern period, as we will see in chapter 4. The goal of this sacrifice is to advance the divine cause. The means once needed to advance this cause included slavery (!), as was the case in ancient Egyptian religion. But even in ancient Egypt worship became progressively dematerialized when Aton, the god of the sun, replaced the cruder Amon. Aton was accessible to all races and to people of all intellectual abilities.[37]

Kazantzakis's similarity to Bergson is especially evident when he notices that all of the world's great religions had their start in the East. The West has received some of these religions and nurtured, refined, and analyzed them, but religious passion itself is an "Oriental" phenomenon. What has been criticized in this chapter as the "traditional view of God" in the Abrahamic religions is actually a particular sort of Western accretion on this basically Eastern phenomenon. As we will see, this point enables us to bridge any supposed gap between Kazantzakis's debt to "Western" religions, on the one hand, and his debt to Buddhism, on the other. That is, both Christianity and Buddhism are species of Oriental madness (in the honorific sense of the term), for Kazantzakis. Ultimately Kazantzakis is a Western-Eastern monist who believes that there is a great deal more of matter in spirit than (overly Eastern) "idealists" imagine, just as there is a great deal more of spirit in matter than (overly Western) materialists imagine.[38]

At one point during a visit to the Sinai, Kazantzakis stipulates that it is time itself, with a rhythm like that of an undulating camel, that transubstantiates matter into spirit, a process that we will isolate in the following chapter. This divine process of transubstantiation is relentless and often destructive because Kazantzakis's God is not so much pretty as sublime:

> The true God disdainfully passes over human virtues, the
> daughters of fear. He is the God of destruction. . . . God is
> the dark unknown all-probable explosive power, that breaks
> out even in the smallest particle of matter.[39]

I will later try to reconcile this quotation with the view of God as the greatest conceivable being; here I wish to emphasize that the Bergsonian and Kazantzakian hero is the most perfect expression of God, of spiritualized, transubstantiated matter in any age. For Kazantzakis the hero answers the metahuman Cry, the Impossible, a response that has implications for the "sacred, lofty" meaning that should come about in the meeting of two human beings.[40]

During Kazantzakis's visit to the Sinai, a tension becomes apparent in his view of God that will be with us for the remainder of this book. On the one hand, God is sometimes, for Kazantzakis as well as for Bergson, a personal being who cares for humanity (or a benevolent panentheistic presence). And, on the other, God is sometimes, for Kazantzakis if not for Bergson, an indifferent and frightful presence or the "unblooming, all-granite one." Or, as Kazantzakis puts the point, "God is a quiver *and* a gentle tear" (emphasis added). It is this harsh, Sinai version of God (the quiver) that Kazantzakis very often refers to as a consuming fire or as an enormous hand that whirls human beings about. It is Yahweh, God the Father, or Allah (Kazantzakis held out a suspicion that he was part Bedouin) that Kazantzakis very often, but not always, means by "God." But because Kazantzakis is interested in the *contemporary* face of God he refines his view as follows:

> The contemporary face of the unfathomable is neither the
> tenderly sweet face of Jesus, that blossomed in idyllic Galilee,

nor the face of the tribal, merciless Jehovah that was forged in
the Sinaitic wilderness . . . a new face of the unfathomable. . . .
It must be like the Laborer who is hungry, who works and rises
up in revolt. This face must no longer be the leader of one
tribe, but of the entire human race.[41] (emphasis added)

Here we can see that Jesus, on the one hand, and Yahweh/God the Father, on
the other, are put on a par in that both of these are mere suggestions as to how
we should think of God-in-process today. Such is Kazantzakis's Bergsonian fear
of reification:[42] "If God at one time took on the form of Dionysos, Jehovah,
Christ, Ariman, and Brahmin, it is only of historical value today. His contemporary form is whatever wrenches our heart with blood and tears.[43]

However, not even this form—the one that wrenches our heart with
blood and tears—stops the divine process. This is because the period in history
through which we are living, a period in which much of the dead wood in
religion needs to be cleared away, is transitory. The blur is due not only to the
fact that time flies, but also to the fact that at any particular time the erotic
passion that accompanies the transubstantiation of matter into spirit will make
exact boundaries among eroticisms toward God, ideas, and women hard to
draw, as Plato also well knew in his *Symposium.* Kazantzakis asks for God's *help*
(which again indicates that the violent images of God do not tell the whole
story of Kazantzakis's theism) in elevating himself above even joy. It can safely
be said that God, for Kazantzakis, was still fermenting.[44]

One can understand the calm of some Abrahamic believers, say the calm
of a Muslim who is convinced that all is in the care of an omnipotent,
omniscient, and omnibenevolent Allah. But this calm is due to a false sense of
security created by a problematic (Western) philosophical concept of God. At
the heart of the Abrahamic religions is an Eastern restlessness, a Jewish battle to
ceaselessly upset the balance that is the goal of those who have inherited from
the Greeks the tendency to harmonize opposite forces. In this regard
Kazantzakis's theism very much resembles Christianity in general: a peculiar
combination of this Hebraic restlessness with a Greek sense of harmony. From
the very start Christianity has exhibited this peculiar mixture. To the extent
that Christianity pays attention to its Asian, as opposed to its Greek, roots it
will preserve a hatred of all tyranny and complacency, a hatred born in the Jews
as a consequence of many centuries of persecution. (Kazantzakis saw Zionism in
the 1920s as a sort of complacency, analogous to that of Homer's Odysseus when
he returned home.) Kazantzakis's thoroughly Bergsonian way of describing the
tension here is as follows:[45]

I could clearly feel the two great torrents struggling within
me: the one pushes toward harmony, patience and gentle-
ness. It functions with ease, without effort, following only

the natural order of things. You throw a stone up high and for a second you force it against its will; but quickly it joyfully falls again. You toss a thought in the air but the thought quickly tires, it becomes impatient in the empty air and falls back to earth and settles with the soil. The other force is, it would seem, contrary to nature. An unbelievable absurdity. It wants to conquer weight, abolish sleep, and, with the lash, prod the Universe upward.[46]

Journey to the Morea

A third source for Kazantzakis's Bergsonism is *Journey to the Morea*, a work that details his journeys to the Greek provinces where the "dead gods" find their final refuge. Here he comes to grips with the realization that if civilization means discipline of primordial instinct, then it has value only when the disciplined instinct serves some purpose greater than any individual. In one of the most moving passages in the Kazantzakis corpus, and a neglected one at that, Kazantzakis indicates that provincial life is not only the home of the dead gods and closed religion, but is also the best place to look for religious heroes who will open religion up once again:

> Spiritual and ethical *decency*, the priceless bashfulness of youth, the sacred "down" of spiritual purity, finds shelter only in the provinces. In a great city the child is born without this down, his eyes and ears are soon corrupted, and this precocious maturity deforms his soul. In the provinces, amid silent lanes, in spotless flowerpot-filled courtyards, on peaceful country strolls, in the craving of expectation and the difficulty of satisfying every aspiration, the youth finds time to desire. A great distance exists between desire and the realization of that desire, and in traversing this distance, a youth belabors and stimulates his highest abilities. For a short while natural youthful elation for the higher things manages to endure, and in living for that short time it matures, is strengthened, and is less easily compromised. So, as the capitals have lost their innocence, the only remaining hope for the renewal of the Earth's virginity has taken refuge in the modest, languid and enchanting province.[47]

Each of us, however, is a potential source of open religion in that the divine indwelling in each of us is protected by what Kazantzakis calls a fortress, like St. Teresa of Avila's interior castle. This divine indwelling is the last refuge of conscience, self-respect, and courage.[48]

Immortality, for Kazantzakis (and here he departs from Bergson), consists in making the most, indeed making an eternity, out of the single instant at our disposal. It is in this way that each of us is a possible source for open religion even if it is great artists, in particular, who glimpse timeless, changeless symbols *in the flow of* everyday reality. For example, the trained eye discerns a prior movement in a fresco and even in a statue, one that reigned supreme in the works of a preceding generation and one that future generations will take: the statue, in a way, moves through and carries tradition. In an instant even a statue balances the tripartite current of time; such could also be said of any particular view of God. By concentrating on a great soul, especially in moments of historical dissolution, we can learn how to become oracles for open religion, and how to transubstantiate matter into spirit, according to Kazantzakis. By keeping in mind Heraclitus's dictum, that one cannot step twice into the same river, and by realizing that the "river" in question is within us, we can always keep alive the hope that spiritual progress is possible.[49]

One religious hero whom Kazantzakis admires precisely because of his *élan vital* is Gemistos Plethon, a passionate defender of Plato who tried to show that tradition is worthy of respect, but that a living human being is not obliged to obey it blindly. This is especially true regarding traditional conceptions of God because the stakes are so great when dealing with views of ultimate reality. But Gemistos is just one among many of those who have suffered and struggled much in their lives; ephemeral things could not subdue them *because of* their belief in God. There is no huge gap in Kazantzakis between *élan vital* or animal-like passion, on the one hand, and religious struggle or God, on the other. Despite the fact that Kazantzakis divinizes passion (at least when passion is intent on spiritualizing matter), he nonetheless can at the same time feel guilty about passion. For example, he relates how he once was in an impressive church in Monemvasia and he opened at random a Gospel on the altar. Whether by coincidence, as is claimed in *Journey to the Morea*, or by design, so as to heighten the literary effect of this incident, Kazantzakis finds the same message St. Augustine received in his *Confessions* when he also fell upon the Bible at random: revelry and intoxication lead one away from the major concerns of life.[50] The issue in Kazantzakis is not reason versus passion or the West versus the East, but how to bring together the best in each element in these pairs.

It is one of the theses of the present book that Kazantzakis is no more opposed to intellect (or the West) than Bergson; rather he is interested in putting it in its proper place. What bothers both of them is a hegemonic intellect that crowds out (Eastern) mysticism. Western (or, more precisely, Greek) reason, as discovered by Socrates in quest of metaphysical truths, is a great advance over the idle gossip and curiosity that preceded it. The goal for both Bergsonian and Kazantzakian reason is to build on, not supplant, the warm, dark, rich substratum provided by instinct (or the mystic intuition of the "Orient"): "We can deny neither East nor West." An ostensive definition of what Kazantzakis means by the hegemony of the intellect or of the West is when he points out a defect found among learned Germans: if given the choice between two doors, on the one written "Paradise" and on the other written "Lecture about Paradise," they would rush to the latter![51] That is, despite his Bergsonian critique of hegemonic reason, as indicated in this image concerning the fondness some have for academic lectures, Kazantzakis himself is a highly intellectual writer.

It is *because* of the fact that Kazantzakis is such an intellectual or philosophical writer that we must consider carefully what he means by the aforementioned violent images of God, images that have been treated with care in some articles by Darren Middleton and by the famous process theologian John Cobb.[52] The key point to notice here is that Kazantzakis's Bergsonian opposition to reification of the spiritual life, and his opposition to reification of God, means that *at times* we should be shaken—forcefully shaken—out of our complacency when reification begins, when the divine film starts slowing down to the point where we can imagine it a snapshot. The "Cry" of God serves as a call forward to new possibilities, some of which may in fact strike us as terrifying. For example, in order to show "forgetfulness" of self, we might be asked to kiss a leper, as was St. Francis. Each of us, at least some of the time, and perhaps most of the time, wants to continue essentially as we are, and it is this security that is shattered by the Cry. But our response to the Cry is for the sake of some things that are good for us: life *in extremis*, heightened consciousness, expanded freedom (as defined above by Kazantzakis), and, in some cases, more extensive and more sensitive love. As Cobb emphasizes, however, the way to these often lies through the valley of the shadow of death. Bergson's God of love and Kazantzakis's dark divinity do not contradict each other; rather, they are mutually reinforcing correlatives.

The "Cry" passage from Kazantzakis treated by Cobb is important because it touches on most of the issues to be treated in the present book: transubstantiation, panexperientialism, a dipolar God in process, a love/hate relationship with traditional religion, and so forth. Hence it is worth quoting at length:

> Christ's every moment is a conflict and a victory. He conquered the invincible enchantment of simple human pleasures; He conquered every temptation, continually transubstantiated flesh into spirit, and ascended. Every obstacle in His journey became an occasion for further triumph, and then a landmark of that triumph. We have a model in front of us now, a model who opens the way for us and gives us strength.
>
> Blowing through heaven and earth, and in our hearts and the heart of every living thing, is a gigantic breath—a great Cry—which we call God. Plant life wished to continue its motionless sleep next to stagnant waters, but the Cry

leaped up within it and violently shook its roots: "Away, let go of the earth, walk!" Had the tree been able to think and judge, it would have cried, "I don't want to. What are you urging me to do! You are demanding the impossible!" But the Cry, without pity, kept shaking its roots and shouting, "Away, let go of the earth, walk!"

It shouted in this way for thousands of eons; and lo! as a result of desire and struggle, life escaped the motionless tree and was liberated.

Animals appeared—worms—making themselves at home in water and mud. "We're just fine here," they said. "We have peace and security; we're not budging!"

But the terrible Cry hammered itself pitilessly into their loins. "Leave the mud, stand up, give birth to your betters!"

"We don't want to! We can't!"

"You can't, but I can. Stand up!"

And lo! after thousands of eons, man emerged, trembling on his still unsolid legs.

The human being is a centaur; his equine hoofs are planted in the ground, but his body from breast to head is worked on and tormented by the merciless Cry. He has been fighting, again for thousands of eons, to draw himself, like a sword, out of his animalistic scabbard. He is also fighting— this is his new struggle—to draw himself out of his human scabbard. Man calls in despair, "Where can I go? I have reached the pinnacle, beyond is the abyss." And the Cry answers, "I am beyond. Stand up!" All things are centaurs. If this were not the case, the world would not rot into inertness and sterility.

As I walked hour after hour in the desert surrounding the monastery, God gradually began to liberate Himself from priests. Thenceforth, the Lord for me was this Cry.[53]

This divine Cry is much like Whitehead's "primordial nature of God," an aspect of God that is, when considered together with God's more concrete "consequent nature," better able than the God of traditional theism to account for the cosmic advance described by Kazantzakis in the above quotation. (This dipolar view of God will be explored in detail later in the book.) Whitehead sees the primordial nature of God in *Adventures of Ideas* as the *erōs* of the universe, the appetitive urge to realize, to as great an extent as possible, the eternal objects or possibilities (much like Plato's forms) for our world.

TRANSUBSTANTIATION

There have been several efforts in recent years to understand the Eucharist in Christianity. The official explanation of the sacrament in Roman Catholicism and Eastern Orthodoxy leaves the change from bread and wine into the body and blood of Christ as a mystery. Somehow or other a change of substance (transubstantiation) is enacted. Most Protestant explanations of the Eucharist are able to strip it of mystery, but at a great price: the Eucharist is a mere symbol of, or better, a sign of, Christ, without the "real presence" of God preserved.[1]

The work of Kazantzakis powerfully illuminates transubstantiation in at least three ways:

1. Kazantzakis presents transubstantiation as a natural *process* rather than as an instantaneous act of "hocus pocus."
2. He nonetheless indicates the *real presence* of God (indeed the creation of God) in the process of transubstantiation, albeit tempered by Kazantzakis's own conception of deity.[2]
3. Kazantzakis not only uses Eucharistic themes in his works, as do many other authors, but he also sees transubstantiation as *the key to his writing*.

That is, the sublimity of the transubstantiation that occurs in the Eucharist is spread across the whole of human life, indeed across the whole cosmos. There is no other modern writer concerning whom one could make this claim. Words like *metousiosis* (transubstantiation or transmutation) and *metabole* (change)— and their cognates—proliferate in Kazantzakis, and for good reason, as we will see.

Transubstantiation as the Key

Several commentators treat transubstantiation in Kazantzakis, but Theodora Vasils is one of the few to note its centrality in Kazantzakis's universe, and even she only notes this fact without explaining its depth. Vasils sees that even in Kazantzakis's early work *Serpent and Lily* we can see his struggle to liberate spirit from flesh, a struggle that engaged Kazantzakis throughout his life.[3] It is odd that many interpreters of Kazantzakis treat transubstantiation as a centripetal concern in that Kazantzakis himself alerts us to its prominence. He explicitly tells us that higher even than morality or truth or beauty is our highest obligation (*anotato hreos*): to transubstantiate matter into spirit, as exemplified, say, by St. Francis.[4]

The same hierarchy is implied by the boss in *Zorba the Greek*, in a scene late in the novel after the boss has learned to more fully appreciate Zorba's Dionysian spirit:[5]

> I think, Zorba—but I may be wrong—that there are three kinds of men: those who make it their aim, as they say, to live their lives, eat, drink, make love, grow rich, and famous; then come those men who make it their aim not to live their own lives but to concern themselves with the lives of all men—they feel that all men are one and they try to enlighten them, to love them as much as they can and do good to them; finally there are those who aim at living the life of the entire universe—everything, men, animals, trees, stars, we are all one, we are all one sub-stance involved in the same terrible struggle. What struggle? . . . Turning (*metousiosei*) matter into spirit.[6]

Finally, in Kazantzakis's "Credo," written late in life, he tells us that:

> [S]uddenly a great light was born within me: the trans-mutation of matter into spirit. Here was the great secret, the red ribbon followed by the Combatant [that is, Bergsonian *élan vital*]. Though he had freed himself from inorganic matter and leaped into the living organism of plants, he felt himself smothering, and therefore leaped into the life of

animals, continually transmuting more and more matter into spirit. But again he suffocated, then leaped into the contemporary Apeman whom we have named "man" too soon, and now he struggles to escape from the Apeman and to be transmuted truly into Man. I now clearly saw the progress of the Invisible, and suddenly I knew what my duty was to be: to work in harmony together with that Combatant; to transmute, even I, in my own small capacity, matter into spirit, for only then might I try to reach the highest endeavor of man—a harmony with the universe.[7]

Communion Metaphors

Obviously it is not enough for Kazantzakis to say in one of his critical essays that transubstantiation is the key to his writing. Whatever genius he has as a writer must exhibit itself in the artistic texts themselves, and indeed transubstantiation is not just mentioned but has a strong mode of ingression in most of Kazantzakis's works, novels as well as travel books and plays. The easiest passages to identity are those where Kazantzakis explicitly uses communion metaphors or describes the distribution of communion.

At several points in *The Fratricides* Kazantzakis has Fr. Yanaros administering communion to those dying in the Greek civil war.[8] The communion itself (according to Fr. Yanaros' theology, at least) is bread transubstantiated into the body of Christ, but the act of receiving the host is part of the soon to be realized change from murderous fratricide to penitance, from the frantic activity of war to rest, from living bodily substance to death, from despair to hope and salvation, from strife to peace. Not all soldiers accept these transubstantiations, however, as is symbolized in the case of the soldier who vomited up the body and blood of Christ when delivered communion by Fr. Yanaros. This event should come as no surprise, given Kazantzakis's love/hate relationship with Christianity.

In order to put the value of transubstantiation in sharp relief, it is helpful, in Kazantzakis's Weltanschauung,[9] to fast before communion so that one can be fully cognizant of the process of transubstantiation as it occurs. For hungry people it is not even necessary that the bread and wine be consecrated in order to appreciate the holiness of eating, that is, to appreciate the process whereby food gives the soul strength to grow wings.[10] Wine in particular has the ability to rise like the sun and convince one that he is part of God, or as Jesus tells Nathanial, that he can "become mine." In Kazantzakis's description of the Last Supper in *The Last Temptation of Christ*, the disciples taste wine that seems thick and salty, like blood, and that makes their minds reel; they also taste bread that descends into their bowels like a burning coal, a coal that devours their entrails.[11] Even the crusty Captain Mihalis in *Freedom or Death* could not resist receiving communion (*metalave*) on Thursday of Passion Week due to its transubstantiating power, to its ability to transform body into cloudlike paradise.[12]

The thesis of this chapter of the book, however, is that transubstantiation is not a mere theme among other themes in Kazantzakis's writing, but a dominant theme around which cluster the notes of many subordinate themes that run counterpoint to it; or better, that transubstantiation establishes a family resemblance among the major issues related in Kazantzakis's universe. Consider how he extends communion metaphors to illustrate topics as diverse as sex and animal maturation. Kazantzakis's first wife, Galatea, was replaced by a new seductress, the Holy Chalice of spirituality. At one point Kazantzakis desired the sanctuary of his wife's flesh and the communion of her body, but this was not the "Great Holy Communion" he later desired, although this, too, as we will see, involved a Buddhist emptiness.[13] There is no incompatibility, in Kazantzakis's view, between transubstantiation and Buddhist "abyss" in that wine being changed into blood, and blood in a living organism being changed into something radically different in a corpse, are analogous; and both of these are analogous to a flame changing the reality of a burnt substance (that is, it is transubstantiated into air).[14]

It should now be obvious that Kazantzakis is willing to take transubstantiation outside the orbit of Christianity. Even in *The Odyssey*, which deals with a pagan hero, he has Orpheus proclaim that:

> I've often pondered on the world, but my mind quakes!
> The earth's so wide no man's embrace can hold her all,
> but if we sip red water or eat a strip of meat,
> earth nestles on our bosoms like a trembling maid.
> If there's a God in truth, he's made of meat and wine!
>
> . . . In Orpheus' loins the wine grew strong and turned to
> blood.[15]

In fact, although the concept of transubstantiation originated in Christianity, it may not be able to allow within its borders a full understanding of the earthiness from which transubstantiation arises. An ancient archon complains in *The Odyssey* about those who talk "too much of God and pass him through too fine / a sieve until there's nothing left of him to eat."[16]

Eating

The two sorts of transubstantiation discussed above (bread and wine transubstantiated into the body and blood of communion, and communion transubstantiated into penitance, rest, salvation, peace, paradise, God, empti-ness) are often collapsed into one. Eating *any* food makes transubstantiation possible, as we will see in detail later. In one of Kazantzakis's most imaginative passages, he has Zorba say to his boss:

> Tell me what you do with the food you eat, and I'll tell you who you are. Some turn their food into fat and manure, some into work and good humor, and others, I'm told, into God. So there must be three sorts of men. I'm not one of the worst, boss, nor yet one of the best. I'm somewhere between the two. What I eat I turn into work and good humor. That's not too bad, after all! . . . As for you, boss, . . . I think you do your level best to turn what you eat into God, but you can't quite manage it, and that torments you.[17]

The boss learns from Zorba that eating is a spiritual function (*psihiki*) and that bread and wine are the raw materials from which mind is made. Each person has an element of the divine whirlwind that allows the transub-stantiation of bread and water into thought and action. The boss is tormented because he wants to be transubstantiated into Buddha itself.[18] Although it is true for Kazantzakis that it is only (*horis*) with bread, wine, and meat that one can create God, these are the necessary but not sufficient conditions for spiritual perfection.[19]

As before, not all of our food is turned into dung. Some of it, as Zorba noticed at Easter, is resurrected into good humor, singing, and dancing.[20] The paschal lamb and Easter cakes can and should be transubstantiated into love songs.[21] At other times of the year, however, eating lamb with wine tran-substantiates one into a lion; not a vicious beast, but a noble lion symbolic of the fact that the beastly and the human both contribute to the everlasting whole of things.[22]

Those close to Kazantzakis always said that he was not, like Zorba, a voracious eater. Yet he was quick to see the spiritual significance in the little food he did in fact eat. A meal takes on "great mystical value" when one notices that, along with the rabbi who once made this point to Kazantzakis, "when a virtuous man is eating he liberates the God who is in the food!"[23] Andrew, for example, in *The Last Temptation of Christ* liberates Dionysian *élan* when he transubstantiates (*metousione*) bread into love and laughter.[24] By way of con-trast, Kazantzakis describes a scene in England that

> made me feel indescribably bitter and certain that we have reached the end. One poverty-striken young girl, wasted away from hunger, had pressed her little face against the well-stocked window of a butcher shop. Desire shown in her

eyes as she stared greedily at the meat. Through some mystic
transubstantiation, all this horrid meat might become yellow
hair, fluffy curls on the nape of the neck, red lips. But where
could this half-starved little girl find the money to undertake
the divine transubstantiation? And so the little girl withered
and the meat rotted, and the union never took place.[25]

Evolution as Transubstantiation

The naturalized transubstantiation that is found in eating (which will be
discussed in detail in chapter 3) actually occurs throughout the physical world,
for Kazantzakis. Human transformation of mundane existence into a glorious
reign, into God, follows from the caterpillar who becomes a butterfly, from the
fish who leaps into the air, from the silkworm who turns dust into silk.[26] The
silkworm in particular exhibits a mute agony when the mulberry leaves it has
eaten are finally transubstantiated inside it and turned into silk; mystic wisdom
knits precious substance (*ousia*) into its golden coffin.[27]

Kazantzakis's asceticism is not life-negating, nor does it indicate ashamed-
ness of animality, but rather it recalls the ancient, pre-Christian meaning of
ascēsis as healthy bodily training as if for an athletic event. The adventures of
the human soul and those of a bat are similar. Both are mythically descended
from a mouse, in Kazantzakis's view, a mouse that ate Christ's body and
developed wings:

> I know of no animal more disgusting than the mouse, no
> bird more disgusting than the bat, no edifice of flesh, hair,
> and bones more disgusting than the human body. But think
> how all this manure is transubstantiated (*metousionetai*) and
> deified (*theonetai*) when God is embedded in it—the seed
> which develops into wings.[28]

The creatures that bewitched or mystified Kazantzakis (the caterpillar-
butterfly, the "flying" fish, and the silkworm[29]) are all heliotropes. The world, in
general, crawls:

> like a worm to sun,
> and thus the mind, in time, bursts like a withered husk
> from which there spring, time after time, new finer thoughts.[30]

Kazantzakis himself, like a silkworm, nodded his head left and right as his
precious essence was produced in his vitals and then was solidified in mid-air.[31]
Or better, Buddha, "that huge silkworm," has "nibbled the whole mulberry tree

of the world,"[32] which indicates that the ultimate goal of transubstantiation would seem to be an Oriental repose, but that this goal (if it is Kazantzakis's goal, which is doubtful) can only be achieved after the effort not just of a single lifetime, but of a whole cosmic epoch.

The difficulty of Kazantzakian ascent is indicated through myth, specifically a Cretan myth through which Kazantzakis could "transubstantiate his own experiences into art."[33] (Kazantzakis treats the subject of transubstantiation in his art, but the artistic process itself is an instance of transubstantiation.) He has Theseus tell King Minos in the play "Kouros" that by transforming the bull into a Minotaur he has brought harmony from chaos, and all of this is a preparation for the transition from soul to air. Likewise, Minos's daughter Ariadne uses her seductive powers to transform the terror of the abyss into love.[34] The inspiration for this myth comes from the bullfights painted on the walls at Knossos:

> I gazed at the bullfights painted on the walls. . . . Thus the Cretans transubstantiated horror (*metousiosan ti friki*), turning it into an exalted game in which man's virtue, in direct contact with mindless omnipotence, received stimulation and conquered—conquered without annihilating the bull, because it considered him not an enemy but a fellow worker.[35]

It should not surprise us that Kazantzakis was fascinated by the same sort of transubstantiated game when he witnessed a Spanish bullfight, "this primitive Holy Communion, with real flesh and real blood . . . this bloody pantomime between God and man . . . this violent contact with God."[36] Blood in particular arouses "primeval mysterious intoxication . . . overpowering giddiness; an animal pleasure that is eternal and human."

My purpose here, however, is to indicate that transubstantiation, for Kazantzakis, is a process found not only in communion, eating, or in the striving of animals, but throughout the whole of evolutionary process. Myros in *Symposium* is correct that eating a goat creates blood and human flesh, and hence thought and hope (that is, a transubstantiated holy communion full of mystery and awe).[37] But further "down" the evolutionary scale we can also see how trees, for Kazantzakis, transubstantiate mud into flowers:

> All the soil was stirring, full of living things and working, and I could feel the tree upon which I leaned raising sap to its peak, struggling to transubstantiate the mud, stone, water, air and sun and make them into blossoms. I was watching matter, the great harlot, with the broad haunches, falling at feet of Christ, like Mary Magdalene, weepingly being transubstantiated.[38]

The cyclicism of nature is illustrated well when we consider that God as transcendent can reverse the process of transubstantiation by becoming imma-nent through "deaf lightning" and "erotic rain," which then merge with Demeter on the plowed field, creating the mud transubstantiated by the afore-mentioned tree on the ascent back to God as transcendent.[39] Trees play their parts well in the cosmic drama because they unconsciously transubstantiate mud; human beings, however, may or may not transform fallen earth into paradise.[40] The possession of freedom makes human beings either superior or inferior to subhuman creatures. They are superior if they, like Odysseus, dig with bare nails into the earth to free God.[41] In any event, with or without human beings "stones, water, fire, and earth shall be transformed to spirit / . . . heavy soul, freed of its flesh / shall like a a flame serene ascend and fade in sun."[42]

Human beings find their glory in hastening the process of transub-stantiation by freeing matter from slavery; they commit mortal sin if they myopically concentrate on the petty details of their lives.[43] Indeed, the essence of God, for Kazantzakis, is the struggle for freedom itself.[44]

History as Transubstantiation

Kimon Friar is correct in implying that in addition to Kazantzakis's obvious exposure to the Greek Orthodox religion and to Catholicism—he was educated by Franciscans—the other main sources for his interest in transub-stantiation were Bergson and, surprisingly, Nietzsche. As we have seen, Bergson enabled Kazantzakis to disburden himself from agonies that tormented him early in life regarding God; from him Kazantzakis learned that God is the "agonized transmutation of matter into spirit." And from Nietzsche he learned to "transubstantiate unhappiness, sorrow, and uncertainty into pride."[45] That is, despite the fact that the process of transubstantiation is spread across the cosmos, it is primarily and quintessentially a human process, analyzed by Kazantzakis under the influence of these two sources.

The locus for this process is history. Regarding the first human beings, Kazantzakis says:

> Now, for the first time since the world was made, man has
> been enabled to enter God's workshop and labor with Him.
> The more flesh he transubstantiates (*metousionei*) into love,
> valor, and freedom, the more truly he becomes Son of God.
> . . . This ancestor is the bulky, unwrought beast given me to
> transubstantiate into man—and to raise even higher than
> man if I can manage in the time allotted me. What a fearful
> ascent from monkey to man, from man to God![46]

Civilization is not a supernatural flower suspended in mid-air, but is like a tree rooted in the earth that, once again, consumes mud so as to produce its flower.[47] And ancient civilizations are like youthful individuals (ontogeny recapitulates phylogeny). The road to fulfillment, for Kazantzakis, is never to deny one's youth, that is, never to give up the battle to transubstantiate adolescent flowering into a fruit-laden tree.[48]

Quite understandably, the most specific locus for Kazantzakis's historical drama is Greece, or better, the modern "Greek problem," which surfaced most explicitly during the civil war: "And therefore, every Greek, in order to justify his own existence, is duty bound to struggle to transubstantiate this blood and these tears into spirit."[49] The misfortunes of civil war and forced migration can be transubstantiated into either "the destruction of this Hellenism or to ascension, a new blooming within the blood and tears of a cry. Both are good. To break comfortable habits, to renounce happiness, is indispensible; it is a pre-requisite, I would say, for all ascension."[50] The transubstantiation of the struggle for justice into faith is necessitated, according to Kazantzakis, by "the invincible rhythm of human history," although the fervant desire to prevent human suffering can hasten the process.[51]

The differences between "primitive" transubstantiation (as when Odysseus witnesses an atavistic communion where raw flesh and blood bring merger with God[52]) and modern varieties of transubstantiation (as in the cinema—which, for Kazantzakis, was the most modern expression of "the spirit"—where abstract conceptions are transformed into simple, clear images[53]) are not absolute differences. Primitive intuition and advanced intellect, as Bergson also argued, have a common ancestry:

> They are not successive degrees of evolution . . . they are
> simply directions which the same fermentation took.
> Difference of quality and not of quantity exists between
> instinct and intellect. Instinct knows things, intellect the
> relationship between things. Both are cognitive faculties. . . .
> Intuition has the advantage of entering into the very essence
> of life, of feeling its movement, its creation. But it has one
> great disadvantage: it cannot express itself.[54]

The commonality between instinct and intellect is often hidden from us because of the turtle-like pace whereby there is "transubstantiation of the thickest mud into the lightest song." This measured pace is "the invincible charm of China,"[55] in contrast to the frightening power of the will in Mussolini, which instantly "transubstantiates reality."[56]

Procreation provides the transubstantiating process continuity from one century to the next, or, as Kazantzakis puts it, a man on his wedding night has God in his guts.[57] Or again, "God's roots might eat and sprout in great-great-grandsons."[58] But the growth of historical institutions can, at any particular moment, be either progressing or regressing. Like Li-Te in *The Rock Garden*, history is sometimes like a cunning leopard who delights in human flesh, at every moment transforming hunger into smiles.[59] Kazantzakis's point, however (which forms the basis of his theodicy), is that apparent regress often is for the purpose of progress, as in Odysseus's abduction of Helen and her subsequent intercourse with the barbarians:

> Helen is the Beauty of the Achaeans which creates the Greek civilization by mingling with the Dorian barbarian. As soon as Odysseus sees that this purpose is fulfilled—i.e., when he saw Helen in the barbarian's embrace—he goes away, leaving Helen to accomplish her mission: to breed, to transubstantiate within her womb the barbarian seed, and to bear a son.[60]

These moments of apparent historical regress are keenly noticed by Kazantzakis largely because of his own psychological disposition:

> There is much darkness in me, much of my father. All my life I have fought desperately to transubstantiate (*metousioso*) this darkness and turn it into light, one little drop of light. It has been a harsh struggle without pity or respite. . . . Virtue, for me, is not the fruit of my nature, it is the fruit of my struggles. God did not give it to me, I have had to labor in order to conquer it by the sword. For me, virtue's flower is a pile of transubstantiated (*metousiomene*) dung.[61]

The Transubstantiation of Personal Life

We have seen that for Kazantzakis transubstantiation works its way through evolutionary process, particularly through the process of human history. But none of us as finite individuals lives temporally across a vast cosmic epoch, nor do we as fragmentary individuals live spatially across the expanse of the universe. If transubstantiation is to really have an impact on us it must be finite and fragmentary individuals who *feel* transubstantiation at work:

> I know that each person transubstantiates his temporal life in his own particular way; however, it is good to confess our struggle, to expose the method of our own soul, and to take aim at our new hope.[62]

It should not surprise us that Kazantzakis is a master at portraying individual struggle. Only at the end of *Saint Francis* does Francis's face become transformed into the radiant calmness of beatitude.[63] Throughout most of his life Francis was tempted by "Lucifer," who symbolizes the subtle evils of this world that are only gradually transubstantiated from terrible darkness into light.[64] Prayer, for Francis (which is really transubstantiated food[65]), is the key tool in the transubstantiation of Lucifer into an archangel.

Some, like Mary Magdalene, have their lives weepingly transubstantiated into an inarticulate dignity,[66] others must transform internal chaos into cosmos through articulate language:

> When a thing is said in a perfect and vivid way, I reflected,
> it can fool even the most alert mind, so that a beautiful
> image becomes metamorphosed into an intellectual or moral
> certainty. There is a point where the form, if it is perfect,
> can create the essence.[67]

Others, unfortunately (the technocrats, the bourgeoisie), do very little to transubstantiate matter into spirit; these are the true nihilists, even if their positivist slogans suggest otherwise.[68]

It must be admitted that turning illness into spirit is difficult, but some such sublimated alchemy, whereby love transubstantiates this ephemeral life into miracle, is necessary in order to achieve happiness:[69]

> My friends believe me happy, because they do not know the
> struggles preliminary to every victory; because they do not
> know that my happiness is the supreme flowering of my own
> despair and my scorn for all things "terrestrial." I am not a
> Romantic in revolt, nor a mystic scorning life, nor an
> insolent belligerent against substance. I love life, the earth,
> man, animal, ephemeral things. I know their value very well,
> and yet their limits, too.[70]

Kazantzakis calls on us to engage in a Nietzschean laughter as we sprout wings from muddy entrails, a process that is all the more difficult if one is not, like Odysseus, born into the purple but rooted in grinding poverty.[71] For the destitute, quest for spiritual perfection is often like a butterfly that tried to rise but

> its great downy wings,
> prismatic and mud-splattered, fluttered and fell to earth,
> and a nude worm emerged and slowly sank in mud.[72]

But even the most lucky human beings die. Or, as Kentaur instructs Odysseus:

return

from whence you came, that holy darkness filled with light,
and build your mansions with blood, water, sweat, and tears.[73]

God

In a way, everything said in this chapter deals with God as transubstantiating process, but a concluding section dealing explicitly with God will make clearer why I have claimed in this chapter that transubstantiation is at the heart of Kazantzakis's writing. God is the alpha of Kazantzakis's universe because, as far as we can tell, the material world has always been involved in the process whereby the divine breath has allowed earth to blossom into spirit.[74] Within Christianity, this eternal process of transubstantiation is focused on Christ:

> There is no other way to reach God but this. Following Christ's bloody tracks, we must fight to transubstantiate the man inside us into spirit, so that we may merge with God.[75]

Christ is central because:

> He conquered every temptation, continually transubstantiated (metousione) flesh into spirit, and ascended. Every obstacle in His journey became an occasion for further triumph.[76]

Christianity is only one vehicle among others, however, in the attempt to understand God. In fact, Kazantzakis's favorite definition of God is remarkably ecumenical:

> Of all the definitions of God, the one I like best is this: Dieu est un coeur debout à son heure! (God is a heart that is upright at the given hour!)[77]

From this quotation, however, it would be misleading to suggest that Kazantzakis's God is merely humanity itself, but spoken of in a loud voice:

> My deepest joy is to see how the mysterious force seizes hold of man and shakes him like a lover, an epileptic, or a creator. Because, as you know, what interests me is not man himself, but the being that I so imperfectly designate as "God."[78]

Although Helen Kazantzakis refers to herself and Nikos as "atheists"[79] (which may mean only that their views on God were not conventional, as when Socrates was accused of atheism), Nikos Kazantzakis is quite clear that

> God is with us, because we are with Him. Work, laughter, evening talks in front of the sea, the sky above, the earth at our feet. The eternal moment will assume its genuine essence—eternity. . . . The major and almost the only theme of all my work is the struggle of man with "God": the unyielding, inextinguishable struggle of the naked worm called "man" against the terrifying power and darkness of the forces within him and around him.[80]

In her introduction to Kazantzakis's letters to Galatea, Katerina Anghelaki Rooke claims that Kazantzakis's transubstantiation of matter into spirit is not a movement from man to God but "signifies man's victory over a non-God."[81] But Kazantzakis emphasizes that behind human appearances there is a struggling essence,[82] that, although often apprehended as a mirage when human beings are under the sun-heat of life's pressures,[83] can also be understood truly by those who locate not this or that creation but the creative process itself. Writers have a privileged access to divine creativity because God creates, according to biblical myth, by *saying* the correct word.[84] "We're each part of God,"[85] Odysseus tells Kentaur, which is quite different from claiming that God is part of us. It is possible for us to merge with God[86] because we are already fragments of the divine process, of the *universe* conceived as a cosmos rather than as a random concatenation of parts.

Conclusion

From what I have said above regarding God in Kazantzakis, it should be obvious that I oppose those who see him, without qualification, as a *humanist* or as a nihilist. It is a questionable interpretation of Kazantzakis to see the abyss (one of his favorite topics) as the terminus of his philosophy.

For example, in *Spiritual Exercises* he makes it abundantly clear that the abyss should be opened and then transubstantiated into an ascending partner, a constant companion of the person interested in spiritual perfection.[87] There is a family resemblance among ordering the chaos of our lives, cleansing the abyss (*katharisoume tin aviso*), and transmuting darkness into light. By engaging in these processes of transubstantiation[88] we save, at the very least, the issue of God if not God itself in the sense that, and to the extent that, the consequent or dependent pole of the divine nature (to be explained later) is in need of salvation.[89]

This crusading transubstantiation can take myriad forms, not least of which for intellectuals is the fight in the skull, whereby old ideas are killed and new ones are born.[90] Regarding transubstantiation itself, however, Kazantzakis has given phoenixlike novelty to an old idea that has for some time been comatose.

EATING AND

SPIRITUAL

EXERCISES

In this and the following chapter I would like to amplify the thesis defended in chapter 2 that transubstantiation is the key to Kazantzakis's writing and to his thoughts on God. In the previous chapter I initiated a consideration of eating in this regard, and in the present chapter I would like to concentrate on the particular sort of transubstantiation found in eating. Those who are familiar with Kazantzakis's writings are also familiar with his frequent descriptions of people eating, and eating for a spiritual purpose.

The philosopher Paul Weiss once complained in a book titled *Philosophy of Sport* that philosophers (and, presumably, theologians) had mostly preoccupied themselves with a narrowly defined set of theoretical questions, ignoring or denigrating everyday affairs like work, play, or eating. This chapter is an attempt to help fill that gap. I am calling needed attention to two writers who have dealt with the topic in a serious way before: Kazantzakis and St. Ignatius of Loyola from the sixteenth century.

My thesis is that the ascetical treatment of eating by Ignatius in his *Spiritual Exercises* can, in many ways, be purified by the more insightful treatment of eating given by Kazantzakis in his own *Spiritual Exercises* and other writings. In the course of the chapter I at least hope to remove the grin from the reader who initially suspects that the present topic is part of the dessert of one's spiritual meal; I am suggesting (despite the fact that I am a vegetarian) that the issue at hand is a meaty one indeed.

Ignatius's View

There are two important places in *Spiritual Exercises* where Ignatius treats the matter of eating. The first is at the end of the first week when he discusses penance. He suggests that penance is of two kinds: interior and exterior. The former consists in sorrow for one's sins, while the latter is the fruit of the former found in punishment inflicted on oneself because of one's sorrow. There are, in turn, three forms of exterior penance: denial of sleep, chastising the flesh (for example, with cords), and denial of food.

At the outset we should be clear about what sort of denial Ignatius is talking about. Denying ourselves what is superfluous is temperance (*temperancia*), not penance.[1] Penance (*penitencia*) occurs when we deny ourselves what is proper for us to have. But Ignatius makes it clear that penance should also be engaged with moderation, since there are two extremes that should be avoided. To eliminate confusion, I will call temperance in penance "temperance-p" to distinguish it from mere temperance. One extreme to be avoided by the exercitant is the failure to do penance at all (that is, to revert to mere temperance). We *often* fail to do penance because of sensual pleasure or because of a false conviction that human nature cannot bear penance without illness. This may be a kind of self-deception or subterfuge we enact on ourselves when suggesting phrases like "It is medieval," "I am not strong enough," or "It's not for me."[2]

However, *sometimes* we may do too much penance, which also upsets temperance-p. We do this by thinking that our body can bear it. For example, when chastising the flesh we may go so far as to enact "penetration to the bone," doing serious harm to our health. Perhaps Ignatius also had in mind here fasting to the point of malnutrition. This seems to ruin the purpose of penance in that prayer begins to suffer; there is a difference between denying ourselves what is proper for us to have and denying ourselves what is *necessary* for health.[3]

Because doing too much penance only occurs sometimes (*algunas veces*), whereas doing too little penance occurs often (*muchas veces*), it is clear that not doing enough penance is the greater danger to temperance-p. Temperance-p is at least useful, and perhaps necessary, during the exercises because of the three effects it brings: satisfaction for past sins, the taming of sensuality by reason, and the acquiring of grace.[4]

The second place where Ignatius deals with eating is of more concern. At the end of the third week he gives his "Rules to be Observed in the Future in the Matter of Food" (*reglas para ordenarse en el comer para adelante*), where his notion of temperance-p is assumed at the outset. He suggests that there is less need to abstain from bread, for it is not the kind of food that we have an uncontrolled appetite for. Abstinence is more appropriate with regard to drink, taking care to avoid harm to the body and thereby maintaining temperance-p.

But greater and more complete abstinence must be practiced with regard to foods (*manjares*) other than bread,[5] because here temptation is likely to be more insistent and the appetite inclined to be excessive. In order to avoid overindulgence, abstinence may be observed in two ways: eating coarse foods (that is, relying on staples[6]) or eating less if the foods are delicate or rich.

The more one abstains in the quantity of food the better, because one will be able to arrive at the mean of penance (that is, temperance-p) all the sooner. By disposing oneself toward temperance-p one will more frequently feel interior directions, consolations, and divine inspirations that will show one what temperance-p is. This is not so much circular reasoning (although it may be just that) but a process that reinforces itself through self-regulation and divine guidance.

When one eats one should pay less attention to the food or one's sustenance and more attention to Christ by imagining him at the table (the Last Supper?) with his apostles. Or one may want to imagine a scene from the lives of the saints so that one will not be distracted by the food. Above all, one should not be entirely occupied with the food itself; nor should one eat hurriedly, not out of fear of an upset stomach, but rather to avoid the suggestion that one is not master of oneself.

To avoid excess, it is useful to plan our next meal just after we have eaten, this to avoid the temptation of the enemy (that is, Satan) by eating less when we are tempted to eat more. In fact, we must not only resist the enemy, but act against him (*hacer contra*), or even wage war upon him.[7] The value of the rules relating to eating have an application wider than merely to eating; they are imbedded in the twofold trend of Ignatius's *Spiritual Exercises*: the removal of anything that is inordinate and the effort to shape one's life after that of Christ.[8]

A serious problem is apparent at this point. Ignatius has given several reasons why we should not overeat, but he only gives one reason why we should not undereat; that is, it will prevent us from continuing the spiritual exercises. This makes eating merely a means to an end, albeit an admirable end. Kazantzakis, by way of contrast, provides us with some intrinsic worth to eating itself; he gives us a positive conception of food that is propaedeutic to the spiritual life; he gives us something that we can get our teeth into! In order to see how he accomplishes this, I will first have to say something about his notion of the transitional age.[9]

The Transitional Age

The genesis of Kazantzakis's thought lies in his theory of history, but his genius lies in his extension of this theory to an anthropological level. His theory of history, heavily reliant on Bergson, goes something like this: the twentieth century is a transitional age. We have lost the primitive, spontaneous, pristine appreciation of the beauty of the world. We are far too sophisticated for this attitude, which is preserved by more atavistic peoples. But we have also lost the spontaneous, unquestioned faith in the God of the Judeo-Christian tradition, such as that found in Ignatius. In short, we cannot be pagans because Christianity has civilized us; and we cannot be Christians *in the traditional sense*, primarily because of the inability of traditional religious theories to deal adequately with the problems of theodicy and reconciling the existence of God with the existence of human freedom. (Hence Kazantzakis should in no sense be seen as a premodern theist.) The influence of Oswald Spengler's thought on Kazantzakis reinforced his distrust of the authenticity of modern Western civilization. These factors led Kazantzakis to see modern human beings as the melancholy victims of this transitional age, who apparently can only assuage their less than sanguine lots with the heroic pessimism of contemporary Sisyphuses.

Yet Kazantzakis should not be seen as another absurdist existentialist, like so many other European writers of his generation. Kazantzakis is able to bridge the gap between his theory of history and his anthropological theory through this notion of a transitional age. This jump to Kazantzakis's anthropology is found primarily in his own *Spiritual Exercises*, whose title and spiritual theme are obvious references to Ignatius's work. The key insight in this work is that we come from a dark abyss and we end in one as well; life is a luminous interval between these two black voids. Remembering Kazantzakis's theory of history, one can say that life is a transition from one void to another. Bergson's *élan vital* enabled Kazantzakis to avoid pessimism here. This pre-existent life force is a pure energy that wills to become alive. Although it must cooperate with matter in this quest for life, it ultimately tries to separate itself from matter.

In Kazantzakian terms, the void at the "beginning" of a human being is inert, unconscious matter, which is similar to the surd called Necessity or Fate by Kazantzakis's ancestors in ancient Greece; the void at the "end" of a human being is death. Life itself is an evolutionary spiritualization by means of transubstantiation. By "transubstantiation" Kazantzakis means the ability to transform matter into spirit. This need not be, as we have seen, any magical hat-trick, but can be seen in the light of a post-Darwinian view of the world. The evolutionary process has passed from inorganic matter to the capabilities of plants; from plants to the instinctual level of animals; from animals to the intelligence of human beings. Persons, who nonetheless retain their materiality, can rise to self-consciousness and freedom of self-determination. As Kazantzakis put it in *The Rock Garden*, life is a process of rising from rocks to reflection. He adopts this position from Bergson, as his early treatise titled "H. Bergson" indicates:

> According to Bergson, life is an unceasing creation, a leap
> upwards, a vital outburst, an *élan vital*. . . . All the history of

life up to man is a gigantic endeavor of the vital impulse to elevate matter, to create a being which would be free of the inflexible mechanism of inertia. . . . Two streams, that of life and that of matter, are in motion, though in opposite directions: one toward integration and the other toward disintegration. Bergson thinks of the *élan vital* as a seething stream which in its ebullition distills into falling drops. It is these drops which constitute matter.[10]

Eating, for Kazantzakis, is one of the most important ways we can elevate or transubstantiate matter into spirit.

Kazantzakis's notion of transubstantiation refers to a religious process. His works constantly ask the question, "Why are we here?" His response, simply put, is "To save God." In fact, the full title of Kazantzakis's work, *The Saviors of God: Spiritual Exercises*, distinguishes his work from that of St. Ignatius. For Kazantzakis's process theism, God (in addition to being transcendent) is the unceasing creativity of life itself freeing itself from matter. God is never ready-made or mechanical.

Obviously one should not get the impression that Kazantzakis was opposed to asceticism. He was by temperament an ascetic himself,[11] and championed the ascetic's life in many of his works, including *Spiritual Exercises*. However, his asceticism does not exclude the Dionysian side to life, as will be seen. His position can best be understood, I think, at three levels in three different novels: *Saint Francis*, *Zorba the Greek*, and *The Last Temptation of Christ*.[12]

Francis and Eating

The first of these works can be seen as a Kazantzakian panegyric to asceticism, especially to penance as regards eating. For St. Francis, there is a "heaven" within us discovered through hunger, and every person, even the most atheistic, has God deep down in the heart wrapped in layers of flesh and fat.[13] The privilege of poverty enables one to replace food and drink with hunger and thirst, thereby releasing this inner God.[14] In fact, Kazantzakis suggests that St. Francis was "drunk" with God, as is indicated in his three imaginary prayers:[15]

> A. "Lord, bend me, or else I shall rot"
> B. "Lord, do not bend me too much, for I shall break"
> C. "Lord, bend me too much."[16]

In Ignatian terms, the first prayer is that of the temperate person, the second that of the person who lacks temperance, and the third that of the extreme ascetic who violates temperance-p. In the hands of Kazantzakis, if not in reality,

St. Francis was just such an extreme ascetic who was enamoured of the "angelic loaf," one slice of which satisfied hunger for eternity. Or, from another angle, the love of friends nourished St. Francis more than bread and milk.[17]

The person who lacks temperance is a glutton, for Kazantzakis. This person is guilty of the sin of immobility by weighing down prayer with a full belly; the glutton's food turns to lead and prevents him from ascending to heaven. As in St. Ignatius, hunger is seen as the Tempter, for Satan is often in the water we drink *and* the bread we eat (note that not even St. Ignatius would go this far).[18]

But the real value of Kazantzakis's analysis of eating comes when he suggests what the worth of eating is, even in the midst of the ascetic's life. Brother Leo, St. Francis's companion who is the narrator of the novel, constantly reminds St. Francis that those who are hungry for reasons of destitution, rather than freely chosen asceticism, dream of bread, not of God. Or, if they do dream of God, it is of a God who gives bread.[19]

There is a positive worth to eating in that bread, wine, and onions "all turn to soul."[20] This important notion can be taken in three senses

1. St. Francis needs a healthy body if he wants to continue to pray, for dead persons cannot pray, at least as human beings.[21] Even St. Ignatius gives evidence of realizing this much. But Kazantzakis goes further.

2. Food is the very material out of which prayer is made. Speaking in Kazantzakian terms, human beings are highly evolved forms of transubstantiated matter who continually need infusions of matter so that this spiritualizing transubstantiation can continue. Thus, eating is not just a means to the end of prayer; it has an intrinsic ontological worth as one of the constituents of prayer. When the ascetic eats, and eat he or she must, the ascetic might profit from not being distracted from food, as St. Ignatius suggests, but rather revel in the spiritual worth of eating. The implication is that religion is just as much a Dionysian affair as an austere Apollonian one.[22]

3. Finally, food has an aesthetic worth, and since God can just as well be seen as the source of Beauty (albeit sublime beauty rather than pretty beauty, in Kazantzakis's case) as well as of Goodness, we should appreciate the culinary arts as well as those of the painter or writer.[23] It should be remembered that even St. Ignatius suggested that we might want to eat fine foods, provided we ate lesser quantities of them. Unfortunately, he shows no awareness of the positive theological function these fine foods can serve.

However, these insights into the worth of eating are only implied in this work, whose emphasis remains severely ascetic. The following exchange between Brother Leo and St. Francis epitomizes the work:

"The birds must go hungry in wintertime," I said. "That's why they don't sing. Could it be that men are just the same, Brother Francis? Could it be that we have to eat in order to have food to transform into prayer and song?" Francis smiled. "Your mind is constantly on food, Brother Leo. Everything you say is correct for those who do not believe in God. But for those who do, the opposite is the case: prayer, for them, is transformed into food, and their stomachs are filled."[24]

Zorba and Eating

A second level of analysis is found in *Zorba the Greek*. Once again, there are two major characters, but their emphasis is reversed. Whereas in *Saint Francis* the title character dominates Brother Leo, in *Zorba the Greek* the title character dominates his ascetic boss, whose name we never learn. Kazantzakis's glorification of the passionate "Zorbatic verve" is not an encomium to lust or wanton appetite. Gluttony is still denigrated, as in the case of Uncle Anagnosti, whose "epicurean" delight in pig-testicles makes him no better than the animal he eats.[25] Zorba takes the positive insights regarding food and makes their power felt, a feat that Brother Leo could not accomplish.

Zorba is always hungrily reminding his boss that the body is a beast of burden that cannot be stranded in the road due to a lack of food.[26] The boss, who initially exhibits an Ignatian indifference toward food, eventually comes around to Zorba's point of view while remaining an ascetic. He realizes that eating is a spiritual function and that meat, bread, and wine are the raw materials from which the mind is made.[27] As Zorba puts it in a passage that was looked at in chapter 2, but which is worth looking at again:

> Tell me what you do with the food you eat, and I'll tell you who you are. Some turn their food into fat and manure, some into work and good humor, and others, I'm told, into God. So there must be three sorts of men. I'm not one of the worst, boss, nor yet one of the best. I'm somewhere between the two. What I eat I turn into work and good humor. . . . As for you, boss . . . I think you do your level best to turn what you eat into God. But you can't quite manage it, and that torments you.[28]

In fact, when the boss's venture collapses, Zorba invites him to *eat* and to dance, each a way of transubstantiating flesh into spirit. The boss is tormented because he is still torn in two directions—flesh and spirit—and he assumes that the two are opposed. For Kazantzakis, however, they are partners on a continuum, as we will see later in this book.

By example Zorba shows the Kazantzakian way. At one point Zorba bravely saves the lives of his friends in a mine, while risking his own life. His *agapē* is boundless. When he finally appears at the mouth of the cave he shouts, "I'm hungry." Although Zorba often overstates his case (as he is not the ascetic that his Apollonian boss is[29]), he, too, realizes that human beings have an imperishable force that transforms matter into spirit, and that this force is divine.[30]

The fundamental needs of human beings, like food, are never exhausted in Zorba's robust and eager body.[31] Yet when his brutish human element is sublimated into an abstract idea he becomes a rarefied, saintly being. For Zorba, not all of our food turns to dung; on Easter he proclaims that some of it is resurrected into life, good humor, dancing, and even prayer.[32]

The Miracle of Food

I previously promised a third level of analysis taken from Kazantzakis's novel, *The Last Temptation of Christ*. It is here, I suggest, that the most subtle treatment of the problem is found. St. Francis, Brother Leo, Zorba, and the boss are all divided inside themselves. To greater or lesser degrees (much lesser in the case of Zorba) all feel the pangs of the split between body and soul, and their desire for food sharply exhibits this split. Wholeness is most fully achieved in the figure of Jesus. At times in his life (for example, in the desert) he shows himself to be an ascetic who is more filled with hunger and thirst for justice than hunger for loaves and fishes. Yet Jesus had his Dionysian moments as well. He lacks the sternness of Judas, whom Kazantzakis sees as a puritanical zealot who neither drinks wine nor eats food for pleasure.[33] Jesus, however, can enjoy the conviviality of his friends (for example, at Cana) without compromising his empyrean standards. In his character a simple meal is merged with the profundity of God:

> The son of Mary felt calmed. He sat down at the root of the ancient olive tree and began to eat. How tasty this bread was, how refreshing the water, how sweet the two olives which the old lady had given him to accompany his bread. They had slender pits and were as fat and fleshy as apples! He chewed tranquilly and ate, feeling that his body and soul had joined and become one now, that they were receiving the bread, olives, and water with one mouth, rejoicing, the both of them, and being nourished.[34]

I cannot help noticing at this point what should be obvious, but is often obfuscated by a too etherealized theology: the transubstantiation that occurs at the Last Supper and in the Eucharist is a matter of eating and drinking. It may be more than a meal, but it is a meal. Speaking derivatively of transubstantiation in Kazantzakian terms, we can say along with Zorba's boss, "Food has worked its wondrous miracle (*thama*)!"[35]

THE NEW

MIDDLE AGES

It is a commonplace in the writings of Kazantzakis that we are passing through a new Middle Ages, a transitional period that will last a very long time, perhaps two hundred years. The barbarians had penetrated to the core of modern Western civilization at least by the time of the Spanish Civil War, if not before, a penetration that made Kazantzakis pessimistic regarding the near future.[1] Wars, shadows, pogroms, selfish individualism, and bureaucratic management are the tangible results of our age, results that tend to overpower the efforts of the few magnificent, fiery hearts left in the world. In the desert of contemporary culture, one's duty is to remain faithful to the flame.[2] The purpose of this chapter is to explore why Kazantzakis sees Western civilization as barren, to determine what he means by the flame, and to ascertain how this flame illuminates Kazantzakis's religiosity and his peculiar admiration for the Middle Ages. Throughout the chapter I will indicate how the above purpose is related to the theme of transubstantiation, a theme that has been my major concern in the previous two chapters as well.

In a preliminary way it can be stated that the above-mentioned flame refers to authentic human life between two black voids. In *Spiritual Exercises* Kazantzakis claims that we come from a dark abyss and we end in one as well; life is a transition from one abyss to the other. This life of *élan vital*, symbolized by the flame, consists in a spiritual energy that tries to separate itself from matter, just as a flame consumes the wax in a candle. Human beings are lumps of matter infused with the possibility of living vibrantly, with Zorbalike zest, wherein it is possible to burn up one's material substance in the effort to transform it into spiritual light. Kazantzakis sometimes switches his imagery to make the same point in terms of a hydraulic metaphor. In an early treatise on Bergson (1912), we have seen Kazantzakis say that life is an unceasing creation where there are two streams: one like water that spurts into the air as steam when it is heated and one that, in its ebullition, distills into falling drops. It is this latter stream that constitutes matter.[3]

If one imagines Kazantzakis writing in mid-winter 1938 about Germany, one can easily understand his pessimism, his fear that a tiny lighted candle could easily be blown out by the winds of change, hence his belief that the best we could do is to daydream, plan, and work for the coming civilization.[4] But Kazantzakis's cosmology, and not just his cultural critique, made him something of a pessimist, as in the above-mentioned claim that "We come from a black abyss; we end in a black abyss." The trick is to render this pessimism compatible with an equally obvious feature of Kazantzakis's writing, that is, his tragic optimism, as in his exhortation to us to act as though the future depended on us even though the new Middle Ages, the postmodern era, may be with us for the next several centuries.[5]

Similarity to Berdyaev

As early as 1906 Kazantzakis was aware of the "sickness" of our age, an awareness that was amplified in 1929 when he ordered a copy of Nicholas Berdyaev's *Un Nouveau Moyen-Age*.[6] It therefore seems fair to conclude that Kazantzakis's own desire for a new Middle Ages was lifelong. A consideration of Berdyaev's thoughts on the new Middle Ages will help to prevent misunderstanding regarding exactly what Kazantzakis's hopes were for this period.

Berdyaev and Kazantzakis are quite clear that there is a rhythm in history as there is in nature, and that it is our lot to live in a period of transition.[7] Our epoch is the end of the modern period, which has reached its senility and is in the process of decomposition, and the beginning of a new Middle Ages. We have passed from an era of light to an era of darkness, but night is not less wonderful than day. In fact, night may well be closer than day to the abyss and hence to divinity. Berdyaev's appeal to St. John of the Cross and Kazantzakis's appeal to St. Teresa of Avila are indications of the fruitfulness of the "dark night of the soul."[8] That is, the common use of the phrase "medieval darkness" misses the deeper, ontological sense that Berdyaev and Kazantzakis have in mind when they refer to the new Middle Ages.

At the time of the fall of the ancient world it was "reactionary" to defend the principles of civilization, in that such a defense could easily be interpreted as an apologia for late Roman decadence. Likewise, contemporary defenders of "progress" are more reactionary than the true progressives in our culture, those who welcome the new Middle Ages, its interiority, and its possibilities for spiritual growth. Neither Berdyaev nor Kazantzakis has in mind a resurrection of the temporary and accidental in medieval culture. They intend a phoenixlike resurrection of that which is eternal. Or, as before, they intend a faithfulness to the flame; that is, an opposition to selfish individualism, imperialist politics, the dominance of *technē* over *sophia*. And they have a fascination for the issue of God. Nor do Berdyaev and Kazantzakis desire to ignore the mighty heralds of human freedom in the modern world. Rather, they want to place the accomplishments of such heralds within the cosmic whole and to strip such accomplishments of the barnacles of commodification that hide their luster. That is, there is a difference between going back to the old Middle Ages and going forward to a new Middle Ages.[9]

In the new Middle Ages, as Berdyaev sees it, the advantages gained through modern political freedoms would be preserved, but they would be given resonance by being heard against the background of divine, cosmic inclusiveness. To be an individual is not yet to be, in the fullest sense of the term, a person. Because decay precedes a Middle Ages, there is a tendency to wish the decay process to speed up so as to be done with it more quickly (as Claudius thinks in Robert Graves's *I, Claudius*). It is in this light that we should consider Kazantzakis's admiration for Lenin. It was Kazantzakis's hope that communism would hasten the end of the devouring and overwhelming lust of capitalism, but the former, as he well knew, had its cheap prophets of materialism and incapacity for interior recollection.[10] The end of the modern period signals the end of capitalist-communist hegemony. Private property should remain, as Berdyaev and Kazantzakis see it, but with a spiritualized application and without scandalously huge private fortunes and aggressive financial speculation. Modern nationalism must also give way to international solidarity among peoples, indeed among sentient beings in general. Religious universalism (as in Kazantzakis's interest in the Hebrew prophets, Mt. Athos, Saints Francis and Teresa, Islam, and Buddhism) is central in the move away from nationalism.

The new Middle Ages is a figure of speech for Berdyaev and Kazantzakis, hence there is no need to idealize the real Middle Ages of the past, as in Pre-Raphaelite painting. Serfdom, ignorance of nature, and fear of hell are, in fact, as the moderns have claimed, examples of primitivism.[11] To "return" to the new Middle Ages is to hope for a better religious type without dogmatic religious hierarchy. Berdyaev and Kazantzakis turn to religious issues not to find the autonomy of religious institutions but to find liberty in the religious quest itself,[12] to find a spiritual core to the intellectual life. The desire for God should not be, they think, merely an isolated department of culture. If there is such a thing as a Kazantzakian aristocracy, it is a leadership through the spiritual best (*aristos*), although the term "saint" is broadly conceived by Kazantzakis.

"The Sickness of the Age"

Kazantzakis's early essay with this title clearly indicates his belief that modern civilization is dying, but it is only implicit in its enthusiasm for the Middle Ages, an enthusiasm that becomes explicit, as we have seen, a few decades later, especially after his awareness of Berdyaev's essay.[13] This early effort is nonetheless important because it directs us to Kazantzakis's fascination with St. Teresa of Avila and the tradition of Christian mysticism, as well as to the silkworm metaphor that he used at several places throughout his career.

In the childhood of the human race there was no trace of spiritual sickness. For simple people Nature smiles and unfolds in a miraculous way; indeed divinity communicates with the earth through the magical ladder of simplicity.[14] Plato's *Symposium*, which Kazantzakis never tired of reading, exhibits the perfect combination of body and soul, of a flight to the divine in a religion of the beautiful, a flight that is nonetheless grounded in earthly passion.

Within Plato's dialogues, however, we can see the beginnings of a poisonous type of reasoning (that is, a use of *technē* to achieve dominance over an opponent, as opposed to a quest for *sophia* or *phronēsis*) that quickened the diseased state of ancient civilization, a diseased state that culminated in Stoic dispassion and the debauchery of the derailed followers of Epicurus.[15] Seen against this background, the Middle Ages can be looked at in either a positive or a negative light. Negatively it brings an oppressive incense over the world, a world-negating nostalgia for a Higher Jerusalem or an Eternal Chimera that never really existed. The barbarians from the north who sacked Rome are to be praised for hastening the fall of the ancient world and they are to be denigrated for introducing an atavism into medieval culture that would eventually culminate in the Inquisition. Because of these negative features of the Middle Ages, it is perhaps accurate to claim, as does Peter Bien, that the true "virtue" of a medieval period lies in the degree to which it prepares the way for the age that follows it where life is creatively pushed upward. It should be obvious that Kazantzakis's version of the decline of the classical world and of the inadequacies of medieval Christendom relies heavily, as many have noted, on Nietzsche. Kazantzakis also relies on Nietzsche in comparing the late modern period to late antiquity: both exhibit the "triumph of the treacherous" in that we know everything (in technical detail) yet know nothing (of wisdom). We have exposed everything, leaving nothing in its virginal state.[16]

Playing counterpoint, however, to the dominant theme in this essay is a subtle praise for the Middle Ages.[17] That is, unlike the modern period, the Middle Ages produced real devotion in people, literally a vow to strive for perfection, and real ecstasy, literally a standing outside of one's natural place so as to see where one should be going in life. Paradoxically, however, these religious ecstasies are not necessarily otherworldly because they were often produced by an intense love of Christ *in the flesh*, as in the mystical visions of St. Teresa. Conversely, as one might expect from the author of *Zorba*, Kazantzakis claims that many of the monks in the half-lit, silent churches of the Middle Ages continued in their devotions because they were enamored of the pale beauty of the Madonnas, as we will see once again in chapter 6.

St. Teresa and the Silkworm

Kazantzakis's admiration for the Middle Ages is perhaps best seen in one of its latest blooms in the sixteenth century, St. Teresa, whom Kazantzakis views in his book *Spain* as the mystic wife of Don Quixote.[18] Just as Quixote tried to bring virtue back to knighthood, so St. Teresa tried to bring virtue back to the monasteries, to extend the best of the Middle Ages for a little while longer. She at least partially succeeded, as is evidenced by her continuing impact on the Carmelite tradition in Catholicism, but in general her spiritual castle was dismantled by the forces of "progress" and modernity, a dismantling that Kazantzakis thinks is fitting for the great antinomy of the Spanish spirit: passion *and* nonentity.

Teresa is not the victim of Kazantzakis's (Nietzschean) invective because for her the holy life is not an attempt to escape from the world; rather, it is a patient, hard-working life of love. The four horses that pull Teresa's spiritual carriage are patience, logic, gaiety, and love. This carriage, as Kazantzakis sees it, follows one of the many roads to spiritual system, all of which climb to a region higher than ourselves. Teresa's road is one where matter and spirit are interchangeable due to the transubstantiation of matter into spirit, just as wine is transubstantiated into the blood of Christ in the Eastern Orthodox and Catholic Eucharist. Her positive Dionysian qualities lead Kazantzakis to suggest that in Presocratic days she would have been a zestful poet, but in our age she would only notice injustice and pain. At the end of the Middle Ages the breath of religion, which had risen like a fire due to people like Teresa, died down to embers.[19]

Mysticism is not escapism if it is, as it was in Teresa's case (and in St. Ignatius of Loyola's case), the product of a solid, simple, common mind.[20] One of the defects of late Greco-Roman civilization and of late modern civilization (and here Kazantzakis is in agreement with Unamuno[21]) is that mysticism has been trampled down by a technically precise mind, a mind that now must rest so that we can once again learn to believe in myth, he thinks.

It is not illegitimate to suspect that it is from Teresa that Kazantzakis borrowed the metaphor of the silkworm-butterfly to illustrate transubstantiation, religious purification, and the Middle Ages. In her classic work, *The Interior Castle*,[22] Teresa develops the idea that God is like the cocoon where the silkwormlike personality of a human being dies and then brings forth the butterfly of spirituality. She notices that silkworms start out the size of a grain of pepper, then through eating mulberry leaves the silkworm develops the strength to spin silk so as to construct the cocoon. Teresa in effect chides our modern, attenuated version of rationality by asking who, from the perspective of *technē*, could possibly believe this story of how a fat and ugly worm could be transubstantiated into a beautiful white butterfly?[23] But this is exactly what happens.

What seems to make Teresa appealing to Kazantzakis is that she does not use this story as an allegory for personal immortality, where the soul flies away completely from the body. Rather, the story symbolizes union with God in *this* life, a union that is temporary, like sexual intercourse. Teresa is generally skeptical of those who claim to have a lifelong marriage with divinity without distraction. The "butterfly" of spirituality, for Teresa, as well as for Kazantzakis, is not freed from human concerns, but exhibits restlessness because, once given a taste of God, its increasing desire is to be drunk with divinity.[24] This restlessness, however, is not to be construed as a desire to return to wormhood, but rather as an indication that the restless individual still needs to learn much about Ignatian-Carmelite-Buddhist detachment in the midst of activity.[25]

It is as necessary for the silkworm to die in Teresa as it is for civilization to die in Kazantzakis.[26] In fact, Kazantzakis at times indicates that we must actively put it to death so that the remaining silkworms of modernity do not gnaw away at what remains of virtue. The new Middle Ages is the dark cocoon out of which, eventually, a new civilization will arise; or, in other words, a butterfly in chains should not be pitied.[27]

The Blond Barbarians

Kazantzakis has rightfully been compared by James Lea to Oswald Spengler in believing that civilizations (or cultures, as Spengler uses the term) are living organisms that pass through several stages of aging until they die; then the process of planting another organic civilization begins. The destruction of enlightenment and positivist optimism was ushered in by World War I, a destruction that made it possible for Spengler and Kazantzakis to claim that there would be a revival of faith, but "faith" broadly conceived.

I would like to emphasize once again that in order to understand Kazantzakis's attitude toward Marxism or Leninism or communism one must see these "isms" as anticipatory of the new Middle Ages. Bien and Lea rightly see communism as only a temporary victor in Kazantzakis's universe. Although this victory carries with it frightening dangers, these dangers are really part of a more pervasive problem: the ascendance of *technē* over spiritual development. A true civilization must be based on moral and spiritual maturity, a maturity that was approximated in the Middle Ages. In fact, the medievals erred in the other direction, according to Lea, by exhibiting a moral development that outdistanced *technē*.[28] Lenin, Gandhi, and Mussolini (a strange threesome) offered different roads to Kazantzakis. He alternated among these roads on the way out of the modern era and toward the new Middle Ages, as Kazantzakis makes clear in the essay on Mussolini in *Journeying*. The presence of Gandhi in this trio is indicative of the fact that politics, for Kazantzakis, as important as it is, is nonetheless not a consummatory good but an instrumental one.

As we have seen, barbarian hoards put the nails in the coffin of ancient civilization, just as rampant "technicism" is the new barbarism with which we must contend (or, in a peculiar way, for Kazantzakis, which we must welcome). It is in transitional times such as ours, as Lea notes, that God's survival is particularly perilous,[29] just as it was in the ninth century when Irish monks on the fringes of Europe saved the sacred texts. Kazantzakis himself was impressed by this fact when he witnessed God's salvation by human beings enacted by the monks on Mt. Athos.[30] It is true that Kazantzakis exposes the hypocrisy of certain types of monasticism in *Zorba the Greek*, but it is also true, as Bien emphasizes, that Kazantzakis himself often retired to monasteries, and that he spent an extremely meaningful period at Mt. Athos in 1914—and this despite the parody of Mt. Athos in *Report to Greco*. What Kazantzakis thought we needed in the twentieth century was a combination of chaotic, barbaric forces and a new, secular monasticism with an asceticism in the original Greek sense of *askēsis* as bodily training, rather than as world-negating and body-hating.

The "blond barbarians" from the north have actually enacted their constructive destruction three times in Europe. The first instance was the prehistoric Dorian invasion of Greece, Knossos, and Egypt, an invasion that, like a helpful forest fire, burned out the old growth so as to make it possible for the new shoots to grow into what eventually became the flowering of civilization in fifth century B.C. Greece. It is this horde of barbarians that Kazantzakis describes in *The Odyssey*, and that provides the example for how we should view the second horde (at the fall of Rome) and the third (contemporary Russia).

The first invasion hastened the transition from the Bronze Age to the Iron (book III of the *The Odyssey*), a transition invited by the opulent Menelaos, who let his people starve. A reader of *The Odyssey* is perhaps surprised to learn (book VIII) that Helen, for Kazantzakis, should be impregnated by one of these barbarians so as to pass on the virtues both of ancient beauty (Helen) and of the violent destruction of the inequalities that made it possible for that beauty to continue to flourish (the barbarians), inequalities such as the ancient Greek institution of slavery or the brutal methods involved in the building of the pyramids. Given what I have said, however, it should not be surprising that Kazantzakis has Odysseus side with the barbarians in Egypt, even if they were doomed to lose their fight (book XI). It is significant that Odysseus leaves Egypt to become (of all things, for Odysseus) an ascetic and a mystic in the last books of *The Odyssey*.

Greece and the New Middle Ages

The "Cretan glance" described in *Report to Greco* makes it obvious that Kazantzakis has always distanced himself to some degree from Western civilization. That is, he has always had only one foot (or eye) on Europe and the other on Asia-Africa. Hence it is important for him to determine the implications of the new Middle Ages for Greece, or more specifically, for Crete. Morton Levitt points out that Kazantzakis was aware that the ancient Greeks are now the inheritance of the whole world, in general; the West, in particular; and especially contemporary Greece (Crete).[31] Kazantzakis feels a special kinship to Homer and a particular pain when thinking of ancient Mycenaean decay, a Mycenae that had to be destroyed in order to be renewed.[32]

In *Journey to the Morea* Kazantzakis uses his visit to the Peloponnesian Peninsula as an occasion to contrast the ancient commonplace, "Nothing in excess," with the motto of our age, "Everything in excess!"[33] There are certain excesses in our age that Kazantzakis hates. But one needs to be careful here. In one sense Kazantzakis is firmly committed to the latter saying; in fact, he had this motto inscribed on his lintel as his way of showing that he aligned himself with Dionysus rather than Apollo. The issue is complicated, however, when we take into consideration certain passages in *Journeying*, treated above in chapter 1. Here we see a tension in Kazantzakis, a tension that I think is evident in almost all of his writings: he is committed to *both* the ancient Greek (moderate) effort to harmonize opposite forces, to use the dialectical tension between correlative forces as a source of friction and energy to propel himself forward, *and* the Eastern (or Jewish) tendency to be "excessive" and restless and dissatisfied with any supposed harmony.

Ancient Greece provides us with historical and organic closure: from chaos to the Parthenon back to chaos. The riddle of history is to figure out the extent to which the rhythm of history is merciless and inexorable (like ancient necessity—*anangkē*) and the extent to which it is amenable to the plastic control of human or divine *élan* (a control perhaps enhanced by the prophets of freedom in modern civilization), as when Kazantzakis suggests that civilization declines when human beings give themselves over entirely to "realism." Kazantzakis does not seem to think that it was inevitable that Zeus would eventually become a stylish rogue, nor in modernity that individualism would reign supreme.[34] Like Plato's Demiurge in the *Timaeus*, to be discussed in the following chapter, Kazantzakis wants us to take joy in bringing as much order and morality out of chaos *as is possible* given the recalcitrant material we have to deal with. That is, there is always some surd element in history that eludes our grasp, as well as God's grasp. Kazantzakis was quite clear in *Spiritual Exercises* that his God is like Plato's in not being omnipotent.[35]

Modern *hubris* (or immoderation, in the pejorative sense of the term) consists in wanting to conquer this surd, to rip the veil of mystery, even if it is quite beautiful, to demand a technically precise explanation for hidden reality. Although this effort was started at the pinnacle of ancient Greece when Socratic dialogue apotheosized natural curiosity and gossip, ancients like Socrates and Plato nonetheless knew the limits of *technē*, and they knew that beyond dialectic lay a perfect reality that we could apprehend only through *nous*. Kazantzakis thinks that the effort to build a modern Greek civilization, in particular, and a Western or world civilization, in general, depends on *how* we appropriate the ancients.[36] The question is not *if* we will do so, for one of the purposes of the new Middle Ages is to learn how to build on, rather than violently tear down or superciliously ignore, ancient wisdom. Kazantzakis does not intend that we grovel before the ancients like serfs, but rather that we learn to synthesize the best insights of Western civilizations (ancient and modern) with those of the East, a synthesis that would be newer and more exciting than stale and myopic concentration on the various talismans of late modernity—for example, productivity.

MacIntyre's Contribution

Some might try to place Kazantzakis's thoughts regarding the death of modern civilization against the background of the two world wars and the Greek civil war, and hence make his insights less plausible as the memory of these wars fades. But various factors have kept Kazantzakis's thoughts on the new Middle Ages alive, not least of which is the threat of nuclear or biological or environmental annihilation. The tendency now to define our age as postmodern is, in a way, to confirm many of Kazantzakis's claims regarding the death of modern civilization. Kazantzakis, however, would most likely disagree with the tendency within the deconstructive variety of postmodernism (rather than the constructive variety found in Bergson, Whitehead, and Hartshorne) to leave spiritual concerns and philosophical theology in the diseased state in which they were left by modernity.[37] Further, the relativism of deconstructive postmodernism (in contrast to the strong commitment to philosophical ethics found in constructive postmodernists—see Whitehead's *Adventure of Ideas*, Griffin's and Cobb's attacks on nuclearism, and my own defense of animal rights) lacks the ascetical rigor that Kazantzakis thought necessary to spiritualize matter. The Kazantzakian *duty* (elaborated in *Spiritual Exercises* and elsewhere) to extend the scope of one's spiritual concern to the cosmos as a whole is hardly compatible with deconstructive postmodernism.

Much more to Kazantzakis's liking, I think, would be the last chapter in Alasdair MacIntyre's *After Virtue*, a book that may well become a classic in its own right.[38] The chapter is titled "Nietzsche *or* Aristotle, Trotsky *and*

St. Benedict." Because the values of modern civilization (for example, material complacency) had been distorted to the point where they became grotesque, Nietzsche's negative proposal to "raze to the ground the structures of inherited moral belief and argument" contains a certain plausibility for MacIntyre, and an even greater plausibility for Kazantzakis.[39] But this "terrible plausibility," if not seen within the constructive context of a new Middle Ages, leads to atheism and nihilism. To paraphrase MacIntyre, to cry out that the emperor had no clothes was to pick on one person or a class of people to the amusement of everybody else; but to declare that we are all dressed in rags gives no one solace.[40] The attractiveness of Nietzsche's position lay in its coming clean regarding certain fundamental assumptions, but this is only one moment in the moral or religious life. MacIntyre's positive suggestion is to return to Aristotle, or better, to preserve the best in ancient moral thought so as to use ancient wisdom in the growth of a postmodern civilization. There is no point in trying, like Gauguin, to return to a primitive condition where Zorbalike virtues would reign supreme. Nor is there any point in recreating the pedantry of Hellenistic scholarship, whereby Aristotle and the ancients are kept alive in an attenuated sense, or where they are kept alive as stuffed dinosaurs or mummies. Rather, MacIntyre and Kazantzakis encourage us to *embody* ancient wisdom in the new Middle Ages; for example, as St. Francis embodied Aristotelian reverence for nature and empirical detail without a scholarly appreciation for the technical details of Aristotle's philosophy. Rather than hear a lecture on virtue we should learn, in the new Middle Ages, how to *live* a life of virtue.

To accomplish this Herculean task alone would not only be extremely difficult (as it was for Kazantzakis at the end of his life, in exile), it would also play into the hands of modern civilization's dogmatic confidence in individualism. But where can we find communities that foster spiritual growth and habits that predispose us to be virtuous? Not in what are called "communities" in capitalist culture, which are really ersatz mutual defense alliances meant to protect property values or privileges and to ward off crime; and certainly not, as MacIntyre emphasizes, in the barbarous despotism that held sway (and still holds sway, in some cases) in the collective Tsardom of communist countries.[41] With Trotsky we should wonder how the legitimate desire for praxis and community became so perverted in twentieth-century Marxism, a wonder that perhaps can be allayed through a consideration of the following remarkable, and very Kazantzakian, lines of MacIntyre from the end of his book:

> It is always dangerous to draw too precise parallels between one historical period and another; and among the most misleading of such parallels are those which have been drawn between our own age in Europe and North America and the epoch in which the Roman Empire declined into

the Dark Ages. None the less certain parallels there are. A crucial turning point in that earlier history occurred when men and women of good will turned aside from the task of shoring up the Roman *imperium* and ceased to identify the continuation of civility and moral community with the maintenance of that *imperium*. What they set themselves to achieve instead—often not recognizing fully what they were doing—was the construction of new forms of community within which the moral life could be sustained so that both morality and civility might survive the coming ages of barbarism and darkness . . . for some time now we too have reached that turning point. What matters at this stage is the construction of local forms of community within which civility and the intellectual and moral life can be sustained through the new dark ages which are already upon us. And if the tradition of the virtues was able to survive the horrors of the last dark ages, we are not entirely without grounds for hope. This time however the barbarians are not waiting beyond the frontiers; they have already been governing us for quite some time. And it is our lack of consciousness of this that constitutes part of our predicament. We are waiting not for a Godot, but for another—doubtless very different— St. Benedict.

It must be admitted that Kazantzakis was always skeptical of organized religion, even if he was, in fact, profoundly religious. (See his description in *Report to Greco* of his father who, whenever he met a priest in the street, would *cross himself* in order to exorcise the unfortunate encounter.[42]) He was even somewhat skeptical of organized monastic communities, as in his parody of monastic life in *Zorba the Greek*, but, as we have seen, he was ambivalent on this topic. It should be obvious, however, that organized monastic communities are not necessarily the only sorts of spiritual communities, nor are they the sorts of communities that would be likely to flourish in the new Middle Ages. MacIntyre's contribution to the new Middle Ages is to help us think carefully about what the advance to a new Benedictine order would be like. The communities of Kazantzakis-lovers, in particular, and of true lovers of wisdom, in general, are spread across the globe without organization and without roots or a sense of place. But these "communities" nonetheless provide the receptacle within which the darkness of the new Middle Ages can produce its own sublime beauty, a beauty that depends, as MacIntyre suggests, on *local* action and care. Unlike the boss, who merely theorizes about universal humanitarian ideals, Zorba seizes the moment to console this Bouboulina here and now, and saves particular miners there and then.

There are obviously problems associated with Kazantzakis's desire to preserve the best in modern individualism, as found in our heightened enlightenment, universalistic commitment to civil liberties on the basis of the dignity of each person. Exactly *how* can we preserve these civil liberties when they are threatened by both left-wing and right-wing (indeed fascist) "communitarianisms"? This is a difficult question, especially given the fact that Kazantzakis himself was, at times, tempted by both communism and fascism. But Kazantzakis's desire to "return" to a new Middle Ages (or better, to make the most of the new Middle Ages that are already here) is more of a spiritual desire than a political one, and herein lies his genius.

The Last Temptation *and* St. Francis

I would like to conclude this chapter with a consideration of how two of Kazantzakis's most well-known novels—*The Last Temptation of Christ* and *Saint Francis*—illustrate the themes I have elaborated regarding Kazantzakis's views on the new Middle Ages. In *The Last Temptation of Christ* Kazantzakis makes a point about Jesus that is often made, rightly or wrongly, about St. Francis: he was a pantheist, or at least he flirted with pantheism. The saint is the one who can smell the presence of God all around, in wood, rocks, birds, and human beings.[43] This view allows Kazantzakis to take another swipe at traditional religious communities because God is not found only, or even primarily, in monasteries, but rather in homes with husbands and wives and children and petty cares and cooking and arguments and reconciliations. Kazantzakis is, *in a way*, in favor of domestic communities rather than monastic ones, and this despite his personal and lifelong asceticism and his admiration for Mt. Athos.[44]

But it would simplify matters too much to think that one could just step outside on a spring day or into the kitchen when Christmas cookies are being made in order to find God. Perhaps everything is of God, but this ubiquitous presence has two meanings for Kazantzakis, one manifest and one hidden. Those who have not sufficiently developed an interior life only catch the manifest meaning, "but the mind which dwells in God sees what lies behind the visible."[45] "Medieval" minds are those that actively prepare themselves to be in a position to receive divine influence, even if such influence comes like a scorching wind or a flash of lightning.[46] That is, those who float on the surface of religiosity do not consider the fact that divine love is a terrifying precipice and that the divine mind is in certain ways an abyss because God knows *all* of what is and has *always* had such an ability.[47]

In *Saint Francis* itself the same distinction can be made. God is not merely like, but in some way is in a gentle rain, a soft breeze, a geranium, or a human soul. It is perhaps not an exaggeration to say that Kazantzakis's Francis literally believes that, if God is everywhere, divinity can be found under any stone that one could lift. This is the point of the belief that God inter-penetrated with a human creature (the Incarnation). Christians have tended to emphasize that God intersected with a *human* creature whereas Kazantzakis's Francis has God appear as a human *creature*.[48]

It is more accurate, however, to say that Kazantzakis's Jesus and Francis are panentheists (those who believe that all is *in* a God, a God who partially transcends the natural world) rather than pantheists (those who believe that the natural world *is* God without remainder). For Francis all roads lead to some earthly destination, but the abyss leads to God.[49] It is precisely this jump (faith) over the abyss that the new Middle Ages would foster. This is an extreme view, but for Kazantzakis theism itself is an extreme position, and this is precisely its appeal. We need a new Middle Ages, he thinks, in order to appreciate what basically was Francis' lifelong view regarding the three sorts of prayer that were noted before in chapter 3, the third of which was Kazantzakis's own and, on Kazantzakis's interpretation, Francis's own favorite:

> The first: "Lord, bend me, or else I shall rot." The second: "Lord, do not bend me too much, for I shall break." The third . . . : "Lord, bend me too much, and who cares if I break!"[50]

(Here Kazantzakis exhibits his "Everything in excess!" side.) Figures like Jesus and Francis can (usually—think of Jesus in the garden at Gesthemene) withstand the rigors of the religious life precisely because God for them is an unquenchable flame, indeed a fire, that burns in them day and night.[51] It is important to notice, however, that for Kazantzakis there is *ultimately* no dichotomy between the manifest divine presence and the partially hidden one. For the Kazantzakian "medieval" religious believer, there is no such thing as quotidian pain unaccompanied by exultation, and no everyday life without miracles.

THEISM:

TRADITIONAL

AND DIPOLAR

In this chapter I will change direction away from a concern for transubstantiation, a concern that dominated chapters 2, 3, and 4. But in the present chapter I will make explicit what was implicit in these previous chapters: Kazantzakis's thought on God is built on a tension between two poles of the divine nature, poles that will be explicated here.

Everyone who has studied Kazantzakis's thought on God admits that his theism differs from the traditional conception of God in Christianity. But scholars in the English language, at least, and perhaps others as well, often go too far in emphasizing the differences between Kazantzakis's theism and traditional theism. For example, Kimon Friar holds that God, for Kazantzakis, "was not an already predetermined goal toward which men proceed, but a spirituality ceaselessly and progressively created by nature as it evolves toward greater and higher refinement."[1] This is certainly true, but only partially so. Morton Levitt correctly calls Kazantzakis's theism a process theism, and also correctly notes that Kazantzakis was not a pantheist, but Levitt does not state with sufficient precision what *sort* of process theism Kazantzakis adhered to.[2] Is God, for Kazantzakis, *merely* the transubstantiation of matter into spirit? I think not.

My thesis in this chapter is that progress can be made in the understanding of Kazantzakis's thought on God by looking at him as a dipolar theist. The text I will primarily examine is *The Saviors of God: Spiritual Exercises*. Evidence from Kazantzakis's novels could also be used to support my case, but

because most scholars agree that *Spiritual Exercises* forms the core of Kazantzakis's philosophy, I will concentrate on this text. The most important contemporary defender of dipolar theism is Charles Hartshorne. I will use
Hartshorne's thought to explain what dipolar theism is, then I will use this
explanation to examine Kazantzakis's text.[3] At the end of the chapter I will also
treat the first great dipolar theist, Plato.

Hartshorne's Dipolar Theism

Hartshorne fully accepts the goal of traditional philosophers in the
Abrahamic religions—that is, logical analysis is in the service of a higher end.
But he holds that the traditional theist's conception of God is internally inco-
herent. One of the major complaints Hartshorne has with traditional theism
(in philosophy and theology, as opposed to biblical theism) is that it either
explicitly or implicitly identifies God as active and not receptive, a mistake
that Kazantzakis (as a Bergsonian) also notices when he says that *we* in some
way save God. St. Thomas Aquinas's unmoved mover is the most obvious
example of this tendency toward reification of God as active but not receptive, but in general traditional theists in Western and Eastern churches, as
well as various Jewish and Muslim philosophers, see God as a timeless, supernatural being that does not change. The traditional theist's inconsistency lies
in also claiming that God knows and loves. For example, if God knows, God
must be a subject on the analogy of human subjects. And if God is a subject
who knows, God must be affected by, be receptive with respect to, the object
known.

It will be to our advantage to get as clear as we can on what is meant by
the term "God" in the beginning part of this chapter. For Hartshorne, the term
refers to the supremely excellent being. Hartshorne has been the most
important defender of St. Anselm's ontological argument in this century, and
his debt to St. Anselm is evident in this preliminary definition. It closely
resembles St. Anselm's "that than which no greater can be conceived." Yet the
ontological argument is not what is at stake here. Even if the argument fails, the
preliminary definition of God as the supremely excellent being or the greatest
conceivable being seems unobjectionable. To say that God can be defined in
these ways still leaves open the possibility that God is even more excellent than
our ability to conceive. This allows us to avoid objections from Thomists or
Eastern mystics or some Kazantzakis scholars who fear that by defining God we
are limiting God to merely human language. All Hartshorne is suggesting is that
when we think of God we must be thinking of one who surpasses all others, or
we are not thinking of God. Even the atheist or agnostic would admit this
much. When the atheist says, "There is no God," he or she is denying that a
supremely excellent or greatest conceivable being exists.

The contrast excellent-inferior is the truly invidious contrast when applied to God. If to be invidious is to be injurious or blasphemous regarding God, then this contrast (both terms) is the most invidious one of all when applied to God because God is only excellent. God is inferior in no way. Period. To suggest that God is in some small way inferior to some other being is to speak no longer about God but about some being that is not supremely excellent or the greatest conceivable. Hartshorne's major criticism of traditional theism is that it has assumed that all contrasts, or most of them, when applied to God are invidious. Kazantzakis, I will show, agrees with Hartshorne in this criticism.

Let us assume from now on that God exists. What attributes does God possess? Consider the following two columns of attributes in polar contrast to each other:

one	many
being	becoming
activity	passivity
permanence	change
necessity	contingency
independence	dependence
actual	potential
absolute	relative
abstract	concrete

Traditional theism tends toward oversimplification. It is comparatively easy to say, "God is strong rather than weak, so in all relations God is active, not receptive." In each case, the traditional theist decides which member of the contrasting pair is good (on the left) then attributes it to God, while wholly denying the contrasting term (on the right). Hence, God is one but not many, permanent but not changing, being but not becoming, and so on. This leads to what Hartshorne calls the monopolar prejudice. Monopolarity is common to both traditional theism and pantheism, with the major difference between the two being the fact that traditional theism admits the reality of plurality, potentiality, and becoming as a secondary form of existence "outside" God (on the right), whereas in pantheism the divine being includes all reality within itself. Common to both traditional theism and pantheism is the belief that the above categorical contrasts are invidious or blasphemous. The dilemma these two positions face is that either the deity is *only* one constituent of the whole (traditional theism) or else the alleged inferior pole in each contrast (on the right) is illusory. I will show that Kazantzakis avoided these positions.

For Hartshorne this dilemma is artificial. It is produced by the assumption that excellence is found by separating and purifying one pole (on the left) and denigrating the other (on the right). That this is not the case can be seen by analyzing some of the attributes on the right side. At least since St. Augustine, traditional theists have been convinced that God's eternity meant not that God endured through all time, but that God was outside of time altogether and did not, could not, be receptive to temporal change. St. Thomas Aquinas identified God, following Aristotle, who was the greatest predecessor to traditional theism, as unmoved. Yet both activity and receptivity can be either good or bad. Good receptivity is likely to be called sensitivity, responsiveness, adaptability, sympathy, or, as Kazantzakis puts it, God's dependence on us to be saved. Insufficiently subtle or defective receptivity is called wooden inflexibility, mulish stubbornness, inadaptability, unresponsiveness, and the like. To deny God receptivity altogether is to deny God those aspects of receptivity that are excellences. Or again, to altogether deny God the ability to change does avoid fickleness, but at the expense of the ability to react lovingly to the sufferings of others. For Kazantzakis this is too great a price to pay, even if God in Kazantzakis's writings is often the cause of people "suffering" when they are called to a higher level of spiritual perfection than that which they occupy at present.

The terms on the left side have both good and bad aspects as well. Oneness can mean wholeness, but also it can mean monotony or triviality. Actuality can mean definiteness, but it can mean nonrelatedness to others. What happens to divine love when God, according to Thomists, is claimed to be *pure* actuality? God ends up loving the world, but without being intrinsically related to it, whatever sort of love that may be. Self-sufficiency can, at times, be selfishness. The trick when thinking of God, for Hartshorne as well as for Kazantzakis, is to attribute to God all excellences (left *and* right sides) and not to attribute to God any inferiorities (right *and* left sides). In short, excellent-inferior or good-evil are invidious or blasphemous contrasts, but one-many, being-becoming, et al., are noninvidious contrasts. Unlike traditional theism and pantheism, Hartshorne's and Kazantzakis's theism is dipolar. To be specific, within *each* pole of a noninvidious contrast (for example, permanence-change) there are invidious elements (inferior permanence or inferior change), but also noninvidious, good elements (excellent permanence or excellent change).

Hartshorne does not believe in two gods, one unified and the other plural, and so on. Rather, he, along with Kazantzakis, believes that what are often thought to be contraries are really mutually interdependent correlatives:

> The good as we know it is unity-in-variety or variety-in-
> unity; if the variety overbalances, we have chaos or discord;
> if the unity, we have monotony or triviality.[4]

Supreme excellence, if it is truly supreme excellence, *must* somehow be able to integrate all the *complexity* there is in the world into itself as one spiritual whole. The word "must" indicates divine necessity, along with God's essence, which necessarily is to exist. And the word "complexity" indicates the contingency that affects God through creaturely decisions or feelings. But in the traditional view God is solely identified with the stony immobility of the absolute, implying nonrelatedness to the world, contra the Kazantzakian view. For Hartshorne, God in the abstract nature, the divine being, may in a way escape from the temporal flux, but a living God is related to the world of becoming, which entails divine becoming as well if the world in some way is internally related to God. The traditional theist's alternative to this view suggests that all relationships to God are external to divinity, once again threatening not only God's love, but also God's nobility. A dog's being behind a particular rock affects the dog in certain ways, thus this relation is an internal relation to the dog. But it does not affect the rock, whose relationship with the dog is external to the rock's nature. Does this not show the superiority of canine consciousness, which is aware of the rock, to rocklike existence, which is unaware of the dog? Is it not therefore peculiar that God has been described solely in rocklike terms: pure actuality, permanence, only having external relations, unmoved, being not becoming?

In short, the divine being becomes, or the divine becoming is—God's being and becoming form a single reality:

> There is no law of logic against attributing contrasting predicates to the same individual, provided they apply to diverse aspects of this individual.[5]

But the remedy for "ontolatry," the worship of being, is not the contrary pole, "gignolatry," the worship of becoming, as some interpreters of Kazantzakis suggest:

> God is neither being as contrasted to becoming nor becoming as contrasted to being; but categorically supreme becoming in which there is a factor of categorically supreme being, as contrasted to inferior becoming, in which there is inferior being.[6]

The divine becoming is more ultimate than divine being in dipolar theism only for the reason that it is more inclusive. I am constantly changing yet I retain my identity as "Dan" throughout these changes, and this largely because of a Bergsonian memory that I possess; but I will die. God *always* changes and yet *always* maintains a stable identity though these changes as "God." To be an everlasting agent and recipient is in truth incomparably better than being either alone.

A Hartshornean Analysis of Kazantzakis

Like Hartshorne, Kazantzakis is quite clear on the point that God's perfection does not lie in omnipotence. Kazantzakis says that "My God is not Almighty."[7] Kazantzakis also claims that "My God is not All-Holy," or better, all-good.[8] It is imperative to realize that he is not criticizing God here, but pointing out that a process theism entails an evolving concept of perfection. To the rather simple-minded, traditional theistic objection that if God changed God would not be perfect, for if God were perfect there would be no need to change, Hartshorne and Kazantzakis could make this rather obvious reply: God's perfection does not just allow God to change, but *requires* God to change. New moments bring with them new possibilities for Zorbalike or Franciscan heroism, new possibilities for saving God. This, I think, is what Kazantzakis means when he describes God as not being all-good, in that God's goodness, greater than any other goodness, nonetheless depends on the activities, *particularly the struggles*, of others to remain the greatest being. This does not mean that God's earlier existence was inferior, because it was at that particular time the greatest existence. Likewise, God is not all-knowing for either Hartshorne or Kazantzakis, at least not with respect to the future, in that the future is not here yet to be known in minute detail.[9] But this is not a defect in God, for it is only in this way that creaturely freedom can be preserved. That is, if human beings are free (as Bergson, Hartshorne, and Kazantzakis think they are), then God is still the greatest conceivable knower even if God is not omniscient with respect to the future.

These and other similarities between Hartshorne and Kazantzakis can be easily found. But what about dipolar theism? Human beings are dipolar beings. We constantly change, yet retain an identity throughout change. However, we are not dipolar in a supreme or cosmic way, as is God. One has little difficulty in showing that Kazantzakis's God becomes, in that on every page it seems that Kazantzakis reminds us that God needs to be saved. God suffers, struggles, stumbles, recovers, loves, cries out to us, makes (monumental!) demands of us, and so on. Both Hartshorne and Kazantzakis see God as contingently dependent on creaturely decisions and feelings, hence God's concrete reality has potentiality for development (see the right column of the above table). It is these references that have led interpreters of Kazantzakis to see him as a monopolar theist, but of a different sort than the traditional theist. Kazantzakis's worship is of a God who purely becomes, we are in effect told by these interpreters, as opposed to the traditional theist's worship of a God who is pure being.

What has not been much noticed is that there are several passages in *Spiritual Exercises* (and many more in other works) where Kazantzakis indicates that his God is dipolar. The first is in "The Preparation."[10] By accepting "the boundaries of the human mind without vain rebellion, and in these severe limitations to work ceaselessly without protest" (the first duty), Kazantzakis reveals himself at the start to be a Kantian. But the second duty propels him beyond Kantianism, or at least beyond Kant's first critique. Kazantzakis will not accept conceptual boundaries, for he believes that behind appearances there is an essence striving to merge with the human heart.[11] That is, the human mind and body stand in between God as becoming and God as being. Our second duty is to smash these boundaries, to the extent that we can, to rush to the *invisible*.[12]

Although Kazantzakis says our third duty is to give up hope of reaching the noumenal God beyond God's phenomenal becoming, he continually returns to dipolar theism. The greatest sin of all for Kazantzakis is satisfaction, so we should not be tempted to give up the divine struggle for God's essence (or being) too early.[13] Our ancestors' struggles to find God must now depend on our struggles, so when we try to find God we should do so as if we had, like St. Christopher, our whole people, all humankind, or all the earth on our shoulders. One should train one's eyes, Kazantzakis tells us, to gaze on people as if they were moving in great stretches of time.[14] Who is this God who needs to be liberated from matter? God is the liberating struggle itself, for Kazantzakis, but what about that aspect of God already (or everlastingly) liberated, that part of a centaurlike God already released from animality?[15]

We toil for the sake of "Someone Else,"[16] not just for the sake of creaturely struggle. We strive for the divine spirit per se,[17] which can be interpreted not only in terms of a Bergsonian *élan vital*, as Friar reminds us, but also in terms of something eternal or everlasting, as Kazantzakis himself indicates.[18] In short, Kazantzakis also describes God in the sort of terms we would expect to find on the left side of the above table. God's "whole being" is of concern to Kazantzakis, and includes the "power" to escape matter.[19] These divine attributes should be kept in mind when we consider Plato later on in this chapter. God struggles in everything; the divine huddles in every cell of flesh, striving upward toward the light. What light?, Kazantzakis asks. That which is above and beyond everything![20]

Pain is not the only part of the essence of God, for Kazantzakis, and anything that narrows our view of God to one rigidly defined perspective is to be criticized.[21] Traditional theism is one of the myopic views he rejects, but he also avoids the view of God as pure becoming. That is, to say, as Kazantzakis does, that the essence of God is struggle[22] can be taken in two senses: (1) God struggles against matter; and (2) God "struggles" against a purely temporalistic struggle with matter. Evidence of the latter is found in Kazantzakis's mention of the "Great Spirit,"[23] who does not toil within the bounds of human time, place, or causality.[24] We are ecstatic (literally *ek stasis*—out of place) to the extent that we escape the prejudices and limitations of our time and place, and in this regard we are children of God. But God is the "Great Ecstatic."[25] God as invisible is *behind* phenomena; God is *deathless*.[26] Our working with and on phenomena affects God. In that spiritual concerns are always on the verge of being extinguished in our quite profligate world, it is we human beings who, in a way, must save God. But in another sense, the God who is saved is always the same.[27]

The last thing Kazantzakis would have wanted is to be put in a category, hence the words that end his book regarding silence, words that indicate that nothing he has said *really* applies to God. One is reminded of St. Thomas Aquinas' claim on his deathbed that all he wrote was straw. This distrust of completion forces me to be tentative in my dipolar interpretation of Kazantzakis. But it also should force others to resist precluding any divine transcendence or everlastingness in Kazantzakis. As he puts it, the real unbelievers are the satisfied.[28] The essence of God always remains obscure,[29] but one possibility is clear: that agonizing struggle, even divine agonizing struggle, may be inferior to the *real* nature of God.[30] That is, God gazes on the divine struggle, as if from an external point of view; *behind* the ceaseless flux of divine activity lies "an indestructible unity."[31]

The Platonic Background

Because Kazantzakis was not familiar with the religious thought of Whitehead or Hartshorne, it may be objected that the interpretation of him as a dipolar theist is implausible. But he was very much familiar with another process theist, Bergson. And dipolar, process theism is as old as Plato, as has been argued by Hartshorne, if not Bergson, and later in an excellent study by Leonard Eslick.[32] Given Kazantzakis's familiarity with ancient Greek thought (he even translated some of Plato's dialogues), it is not implausible to suggest that his thought on God at least unwittingly continues a long Greek tradition.

Certain Platonic texts are obvious sources. In the *Sophist* (246–49) the Eleatic Stranger develops the mature Platonic metaphysics, which is opposed by both the "giants," who are the materialists who drag everything down from heaven to earth; and the "gods" (or, we might say, the traditional theists) who defend their position somewhere in the heights of the unseen. Kazantzakis also has these positions as enemies. Reality is dyadic, for Plato, and is constituted by anything (being or becoming) that has *dynamis*, the dynamic power to affect or to be affected by something else.[33] Even in the *Republic* Plato avoids what many have assumed to be the Platonic position: unbridled worship of being. The task of the philosopher (501b) is to glance frequently in two directions: first, at the Forms of Justice, Beauty, and the like as they are in the nature of things, but also at this cavelike world, where one must try to reproduce the Forms to the extent that one can.

There are two significant ways in which Plato talks about God. First, he inherited from Parmenides the notion that being is eternal, immutable, and self-same. It is this notion that was the starting point for traditional, monopolar theism. "The extent to which Plato is committed to such an absolute schism between *being* and *becoming* . . . would seem to dictate for him a similar exclusion from divinity of all shadow of change."[34] This tendency is evidenced in book 2 of the *Republic*, the *Phaedo* (78–80), and in Kazantzakis's favorite, the *Symposium* (202–3). However, as Eslick and others hold, there is no textual foundation for the popular identification of Plato's God with the transcendent Form of the Good, nor even with the world of Forms, either as a whole or in part.[35] It comes as a shock to some readers of Plato who have only read the *Republic*, *Phaedo*, and *Symposium* that in the *Phaedrus* (245, etc.) Eros is claimed to be divine. Here Plato discovers, according to Eslick, a new, dynamic meaning for perfection.[36] The perfection that is dynamic is the perfection of life itself, treated not only in the *Phaedrus*, but in book 10 of the *Laws* as well. Kazantzakis's identification of God with love[37] or with struggling soul immediately comes to mind in this regard.

In the *Timaeus* and the *Sophist* both poles in Plato's theism are brought together: the perfection of divine immutability and the perfection of divine life. The former is identified in the *Timaeus* with the Demiurge, who everlastingly and without change contemplates the archetypal models, the Forms. Kazantzakis also refers to God as the Demiurge.[38] The latter perfection is identified with the World Soul—which is close to Kazantzakis's panexperientialism,[39] to be discussed later in the book—whose essence is self-motion, and is depicted as posterior to the Demiurge. The motions of psychic life include both actions and receptions. In fact, in the *Sophist*, as has been noted above, reality itself is identified with dynamic power; specifically, the power to affect or be affected by others. Even Aristotle attests to the fact that reality, for Plato, is the joint product of the One and the Indefinite Dyad.[40] Unfortunately, Aristotle's own notion of God loses the Platonic character of divine immanence, of God as the Kazantzakian soul of the world. Even more unfortunate is the fact that Plotinus, and others who became identified as followers of Plato, were with respect to their descriptions of God really Aristotelians. It is not unreasonable to speculate that Kazantzakis saw the inadequacies of latter day Platonists. Both Plato and Kazantzakis see God as dipolar, both seem to be panexperientialists, and both identify reality with dynamic power.

It is ironic that Aristotle, who generally elaborated a unified scheme of embodied form, ended up in his view of God with a dualism more vicious than any envisaged by Plato. Aristotle's gods are strictly unmoved and removed from those who are not divine. Plato, by way of contrast, generally elaborated a scheme whereby there is some sort of *chōrismos* or separation of form from matter. Yet, in his view of God, Plato ends up with a cosmic monism wherein God (the soul for the body of the world) is infused into all of nature. God, as Kazantzakis is fond of putting it, hides in every cell and in every speck of matter.

In addition to Plato and Bergson and his rather extensive theological readings, Kazantzakis could have been inspired in his dipolar theism by certain oddities in the Christian tradition itself. As we have seen, traditional theistic philosophers and theologians have claimed that God is immutable *and* that God knows and loves the world (and needs it, Kazantzakis would say), but they never made it clear how both of these could be true. Kazantzakis's genius consists in the realization that God is *always* mutable; God's immutability consists in the everlasting divine mutability. The fact that God exists does not change, but *how* God exists does change in light of how the creatures change. Likewise, Kazantzakis indicates in his writings that God must be both active and receptive, just as Jesus could be both confrontational (when he cleansed the temple) and contemplative (in his passion). In each of these pairs Kazantzakis wisely tried to preserve the best in each element. For all the daring in his *neo*classical theism, he is still, in a way, neo*classical*.

I should close this chapter by noting that in one sense Kazantzakis was a very scholarly writer, as is evidenced in his knowledge of the ancient Greeks, various theological writers, Nietzsche, and Bergson. But in another sense he was a writer who eschewed intellectual categories and labels, as we will see in the next chapter on mysticism. The question here is not whether Kazantzakis's thought can be *reduced* to dipolar theism. Rather, the question is whether dipolar theism gets us closer to understanding his view of God than the alternatives: traditional theism, a purely temporalized deity, atheism, agnosticism, etc. My contention is that viewing Kazantzakis in terms of these other alternatives leaves out some significant features of his thought on God that are not left out if we view him as a dipolar theist. It must be admitted that Kazantzakis would probably not have been interested in some of the internecine debates among process theists themselves, debates surrounding the exact status of Platonic eternal objects, the degree to which God is omniscient with respect to "present" events, and so forth. It is clear, however, that he was very much interested in developing a view of God-in-process that was superior to that found in traditional theism, and this so as to avoid the satisfaction or complacency (Kazantzakian sins!) evidenced in most atheists or agnostics.

TWO SIDES OF

MYSTICISM

We have seen that the relationship between Kazantzakis and God is not an easy one to delineate. On the one hand, in some ways it is difficult to refer to him as a theist at all. For example, Katerina Anghelaki Rooke claims that Kazantzakis's transubstantiation of matter into spirit signifies humanity's victory over a non-God, that *Spiritual Exercises* is not theology but anthropology.[1] Helen Kazantzakis referred to her husband and herself as "atheists."[2] And Peter Bien indicates that early in life Kazantzakis admired the socialists *because* of their atheism.[3] On the other hand, Pandelis Prevelakis is surely correct that if Kazantzakis's texts are nontheological they nonetheless have the word "God" contained in them more frequently than in any other writer's works![4] The difficulty can be resolved, however, when it is realized that despite the fact, admitted by Kazantzakis himself, that his ultimate interest is not humanity but God, the God he has in mind is in many ways different from the one normally talked about in the Abrahamic religions (Judaism, Christianity, and Islam).[5] Bien puts the point well when he says that Kazantzakis was not a ζῷον *politikon* but a ζῷον *metaphysikon*, for whom politics was subordinate to the contemplative effort to discover the ultimate meaning of life and death, yet for whom "God" does not exactly refer to the traditional Western conception normally attached to this word, although, as I have argued, this point is often exaggerated by some interpreters.[6]

It makes sense to claim not only that Kazantzakis was a theist, albeit a heterodox one in some ways, but also to suggest that his writings are inspired with (literally, breathed into by) mystical concerns and experiences. In this chapter the designation "mysticism" will be used to refer to two theoretically distinct realities: (1) the immediate experience of an immanent God in transubstantiating activity; and (2) the experience of a transcendent God as ineffable or paradoxical or aw-ful precisely because of God's dematerialized condition. That is, in this chapter I will presuppose Kazantzakis's dipolar theism. Regarding the first sense of the term "mysticism" (mysticism-1), it should be noted that it would be odd if God, as an omnipresent being-in-becoming, could only be known or affirmed indirectly. Most of us are more like unreflective, mechanical, and dull-witted human beings than we usually admit. The most readily detectable data are those that are sometimes present, sometimes not, as in redness or pain. What is always given tends to escape notice. That is, the first sort of mysticism consists in the transubstantiating *activity* of putting oneself in a position to be receptive to the divine or the spiritual as ubiquitous.

Regarding the second sense of "mysticism" (mysticism-2), it is crucial to notice that some human beings intuitively prehend (as opposed to intellectually apprehend) or grasp implicitly that there is some sort of meaning in the world. That is, they *feel* as an inchoate object of experience that they are parts of a meaningful whole, that there is a concrete fact of relatedness between themselves and a personal force at work in the *universe*. That is, the second sense of mysticism consists in the fruit of the labors exerted in the first sense, in prehending and glorying in the fact that we are parts of a mighty whole.[7]

It will be the purpose of this chapter to argue that depictions of mysticism-1 *and* mysticism-2 play prominent parts in Kazantzakis's writings and that we can learn a great deal about both by taking Kazantzakis seriously. It should be emphasized, however, that the two mysticisms are in reality related even if they are theoretically distinct; they are two sides of the same coin, so to speak. Mysticism-1 is the transubstantiating activity of saving God, as Kazantzakis puts it, whereby matter is transformed into spirit. Or better, it is the immediate experience of this transubstantiation. And mysticism-2 is inchoate awareness of dematerialized spirit and of the whole point to transubstantiating activity.

After treating mysticism-1 and mysticism-2, I will: (a) look at Peter Bien's interpretation of Kazantzakis's mysticism; (b) examine three different sorts of terms that can be used when talking about God; and (c) consider the connections between Greek Orthodoxy and Kazantzakis's mysticism. Kazantzakis was an ascetic who intensely desired union with God. His asceticism is continuous with that found in Eastern monastic tradition, as is his belief that it is a human being as a psychosomatic whole who is engaged in the process of dematerialization or deification (*theosis*). But the Bergsonian dynamism found in Kazantzakis's transubstantiation is uncharacteristic of Eastern Orthodoxy. This should not, however, prevent us from noticing the somatic element in Kazantzakis (and this despite his asceticism) that is similar to Eastern Orthodoxy's prayer of the heart. Further, I will briefly treat the tension between apophatic and kataphatic theology in Kazantzakis, a tension that once again reminds us of his Eastern Orthodox roots.

Mysticism-1

Readers of Kazantzakis are familiar with his idea that God is to be found in action, even action replete with mistakes and fumblings if it is persistent. God is not the power that has found eternal equilibrium, as in "the God dressed in cassock, fingering the rosary, unwashed, unmarried, indolent." In fact, Kazantzakis indicates, as we have seen in chapter 2, that of all the definitions of God, the one he likes best is this: "God is a heart that is upright at the given hour!" In the following quotation we can see Kazantzakis denying that he was a mystic who scorned life, implying that he *was* a mystic of some sort:

> My friends believe me happy, because they do not know the struggles preliminary to every victory; because they do not know that my happiness is the supreme flowering of my own despair and my scorn for all things "terrestrial." I am not a Romantic in revolt, nor a mystic scorning life, nor an insolent belligerent against Substance. I love life, the earth, man, animal, ephemeral things. I know their value very well, and yet their limits too.[8]

The value Kazantzakis refers to here is at least partially divine in that God is blowing furiously all around us. Mysticism-1 consists in the ability to discriminate between ordinary reality that is in fact ordinary and "ordinary" reality that is infused with God. In ordinary moments, as in evening talks in front of the sea, one can sometimes find an eternal element that Kazantzakis refers to as the moment's "genuine essence."[9]

The essence of divinity as discovered in mysticism-1 is precisely the struggling, suffering, joy, and hope found in everyday life. Kazantzakis tries to avoid sentimentalism, however, in emphasizing not only the aforementioned talks in front of the sea, but also, and especially, the titanic struggles inside of those who take God seriously. For these heroic individuals God is anything but an abstraction.[10] Rather, for them life is an unceasing battle with God, the winds, snow, and death. "Paradise" for these heroic individuals, *for these mystics*, is exactly this inner fire whereby matter is burned up into spirit. For all we can tell, only human beings have mystical experiences, but the transubstantiating process for Kazantzakis, whereby matter is transformed into spirit, is cosmological and not merely anthropological. Even the manure that fertilizes the fruit is blessed in that it plays a role in the transubstantiating process whereby what is sweet and fresh are produced.[11] For example, the invincible charm of China, according to Kazantzakis, consists in the transubstantiation of the thickest mud into the lightest song.[12]

In one sense, at least, there is something romantic about mysticism-1 in Kazantzakis (despite what he says in the above quotation) in that, like Wordsworth, he has a tendency to believe that heaven lies about us in our infancy. The point is illustrated well by Zorba:

> Zorba sees everything every day as if for the first time. . . . As I listened to Zorba . . . the world was recovering its pristine freshness. All the dulled daily things regained the brightness they had in the beginning, when we came out of the hands of God. Water, women, the stars, bread, returned to their mysterious, primitive origin and the divine whirlwind burst once more upon the air. . . . The universe for Zorba, as for the first men on earth, was a weighty, intense vision; the stars glided over him, the sea broke against his temples. He lived the earth, water, the animals and God, without distorting intervention of reason. . . . God changes his appearance every second. Blessed is the man who can recognize him in all his disguises. At one moment he is a glass of fresh water, the next your son bouncing on your knees or an enchanting woman, or perhaps merely a morning walk.[13]

There is an obvious tension here. On the one hand, blessedness consists in *recognizing* God and, on the other, blessedness consists in *creating or saving* God. It is quite clear, however, which of these two tendencies has the upper hand in Kazantzakis: the latter one. Those moments of rest wherein we can recognize God are parts of a larger whole in which the religious hero or saint seeks the essence of God in struggle.[14]

Kazantzakis describes how he clambered on all fours, covered with blood, up God's rough, unaccommodating ascent:

> God is being built. I too have applied my tiny red pebble, a drop of blood, to give Him solidity lest He perish—so that He might give me solidity lest I perish.[15]

(Here, as in many other passages in Kazantzakis treated earlier in the book and some to be treated later, we can see that God is not purely anthropological.) At this point another tension comes to the fore; or better, the above tension between recognizing God and creating/saving God can be seen in another way. On the one hand, those who recognize God are those who are innocent, like children or primitive people. On the other hand, the religious hero in his or her struggle creates or saves God. These two tendencies are not necessarily in contradiction, however, as the following quotation shows:

> Truly, nothing more resembles God's eyes than the eyes of a child; they see the world for the first time, and create it. Before this, the world is chaos. All creatures—animals, trees, men, stones; everything: forms, colors, voices, smells, lightning flashes—flow unexplained in front of the child's eyes (no, not in front of them, inside them), and he cannot fasten them down, cannot establish order. The child's world is made not of clay, to last, but of clouds. A cool breeze blows across his temples and the world condenses, attenuates, vanishes. Chaos must have passed in front of God's eyes in just this way before the Creation.[16]

In childlike or Zorbalike innocence one sees what is essential, and *in this seeing* the world *is*, in a way, created. Kazantzakis makes it clear that the "childhood" he has in mind does not necessarily refer to those whose chronological years are few in number:

> I thank God that this refreshing childhood vision still lives inside me in all its fulness of color and sound. This is what keeps my mind untouched by wastage, keeps it from withering and running dry. It is the sacred drop of immortal water which prevents me from dying. When I wish to speak of the sea, woman, or God in my writing, I gaze down into my breast and listen carefully to what the child within me says. He dictates to me; and if it sometimes happens that I come close to these great forces of sea, woman, and God, approach them by means of words and depict them, I owe it to the child who still lives within me. I become a child again to enable myself to view the world always for the first time, with virgin eyes.[17]

My emphasis of mysticism-1 in Kazantzakis should not be interpreted as a negation of the obvious eroticism in his writings. In fact, one expression of the dynamism involved in mysticism-1 can be found in erotic passion. Dionysus was, after all, a god. But God has innumerable faces, including those of Ares, Athena, Yahweh, Jesus, and Buddha, who appear in our lives as moods and tendencies with which we must wrestle. The fact that each of these tendencies appears in the lives of others indicates that they are not idiosyncratic, nor, as I have been arguing, exclusively anthropocentric. God does not so much sit on a throne (unless he is appearing momentarily in the guise of Yahweh) as he or she wrestles here on earth with us and in us.[18] In more primitive, childlike ages everything may have been ingenuous, and there is still a need, as we have seen, to keep alive the view that natural beauty is like manna from heaven, a communication from heaven via the magical ladder of simplicity. It is much more likely in our age, however, that we discover God through struggle, but (erotic, i.e., passionate) struggle itself interpenetrates with innocence, as when we again notice the following quotations:

> The soul withdraws into mystic and religious ecstasies. Saint Teresa loves Christ in the flesh. And how many monks in those half-lit silent churches had not themselves been enamored of the pale Madonnas![19]

Teresa of Avila is, for Kazantzakis, as we have seen, the mystic wife of Don Quixote:

> For Teresa the holy life was not a mad fury that sprouts wings and tries to escape from the world. It was a patient, hard-working life of love. . . . Patience, logic, gaiety, love— these are the four mares that pulled the carriage of Saint Teresa and her soul.[20]

She tried to live perfectly her own "tiny individual life" so as to follow a rhythm that is higher than ourselves. She tried, in Kazantzakian fashion, to liberate "Someone" inside of her who was a slave struggling to get free. Or again, religion is a breath that had once, in the Middle Ages, risen like a fire, but which had, in her age, died down; hence her efforts to rekindle this fire. Yet:

> Even the most mystical of Spanish women, Saint Teresa, never lost the sacred mean. And if there is a Paradise, and if they tackle housekeeping up there too, and if there are things up there too that need locking up, surely Saint Teresa, the Spanish woman, will keep the keys.[21]

The eclecticism of Kazantzakis's religiosity can perhaps better be termed his belief in the transubstantiation of matter to spirit as ubiquitous but seldom noticed. Even the bullfight exhibits a primitive Holy Communion, and with real flesh and blood. It exhibits a violent contact with God not altogether different from Teresa's, despite initial appearances to the contrary. For example, the bullfight reconciles us to death, an effort that the mystic would otherwise find commendable. And the bullfight awakens in the spectators a primeval, mysterious intoxication aroused by blood that is not entirely anthropological.[22] The "mystical March" to God is, in a way, dreadful as well as joyous. Kazantzakian religion consists in exploring *all* of the possible means of recognizing or creating/saving God: ascetic, hedonistic, agonistic, and intellectual (the "fight in the skull" is crucial for Kazantzakis as old ideas are smashed and new ones born).[23] Kazantzakis is aware of the mysterious significance of *both* ascetical preparation for "Holy Communion," when one fasts and puts oneself in the proper frame of mind, as well as the pleasure associated with a mouthful of bread and a sip of wine, which can, in certain circumstances and with the right attitude, lead us to think we have grown wings.[24]

The overall point to this section of the chapter is that there are numerous texts in Kazantzakis, from all periods in his career, that attest to the fact that for him certain religious individuals (mystics) "hear God breathing everywhere."[25] This fact is especially confirmed in *Spiritual Exercises* where he says, as we have already noticed, that:

> God struggles in every thing, his hands flung upward toward the light. What light? Beyond and above every thing![26]

It is the job of religious individuals (mystics) to recognize this struggling God *and* to aid in the transubstantiating process whereby earthen matter is molded and liberated:

> My God is not Almighty. He struggles, for he is in peril every moment; he trembles and stumbles in every living thing, and he cries out. He is defeated incessantly, but rises again, full of blood and earth, to throw himself into battle once more.[27]

Kazantzakis's God is not omnipotent. Nor is his God omnibenevolent *in the traditional sense*, where God's goodness is fully actualized outside of the struggles of creatures in time. Some heterodox Christians deny divine omnipotence, but to be *any* sort of Christian, even a heterodox one, seems to require a belief in *some* sort of divine omnibenevolence. Hence even though Kazantzakis's treatments of religious experience (mysticism) rely heavily on Saints Teresa, John of the Cross, Ignatius of Loyola, Francis of Assisi, and others, there will always be some problems in *fully* reconciling his view with Christianity. As we have seen and will continue to see, however, this point can be exaggerated, especially by those under the spell of Kazantzakis's Nietzscheanism. In one sense, for Kazantzakis, God is as great or as good *as possible at any particular time*, but new moments bring with them new possibilities for divine struggle and accomplishment.

We do not proceed from divine unity back to the same divine unity again. Natural processes are not deceptions or multicolored phantasmagoria unrelated to God. Rather, they are condensations of two enormous powers:

One power descends and wants to scatter, to come to a
standstill, to die. The other power ascends and strives for
freedom, for immortality.[28]

Peter Bien quotes Kazantzakis as saying that the transubstantiation of this
"downward" material power into the "upward" spiritual one is

the sole method followed by all organic beings in order to
deliver themselves from inertia, tranquility, and prosperity,
and to throw themselves into danger, adventure, and unex-
pected success.[29] (emphasis added)

And, as we have seen, this transubstantiating process takes many forms.
Kazantzakis even suggests that Teresa of Avila, if she were alive in the
twentieth century, would be a political activist in that this is the contemporary
form taken by the spirit in its struggle to ascend. Kazantzakis's "god," according
to Bien (Bien reserves "God" for the Judeo-Christian deity, using "god" for
Kazantzakis's deity), is the "ever-renewed and ever-refined creative energy
manifested in a process by which the vital force employs materiality in order to
pass beyond materiality."[30]

Prevelakis reports the testimony of Panait Istrati to the effect that
Kazantzakis himself was a mystic whose feet were nonetheless on the ground.[31]
But this is not odd in that mysticism-1 is by definition this-worldly. Richard
Chilson, however, rightly notices that despite Kazantzakis's lifelong desire for
mystic unity with God, dualism remains "the pervasive fabric" of his thought.
Kazantzakis is, in fact, a monist, but this is largely a monism of aspiration. Or
again, mysticism-1 is the periodic or intermittent experience of the divinity that
is always there; most of the time mystics experience the world nonmystically.
Kazantzakis may have personally had an aversion to flesh, but his "whole
philosophy," as Chilson puts it, is expressed through material images.[32] Most of
the time Kazantzakis and other mystics live in and through matter; mysticism-1
consists in those rare situations wherein we realize that God huddles in every
cell.[33] Although, as Bien emphasizes regarding The Last Temptation of Christ,
union with God is the supreme purpose of Kazantzakis's struggle, it is not easy to
achieve this purpose if God is pure or fully transubstantiated spirit. Bien puts
the point well:

This . . . is what The Last Temptation is about: evolution
toward dematerialization. I call it a post-Christian book
because, although it employs the Christian myth, it speaks
to a Darwinian culture, rejecting the idea of a static, everlasting kingdom as the goal of Jesus' endeavors. The spirit
that drives Jesus toward his goal is an eternally dynamic and

cyclical creativity which, no sooner has it found release from materiality, will re-embody itself and start the process anew—which is why the novel's very last words are not "It is finished" but rather "Everything has begun."[34]

Note both words in Bien's phrase "eternally dynamic." Rather than "cyclical," however, we might say "spiral." Kazantzakis seems to be opposed to both the dogmatically linear mode of thinking in most Marxists, say, as well as to the utter circularity or futility of some existentialists. If he was at certain stages of his career a Marxist, it was a Marxism "polluted" by mysticism, as Minas Savvas puts the point.[35] In *The Greek Passion* we hear from Priest Fotis that God is never in a hurry to burn up or transubstantiate matter. Measured against the chronology of God, a human being's life, even a mystic's life, is truly an instant.[36]

The Influence of Bergson, Again

It is not too controversial to claim that Bergson and Nietzsche were the two greatest intellectual influences on Kazantzakis, but it is still somewhat controversial to say that Kazantzakis's universe is much more of a Bergsonian one than a Nietzschean one. This thesis is less startling, however, as a result of Peter Bien's study of Kazantzakis, the best written to date, *Kazantzakis: Politics of the Spirit*. In an analysis of *The Greek Passion* (in England: *Christ Recrucified*), Bien highlights the features of Bergson's influence on Kazantzakis that are crucial for an understanding of his view of mysticism:

> Bergsonism's most subtle presence occurs in *Christ Recrucified*, where it governs the very structure of the plot since the refugees—forever moving, forever producing effects by means of which their own reality expands and transcends its being—are the developed organisms through whom the continuity of genetic energy passes like a current, upwards, toward composition, whereas the established citizens who resist them in the village represent matter's inverted evolution toward decomposition. The meeting of these two streams is the luminous interval called life, the interval between the one dark abyss from which the refugees enter the book at the start (as energy longing to express itself via materiality) and the other dark abyss into which they pass out of the book at the end, defeated in materiality but with their creative potential intact. If we allow the images to guide us to an intuition of duration, as both Bergson and

> Kazantzakis desire, we will appreciate the degree to which
> this remarkable novel is governed in its deep structure by a
> vitalistic theory of the world and of human destiny.[37]

The past is dead, but the future is alive with possibilities, including (on Bergsonian but not on Nietzschean grounds) the possibility of union with God.

Three other scholars who are helpful in the effort to establish a strong connection between Kazantzakis's mysticism and Bergson's are Maurice Friedman, George Pollby, and Andreas Poulakidas. Friedman is correct to point out that Bergson and Kazantzakis found in the Christian mystics an active love that represents one of the highest upward surges (the highest, for Bergson) of the creative force. The mystic passes through a mystical state only to burst a dam and be swept back into a vast current of life. For both Bergson and Kazantzakis it is the creative process itself that is the object of mystical experience-1, a process that Zorba, say, saw with radical amazement.[38] Pollby is right to suggest that even the "even this one does not exist" at the finale of *Spiritual Exercises* is more Bergsonian than Nietzschean. This is due to the fact that it is a positive pointing beyond what might be assumed to be the final word in that book; beyond the finale of this book there are joyous struggle and unknown possibilities.[39] As Poulakidas emphasizes, it is the transubstantiating process that has the upper hand in Kazantzakis. Old terms like *metousiosis*, *metavole*, and *transubstantio* were given new meanings by Kazantzakis, yet they need not scandalize Christians because they serve well to stave off nihilism. There is no need to despair when both Bergsonian instinct and intelligence provide "mystical communications" to the human soul.[40]

Mysticism-2

From all of the above some still might conclude that mysticism in Kazantzakis could still be interpreted strictly in anthropological or at least natural terms. It is the purpose of the present section of the chapter to supplement the efforts in chapter 5 on dipolar theism to dispute this conclusion. Throughout his career Kazantzakis indicated something like the following idea from *Spiritual Exercises*:

> I feel that behind appearances this struggling essence is also
> striving to merge with my heart. But the body stands
> between us and separates us. The mind stands between us
> and separates us. What is my duty? To shatter the body, to
> rush and merge with the Invisible. To let the mind fall silent
> that I may hear the Invisible calling. I walk on the rim of the
> abyss, and I tremble. Two voices contend within me. The

> mind: "Why waste ourselves by pursuing the impossible? Within the holy enclosure of our five senses it is our duty to acknowledge the limitations of man." But another voice within me—call it the Sixth Power, call it the heart—resists and shouts: "No! No! Never acknowledge the limitations of man. Smash all boundaries! Deny whatever your eyes see. Die every moment, but say 'Death does not exist'."[41]

It should not be assumed here that Kazantzakis hopes for personal immortality; rather, it is this Invisible that is deathless. At another point in the same work Kazantzakis refers to this "Invisible" as "Someone Else" for whose sake we toil (note that he does not say "something else"). This Someone Else is a spiritual being who "storms through matter and fructifies it," a spiritual being who, as in Saints Teresa of Avila and John of the Cross, is referred to by Kazantzakis as the Bridegroom of eternity and of the human soul.[42]

Mysticism-2 is an experience of God that is literally ecstatic in that one is transported out of one's normal place into a (partial) union with "God, the Great Ecstatic," to use Kazanzakis' phrase, the being "who gives birth to all things." Other Kazantzakian names for God include "Deathless Abyss," "Mystery," "Absolute Darkness," "Absolute Light," and "Spirit." Clearly God is transcendent in *some* sense for Kazantzakis as well as immanent. The fact that his God does not entirely fit under the old features (as before, Kazantzakis's God is not omnipotent) does not necessarily mean that his God is totally of anthropological origin. Just as each one of us constantly changes yet retains some sort of identity through these changes (my life is still mine and not yours), so also there is a sense in which God is "always the same" for Kazantzakis. God is the *indestructible* rhythm that battles for freedom. He even suggests something close to a divine view of the world *sub specie aeternitatis* when "God gazes on his own struggle." As before, Kazantzakis's deity is much like Whitehead's primordial nature of God, an eternal lure or Cry, who seduces us to advance in our spiritual lives. God can do this because behind the innumerable, ephemeral masks God has assumed there is "an indestructible unity":[43]

> The essence of God is obscure. It ripens continuously, perhaps victory is strengthened with our every valorous deed, but perhaps even all these agonizing struggles toward deliverance and victory are inferior to the nature of divinity.[44]

At times we find Kazantzakis wistfully contemplating God before the creation of the world, a vision so sublime that he aptly compares God to a dark catacomb. He knows that God is an eternal element in that he has inchoate, mystical experience of this fact, but this experience indicates to him that God is "beyond logic in the geometry of the universe." In the following quotation from Helen Kazantzakis's biography, note that Kazantzakis refers to God not only within him but also *around* him:

> The major and almost the only theme of all my work is the struggle of man with "God": the unyielding, inextinguishable struggle of the naked worm called "man" against the terrifying power and darkness of the forces within him and around him.[45]

Behind appearances there is a divine essence, an "Invisible One," and this, as we have seen, must be kept in mind when we interpret Kazantzakis's silence at the end of *Spiritual Exercises*, a work he refers to as "completely mystical." Elsewhere he is quite explicit that by "silence" he does not mean what we normally mean by the term, nor does he refer to a type of despair. Rather, Kazantzakis is worried that without a period of silence, and without a claim that "even this one does not exist," we would end up with a god that looks too much like a human being. Kazantzakis states rather forcefully that "I do not want him!" What he wants is "the big mystery" rather than any small one.[46]

In one sense God, as the transubstantiation of matter into spirit, can be seen, and in another sense God is, as Kazantzakis puts it, "Unseen."[47] Like a Japanese garden, we arrange individual stones in an ephemeral way so as nonetheless to indicate certain elements of (an unseen) eternity.[48] The eternal is not necessarily pretty, but it certainly is aw-ful; to breathe it is to sense its acrid air; it is like a tremendous whirlwind that breaks every harmony, always seeking something higher.[49] Kazantzakian prayer consists in being pushed beyond one's limits to the point where one could break; it consists in moving beyond the masks of God and beyond religious symbols to discern "the same never-changing God." To talk about this God at all obviously returns us to the use of symbols, such as when Kazantzakis refers to this God as "chaos, a terrifying uninhabited darkness," a description that is familiar to those who have read the great Christian mystics. Similar descriptions can be found in St. John of the Cross and in *The Cloud of Unknowing*.[50]

In one sense Kazantzakis makes the claim familiar in mysticism-2 that God does not have a name in that God is too big for names: "A name is a prison, God is free." Hence it makes sense for him to say that silence is the voice of God. There is an almost identical emphasis in the Spanish mystics with which Kazantzakis was familiar, as in St. John of the Cross' "Silent music, Sounding solitude" (*La musica callada, La soledad sonora*). A fine book has been written even about the importance of silence in St. Thomas Aquinas, who talked a great deal about God! The similarities between Kazantzakis's mysticism-2 and Christian mysticism are perhaps nowhere more evident than in the following lines from *Report to Greco*:

> Every man is half God, half man; he is both spirit and flesh.
> That is why the mystery of Christ is not simply a mystery for
> a particular creed; it is universal. The struggle between God
> and man breaks out in everyone, together with the longing
> for reconciliation. . . . God does not love weak souls and
> flabby flesh . . . the supreme purpose of the struggle—union
> with God.[51]

It should be noted that there is a slight difference here between Christian mystics, who tend to desire union with God, and Jewish ones, who are far more impressed with God as *totaliter aliter*, such that their desire is not so much union with God as *devekuth* (loving intimacy). That is, to say that silence is the voice of God is not necessarily to say that God is *totally* beyond human experience and comprehension. The relationship between human beings and God is one of personal contact, although the divine person(s) sometimes initiates such a contact with the force of a lightning flash, one of Kazantzakis's favorite metaphors for mysticism-2. A less violent contact is found when Kazantzakis quotes St. Francis of Assisi's biographer, Thomas of Celano, to the effect that only a thin partition separated Francis from eternity such that he was always able to hear the divine melody.[52]

It is not so much that we are blind with respect to God, as that we do not understand the sublime magnitude of the little that we do see, as when Kazantzakis describes the person who explores God's toenail and immediately assumes that God is hard like a stone. Mysticism-2 at least partially consists in the realization that we are not to measure God by our own hearts, but rather vice versa.[53] Like Teresa of Avila, Kazantzakis indicates that behind all appearances lies a struggling divine essence (the "Invisible") that is striving to merge with our hearts just as the mystic is striving to merge with God's. Nonetheless God's striving is on a cosmic scale such that there is something trivial involved when we push anthropocentric images too far in our description of God. Behind any religious face like Buddha's or Confucius's or Jesus' lies the awesome reality of the Tao or the Great Spirit or God—the Great Ecstatic.[54] Because of the sublimity of God, it seems to be essential in Kazantzakis that mysticism-2 involve ascetical rigor, a discipline fostered by places like Assisi and Avila that are "all stones and saints." We must tame some passions in order to unleash others in Kazantzakis's religious eroticism. But no human passion is sufficient to put God under our thumbs. Kazantzakis defines "God" in *Spain* as "the Power that always gives us more than we are able to receive and always asks for more than we are able to give."[55]

Kazantzakis is very clear about the fact that he thinks there is some "mystic law" at work in the world.[56] The purpose of the present chapter is to determine exactly what this mystic law is in Kazantzakis. It is certainly to be associated with the divine immanence that I have referred to as mysticism-1.

But I think it is misleading to claim that Kazantzakis's mysticism is exhausted by contact with divine immanence in that it is too easy to turn mysticism-1, when seen as self-authenticating and without its connection to mysticism-2, into a species of anthropology. As Jerry Gill puts the point, "the very idea of limits brings into existence the possibility of transcending them." And Gill is correct to draw the following lesson from *The Last Temptation of Christ*: "the ultimate temptation is that of being content to live within the limits of a natural, human existence." It must be admitted that Kazantzakis was at least tempted by nihilism and atheism, but there are too many passages in Kazantzakis, as I have tried to show, where he makes it clear that he does not want a merely human "god."[57] Nor does he want a "god" who would be limited by our puny imaginations. It is those who turn Kazantzakis's partial criticism of (and partial appropriation of!) traditional theism into an agnosticism or an atheism who are unfaithful to Kazantzakis's texts.

My treatment of mysticism-1 makes it possible to incorporate pantheistic *elements* and Buddhist *threads* into one's interpretation of Kazantzakis, but neither a pantheistic nor a Buddhist/nihilist interpretation can bear the weight of Kazantzakis's many writings about God *simpliciter*.[58] There is a sense in which (the traditional) God, for Kazantzakis, had in fact ceased to exist, à la Buddhism, or better, à la Nietzsche. But there is another sense in which God continues to exist as a (Whiteheadean) lure for human beings.[59] The form and function of *Spiritual Exercises*, for example, are emblematic of Kazantzakis's theism in general: the awareness of and ascent toward God—mysticism-1—and then beyond—mysticism-2.

Bien's Interpretation

Peter Bien has noted the similarity between Kazantzakis and William James with respect to their critiques of useless abstractions. But there is another similarity between the two. Both Kazantzakis and James have been interpreted as defenders of a purely immanentist or anthropological theism, whereas both in actuality play a counterpoint to their dominant, immanentist theme. This counterpoint consists in the notes heard by those who pay attention to the *farther side* of the unheard order and to the "More" in religion.[60] It is precisely union with this "More," this "Someone Else," that mysticism-2 is all about.

Two fundamental elements constitute the essence of Christian *and* Kazantzakian sanctity: a disciplined life or asceticism, on the one hand, and union with God, to the extent that this is possible, on the other. And, it should be noted, these two are connected. It is only through a disciplined, transubstantiating life that one can be in a position to achieve union with God. These two elements are also found in Buddhism. That is, we should avoid the view that suggests that Buddhism is simply self-abnegation or nihilism or a religious atheism. Stephen R. L. Clark's quotation of Gautama is instructive in this regard:

> There is an Unborn, Unoriginated, Uncreated, Unformed. If there were not this Unborn, this Unoriginated, this Uncreated, this Unformed, escape from the world of the born, the originated, the created, the formed would be impossible.[61]

Nothing in what I have said entails the claim that Kazantzakis believed in personal immortality. Clearly his belief was that if we are to be apotheosized it is to be in this, our only, life.[62] Rather, with Bien, I am suggesting that, for Kazantzakis, it is God who is "Immortal." What this means is that Kazantzakis is searching neither for heaven nor Nirvana nor *ataraxia*. Kazantzakis believes in matter; or better, in the transformation of matter into spirit and in the attachment of an embodied human being to spirit as if fastened by a nail. The (nonanthropocentric) "God" of Kazantzakis is a name given to a dark force at work in the world that in many ways is more like an agitated Yahweh or God the Father than like an anaesthetic or passive receiver of human woes. In any event, Kazantzakis's theism is Buddhist if what one means by Buddhism includes a consideration of the aforementioned Unborn or Undying, and it is in the Abrahamic tradition *if* what one means by Judaism, Christianity, or Islam is an embracing of mysticism-1 and mysticism-2.[63]

Bien puts Kazantzakis's mysticism into focus when he says that human knowing (*gnōsis*)—"You and I are one, Lord"—is necessarily followed by unknowing (*agnōsis*)—"Even this one does not exist." The former element is reminiscent of the kataphatic tradition of Christian mysticism, otherwise known as the *via positiva*. But the latter element does not necessarily lead to nihilism, as some scholars allege,[64] in that it is part of traditional apophatic theology or the *via negativa*. This negativity is not absolute, but rather is indicative of a psychic renewal consistent both with Buddhism and Christianity (including Greek Orthodoxy). It is a "rest in the life force's evolution toward ever-increasing value." Only silence as part of the *via negativa*, Bien thinks, can "abrogate the differentiation implicit in words" so as to tease into consciousness the wholeness of God.[65]

Religious Language

In order to adequately understand Kazantzakis's language about God it will be useful to be precise regarding three different uses of religious language. What is crucial from a Kazantzakian point of view is that two extremes be avoided: that we can capture deity in some verbal formula devoid of any doubt or obscurity, on the one hand, and that we are totally in the dark in the effort to describe God, on the other.

1. Literal terms applied to God do not deal with matters of degree, but must deal with matters of all or none. That is, literal terms express a purely formal status by classifying propositions as of a certain logical type. For example, the categorical terms "absolute" and "relative" have a literal meaning when applied to God: either God is independent of (that is, is absolute with respect to) creatures for divine existence or not. And either God is related to (that is, is relative to) creatures in the divine actuality or not. God, for Kazantzakis, is literally absolute in existence and relative in actuality or in the mode of divine existence (the latter because God needs creatures, as Kazantzakis often indicates).
2. Analogical terms applied to God, by way of contrast, admit of degree as they apply to different entities within the same logical type. For example, concrete individuals feel in different degrees of intensity and with different levels of adequacy, with God being the supreme example of feeling in that God is intensely affected by and affects all of reality.
3. Any symbolic terms applied to God are used locally and not cosmically to a particular kind of individual in a particular culture, with an even greater degree of specificity than analogical terms, as when God is referred to as a lightning bolt or a king.

There is an obvious distinction between formal and material predication. To compare God with a rock, a king, a shepherd, or a parent is a material description that cannot be literal. Formal or non-material predication is illustrated when one refers to God as noncorporeal or nonrelative *or* when one refers to God as corporeal or relative. That is, when the abstraction "concreteness" or "corporeality" is applied to God one is not identifying God with any particular concrete thing, but is rather contrasting the abstraction "concreteness" with the abstraction "immateriality." The formal (literal) predicates of deity are not exclusively negative. If God's very existence cannot be contingent (God is eternal for Kazantzakis), the question arises: Is God's necessary existence to be conceived as having the ability to be related to creatures (indeed the *need* to be related to creatures, for Kazantzakis) or simply as the absence of relativity? These are two categorically or formally opposite ways of interpreting the proposition "God exists." On either interpretation something literal is being said of God. In between the formal, literal terms (absolute-relative, being-becoming, etc.) and the most material, particular, symbolic ones (shepherd, monarch, lightning bolt, etc.) there are analogical terms (love, personality, etc.). To the extent that analogical terms involve qualitative distinctions of degree they are removed from the all-or-nothing character of literal terms. Who can say literally how divine love differs *qualitatively* from ours? That is, there is a certain amount of Kazantzakian "silence" at work when analogical or especially symbolic religious language is used.

Neither abstractness nor concreteness have been properly understood by theists, overly influenced as they often are by the tradition of negative theology. It is easy enough to say that one is being modest in claiming that human language cannot properly apply to God, hence we cannot speak literally about God. But negative theology itself can be a sort of presumption. Dare we to forbid God to sustain relations with creatures and thus be influenced by them? Traditional theists do precisely this, but not Kazantzakis. When traditional theists say that God may have relations with creatures symbolically, and in effect tell God that such relations cannot be literal, is this not monstrous presumption? Kazantzakis, by way of contrast, does not try to exert this sort of veto power over God.

The modesty of negative theology is somewhat suspect because it puts a human veto on the wealth of the divine life. Kazantzakis is, in fact, influenced by negative theology, but not exclusively so: he *does* say things about God! We can speak literally about the fact that God is relative, that is, is related to (must be related to) creatures. But we cannot speak literally about what it is like concretely to *be* God. Here we must be silent. We can only speak of God in literal terms if we do so abstractly; we can only talk about what it is like to *be* God concretely in, at best, analogical terms. But if there is no sense whatsoever in which univocal meaning or literal terms can be used regarding God, then talk about God is pure sophistry.

The heavy influence of the *via negativa* on traditional theism has created the illusion of safety in what is not said regarding description of God. But overly aggressive negative theologians have typically atoned for their paucity of discourse by an orgy of symbols and metaphors. Kazantzakis is obviously not opposed to metaphor; in fact he implies that religious metaphor has a crucial role to play in moving the emotions toward God. But description of God must be based on *some* literal terms or it is a scandal. Analogy itself, as a comparison between things that are somewhat similar and somewhat different, ultimately rests on there being *some* univocity of discourse so as to secure the similarities. It is true, however, that the contingent or concrete aspect of God (as opposed to the abstraction "contingency" or the abstraction "concreteness") transcends reason and literal discourse in the sense that this reality must ultimately be felt as a sheer fact.

It is one thing to know an individual as distinguished from other individuals. It is another thing to know that same individual in *its* actual mode of existence or in *its* actual state. To know deity in this sense is to know the universe as God knows it. Once again, here we must maintain Kazantzakian silence.

Kazantzakis and Eastern Orthodoxy

Kazantzakis grew up in an Eastern Orthodox culture even if he later was educated by Franciscans and lived much of his life in Western Christian (or post-Christian) cultures. But there is no great need to worry about whether Kazantzakis was more affected by Western or Eastern theism when it is realized that a similar mysticism plays a prominent role in both traditions. Vladimir Lossky is correct to note that the cleavage between Eastern and Western Christianity only dates from the eleventh century, such that all that is prior constitutes a common tradition. The Orthodox church would not be what is is without Saints Augustine and Gregory the Great, and the Roman church could not do without Saints Athanasius or Basil.[66] Hence it should not surprise us that the tension between apophatic and kataphatic theology characterizes both traditions. Saint Thomas Aquinas, the quintessential Western theologian, for example, quotes the largely apophatic pseudo-Dionysus over 1,700 times![67] Regarding some theological issues Kazantzakis is obviously heterodox according to both Western and Eastern standards: his denial of divine omnipotence, his Arian Christology, and his denial of personal immortality. But on at least two other issues, and these surrounding mysticism, Kazantzakis is well within the folds of Western and especially Eastern churches, as I will illustrate in this, the final section of the chapter, where I will compare Kazantzakis to the Orthodox approaches to these two issues.

The first issue concerns the role of the human in mysticism. There is a range of monastic life in Eastern Orthodoxy from the extreme eremitism of St. Anthony of Egypt to the organized cenobitism of St. Pachomius. Although the latter tendency was more committed to the active life—social work, manuscript copying, etc.—than the former, neither tendency exhibits the dynamism found in Kazantzakian/Bergsonian transubstantiation. Yet Kazantzakis's asceticism is continuous with the Eastern monastic tradition, in general, as is his belief that spirituality consists, as it did for the fourth-century monk Macarius, in a human being as a psychosomatic whole engaging in a process of dematerialization or deification (*theosis*). And the tension between Macarius's "prayer of the heart," which depends on its somatic element, and the view of Macarius's contemporary Evagrius, who defended a Neoplatonic stance influenced by Origen called the "prayer of the mind," is found throughout Kazantzakis's writings. That is, the somatic element in Kazantzakis, and this despite his asceticism, is reminiscent of Macarius (and of the seventh-century monk John Climacus, who emphasizes Jesus and the incarnational element in mysticism); and the intellectualism that very often dominates the aesthetic element in Kazantzakis's novels is reminiscent of Evagrius. Macarius (or better, the Macarian Homilies, if not written by Macarius) reverts to a more biblical idea of the human person rather than to the Platonic idea that the soul is imprisoned in the body. Deification here, as in Maximus the Confessor, does not suppress humanity but makes it more authentically human.[68] My point here is that Kazantzakis can be, should be, discussed in the same breath with these monks.

The second issue concerns the tension between apophatic and kataphatic theology, between the way of negation and the way of union, respectively. It is not odd that we find Kazantzakis at different points in his writings traveling down both roads. Some of those who have most emphasized divine transcendence, and hence apophatic theology—Gregory of Nyssa, the pseudo-Dionysus, Maximus the Confessor—also believed in true mystical union with God. The difficulty in Kazantzakis regarding how God can be both knowable and unknowable is typical of Abrahamic religions in general. In Eastern Orthodoxy the kataphatic tendency, wherein God is knowable, is often associated with the hesychasts (*hēsychia* means "quiet"), who devote themselves to inner recollection and private prayer in the effort to experience God directly. In the fourteenth century the hesychasts were defended and given a firm dogmatic basis by St. Gregory Palamas. He was opposed, however, by the more apophatic defender of divine otherness, Barlaam, who thought that God could only be experienced indirectly. It should be noted that hesychasm or quietism has never been officially accepted by the Western Church, even if this tendency has had Western representatives who have at least positively influenced officially recognized mystics like John of the Cross and Teresa of Avila.

These two issues are connected in that the hesychast vision of divine light, which does not necessarily undermine the apophatic doctrine of God, is often produced by somatic "techniques" (a dangerous word) like the constant repetition of the Jesus prayer or carefully regulating breathing in conjunction with this prayer. As in the Macarian Homilies, the hesychast and Gregory Palamas see the body not as an enemy but as a partner of the soul. "Christ, by taking a human body at the Incarnation, has made the flesh an inexhaustible source of sanctification."[69] This emphasis on the body in prayer is obviously not an example of the sort of gross materialism constantly criticized by Kazantzakis, but is rather an effort to remain faithful to the biblical idea of the unity of a human being and to Aristotelian hylomorphism, wherein the soul and the body function together as a unity. (There is nothing wrong with Aristotle's hylomorphism, only his abandonment of it when discussing the gods.) Through somatic/psychic effort we know the "energies" but not the essence (*ousia*) of God, according to Gregory of Palamas and the Cappadocian Fathers, a doctrine that helps us to make sense of Kazantzakis's affirmations regarding God *and* of his emphasis on silence. Or, as Gerard Manley Hopkins put the point, the whole world is charged with the grandeur of God (à la mysticism-1), yet this God is also a partially unknowable Burning Bush (à la mysticism-2). When unguarded, mysticism-1 can lead to a pantheism where God is too immanent;

and when left unchecked, the apophatic tendency makes God too transcendent. Kazantzakis, like the great Orthodox monks, tries to avoid both of these
extremes.[70] As before, despite appearances there is a conservative element in
Kazantzakis wherein he tries to preserve the best in the conflicting forces at
work in religious tradition.

METHOD AND

PURPOSE

Implicit in much of what has been said in the first six chapters of this book is a view of Kazantzakis's method and purpose in the development of his view of God, a method that obviously includes a certain antipathy to method. In the present chapter I would like to make this method explicit. On the evidence I have cited thus far, I think the following twelve points can be safely claimed about Kazantzakis's method:

1. There is a tension in Kazantzakis between Western (specifically, Greek) moderation and Eastern (or Asian) restlessness.
2. Or again, there is a tension in Kazantzakis between the desire to harmonize opposites and the desire to break all harmonizing boundaries in the effort to progress by conquering the weight of the status quo in religion.
3. We can deny neither the Western harmony of opposites tendency nor the Eastern tendency to shatter this harmony, but it is clear that for Kazantzakis the former rests on the latter.
4. Thus, in a sense it is fair to say that all that is worthwhile in the human-divine relationship is ultimately Eastern.
5. Nonetheless there is a symbiotic relationship between Western rationalism and Eastern mysticism such that there is more matter in spirit than many Eastern believers think and more spirit in matter than many Western thinkers imagine.

6. The reason for the derivative status of reason in Kazantzakis is that divinity itself is a whirlwind (as in the Book of Job) who breaks every harmony.[1]

7. This transcendence of rational harmony leads to what Kazantzakis refers to as an abyss or to a transubstantiation of matter into spirit or pure air or nothingness.

8. But this abyss or nothingness is not sheer nonbeing (whatever this might be: to think about it is to turn it into a somethingness, as Parmenides realized), but is one moment in the systole and diastole of the religious life: knowing (gnōsis) shattered by creative unknowing or silence (agnōsis) leading to an attempt to reach a higher sort of knowing and so on.

9. That is, in both Buddhism and Christianity there is an attempt to extol the virtues of the ascetical life so as to achieve union with the Unborn and Uncreated; in both of these religions that affected Kazantzakis so profoundly there is a place for silence and for the claim that "even this one does not exist."

10. As we have seen Bien emphasize, the apophatic way or the via negativa is needed to provide rest or psychic renewal so as to abrogate the differentiation implicit in words (in the kataphatic efforts of the via positiva), a differentiation that prevents the union mentioned above at (9).

11. God is, as the hesychasts with their somatic techniques realized, at least partially knowable, contra those who would assert (strange as this sounds) the hegemony of the apophatic.

12. There is a dialectical tension in Kazantzakis between Bergsonian tendencies and Buddhist ones, but the tension can perhaps best be understood in terms of the inclusion of the latter in the former; once again, silence and the experience of nothingness are but moments in the ongoing and apparently never ending process of the universe. There is no contradiction between (12) and (4) because Bergson, although French, nonetheless defended a view that relies heavily on Eastern tendencies, as was seen in chapter 1.

My effort to make these methodological commitments in Kazantzakis explicit will consist in a treatment of his relationship to various phenomena (Eastern Orthodoxy, ancient Greek religion, Buddhism, Russia) as evidenced in several of his works that I will treat in the later sections of the chapter: the novel *Toda Raba*, the travel book on *Russia*, and several plays: *Buddha, Sodom and Gomorrah, Christopher Columbus, Melissa,* and *Kouros*. The point, however, is that one needs to read a great deal of Kazantzakis to get an adequate understanding of his method in that one can easily think that he engaged in apophatic orgies or that he absolutely hated Western rationality if certain hyperbolic passages are taken in isolation and not within the larger systole-diastole picture.

The Perennial Greek Predicament

In an important article on Kazantzakis and the relationship between contemporary Greece and ancient Greece, Bien makes it clear that for Kazantzakis Greece (and especially Crete) lies between West and East.[2] The ancient Greeks transubstantiated primitive instinct, orgiastic intoxication, and a bestial shout into love and religious worship, just as the ancient Greeks themselves were the transubstantiated product of both the barbaric Dorians and the comparatively civilized Achaeans.[3] But the emergence of reason in ancient Greece did not *have to* culminate in what Bien refers to as the quixotic Western attempt to conquer necessity (*anangkē*). The quintessential example of this attempt consists in the belief in divine omnipotence, where *everything* occurs for a (divine) reason, a belief resisted by both Plato and Kazantzakis. There are some things outside not only of human but also divine control, for example the precise manner in which millions of free agents can act such that they get in each other's way. The perennial Greek predicament is precisely our predicament: how to reap the benefits of rationality without having it poison us?

Nietzsche's response to this question, a response that obviously influenced Kazantzakis, was to criticize the Western appropriation of Greek rationality from the time of Socrates on, praising instead Presocratic balance. Kazantzakis extols the Zorbatic virtue of folly or madness (*trela*) in the face of a hegemonic rationality, but it is not as clear as some scholars think that Kazantzakis's own view is decidedly Nietzschean. For one thing, Nietzsche's (and apparently Heidegger's) view that we have been in a state of intellectual decline ever since the fifth century B.C. is an example of romantic sentimentalism that Kazantzakis would certainly want to avoid. In some peculiar way, Kazantzakis is committed to biological and conceptual and spiritual *progress*, as the above delineation of his method is meant to illustrate. What he *does* inherit from Nietzsche is the latter's invective against the worst in traditional theism as well as Nietzsche's belief that there is something singularly and perennially Greek about the effort to fuse clashing forces (like the Apollonian and the Dionysian), to use Bien's language. But Nietzsche, unlike Kazantzakis, was an agnostic or an atheist; or better, if Nietzsche was not an agnostic or an atheist, he should have spoken more forthrightly on this issue.[4]

To say that the Greek predicament is perennial is to imply that it applies as well to Orthodox Christianity. Indeed in Orthodoxy, as in the Abrahamic religions in general, there is a belief in the possibility of spiritual progress for human beings (as opposed to either Nietzsche's nihilism or to his cyclicism in believing in the eternal return). One is reminded here of St. Paul's (spiritual) race whereby the soul grows by participation in what transcends it. And one is reminded of the spiritual passion praised in the *Song of Songs* or the movement from strength to strength in the *Psalms*. All of this, along with Gregory of Nyssa's (Kazantzakian) belief that the greatest obstacle to spiritual progress is relaxation, indicates that Kazantzakis's predicament, the perennial Greek one, is very much connected to Orthodox concerns. (It is the Orthodox belief that God cannot change, that God is an exception to omnipresent becoming, that is most problematic from a Kazantzakian point of view.) Gregory of Nyssa puts the relevant point as follows:

> In this way the bride [the soul] is, in a certain sense, wounded and beaten because of the frustration of what she desires, now that she thinks that her yearning for the Other cannot be fulfilled or satisfied. But the veil of her grief is removed when she learns that the true satisfaction of her desire consists in constantly going on with her quest and never ceasing in her ascent, seeing that every fulfillment of her desire continually generates a further desire for the Transcendent.[5]

We have seen that there is a distinction in Orthodoxy between the inner reality of God and the energies (or attributes) of God. The latter are not static, but rather are active manifestations of God. The goal of *theosis* is to transfigure or transform or transubstantiate oneself into God, a process that indicates both the reality of communion with God as well as the otherness of God. The important question here is whether, in order to maintain a legitimate belief in divine otherness, one needs to hold, as is the case in traditional thought in the Abrahamic religions, that God is not internally affected by, nor changed by, the creatures.[6] There is something defective about claiming the kataphatic belief that God is being and not becoming, while simultaneously claiming the apophatic belief that God is utterly unknowable. Kazantzakis's alternative seems to be to suggest that there is something *both* knowable and unknowable about *both* God's being *and* God's becoming. In any event, in ancient Greek philosophy, Greek Orthodox theology (say Irenaeus), and Kazantzakis alike there is the familiar difficulty of discerning what is of humanity and what is of God. And regarding this difficulty both mystical intuition and intellect (the Asian East and the West, respectively) are needed if an adequate response is to be developed.[7] To use a phrase from Joseph Flay, Kazantzakis's own response to the perennial Greek predicament consists in an ironic or oxymoronic, but nonetheless logically consistent, "erotic stoicism."[8]

Taking Polytheism Seriously

By trying to preserve the best in Greek Orthodoxy as well as in ancient polytheism, Kazantzakis runs the risk of alienating both traditional Abrahamic believers as well as deconstructive, postmodern Nietzscheans. But his fascination for the best in the Abrahamic religions as well as the best in ancient polytheism is perfectly compatible with a Bergsonian view of God. The point I wish to make in this section of the chapter can be understood through a consideration of three views of human temporal identity as they relate to God. I will be relying to a great extent in this effort on the work of the philosopher Stephen R. L. Clark.

Human identity is a fragile thing even on a moderate view. Three views of the relationship between temporal relations and human identity can be distinguished. One extreme view suggests that all temporal relations are external. That is, the present self is not internally affected by "its" past self, nor is it affected by "its" future self. This "drops of experience" view, defended by many Buddhists, in effect is a denial of a self enduring through time. At the other extreme is the view often held in the Abrahamic religions that all temporal relations are internal. That is, the present self is *substantially* the same through time in that both past and future phases of itself are explicitly or implicitly contained in it, and this largely due to an expansive belief in divine omniscience with respect to the future. A moderate view in between these two extreme symmetrical views is the much more plausible asymmetrical view: One is internally affected by one's past but externally related to the future. According to this view, the past provides necessary but not sufficient conditions for the precise character of the present phase of one's self. We are causally affected by our past but we can only anticipate the future through probability estimates; on this view human identity is left in a rather fragile state with respect to the future, but not as fragile as in the Buddhist view. Kazantzakis obviously rejected the view that all of one's temporal relations are internal in that the value he placed on human freedom and his denigration of divine omniscience *with respect* to the outcome of future contingencies are incompatible with this view. His own stance seems to waver between the Buddhist view and the asymmetrical one. Odysseus, for example, *constantly* changes his identity, but Captain Mihalis, Zorba, Fr. Yanaros, and so on, do not, even though they do change *somewhat* in the course of the novels in which they appear.

Belief in the asymmetrical view of human identity is conducive to a William Jamesian or Kazantzakian healthy-mindedness in religion in that when melancholia interrupts healthy-mindedness it is possible for a partially new self to come to be. But this view also alerts us to an important question: how is it that we are not always changing, always trading in our old identity, but in some sense acquire a stable character? Both the breakdown and the preservation of human identity must be incorporated in any adequate theory of human identity. Clark, relying on Wordsworth, puts the matter this way:

> We are more likely to fear this breakdown, and so defend ourselves against it more fiercely and rigidly . . . if we think that our chosen identity is indeed an attempt to freeze a wave of the sea, to make solid sculptures out of butter on a warm day. We shall be less fearful of collapse if we conceive that the sea itself is the real shaper of our standing wave, that it was the former identities that were the momentarily aggregated flotsam that the waves have swept away. A stable identity, in short, is likely to be one which is believed to be the manifestation of an underlying reality . . . in touch with "something far more deeply interfused." Those who believe that their identities are maintained by their own endeavors, by their own disciplined insistence on being as they were, are very likely not to last the course.[9]

Both continuity and change are problems, but Clark the conservative thinks that the modern tendency to switch identities as we do clothes has led moral philosophers and theologians (and, it might be alleged, Kazantzakis) to prefer a smorgasbord of values, a wardrobe of differing costumes. The traditional emphasis on divine eternity, as opposed to the (Kazantzakian) process theologian's emphasis on divine change, has consequences for philosophical anthropology. Everyone wants a balance between continuity and change, yet Clark sees the latter as the greater danger. Hence he thinks it crucial to emphasize that activity of an expected kind serves as a code to others to summon up one identity or god rather than another. Nonetheless,

> the sudden emergence of a forgotten self—an emergence made easier by social ritual and the consumption of a mild drug (usually alcohol)—may be experienced as a joyful rediscovery or an humiliating possession by something quite at odds with waking values. . . . Religion is the collective noun for all such practices, whereby our changing selves may move in time to some unknown tidal motions, without driving us insane.[10]

These passing moods and styles of action are sometimes hostile to each other. In this contest between alien powers each must be given due respect: this is the lesson to be learned from polytheism, a lesson that Kazantzakis himself obviously learned.

It is a mistake to adopt a view of the self as substantial in the sense that the I "has" momentary moods. The ego is more of a demand or a postulate than a plain discovery; it is something that we can see *beneath* the many moods and personalities that play themselves out in everyday life. There is some truth to the familiar criticism that the ancient Greeks had no clear conception of the unity of the human subject. But there is also some truth in the polytheistic belief that each "individual" is a medley of competing parts and loyalties; this truth is corroborated by the fact that contemporary readers do not find Homer's heroes altogether unlike contemporary human beings. Further, the moods and styles encountered by the ego cannot be mortal, as the ancient Greeks knew, because they are confronted again and again not only in the life of the ego but also in the lives of other egos, and they cannot be resisted: "Those who try to proclaim their own immunity to Aphrodite find that she is raised up against them."[11] It is precisely this Aphrodite who was the transubstantiated product of instinct (Astarte), as we have seen Bien emphasize regarding Kazantzakis's view in *Report to Greco*, and who was the irresistible force in Zorba's life.

Religious experience is an entry into the world of religious tradition; it consists in being seized by the inwardness of such tradition. Only those who misunderstand this inwardness go out of their way to insist that there is really no Aphrodite. She *is* a real presence or mood in the world, as Kazantzakis often attests, and religious tradition is built out of this and other presences. Some of the things that we think are unreal or dreams are in fact drowsy awakenings to the real.[12] It is a crucial feature of many religions that the phenomenal universe is the actualization in time of an ideal project that is best grasped as a cosmic community united in love (for example, by Aphrodite). On this view human beings can be seen in at least two different lights: there is the ordinary life of competitive individualism and material interest and there is the "original" life of divine conciliarity. We can blaspheme Aphrodite, for example, through alcoholism or through academic infighting. But avoiding such blasphemy does not necessarily mean that we should naively preach that Aphrodite is, or even could be, ubiquitous, as Kazantzakis well knew. As Clark puts the point:

> The ancients reminded us that even when kissing our child
> we should remember that she too is mortal. . . . That hard
> advice is now seen as a betrayal of "love," a refusal to be
> besotted, as if such love were the only real thing in an empty
> world.[13]

Ares is also alive and well in the contemporary world, and a primary devotion to him is certainly to be denigrated:

> Those who fight for killing's sake, the servants of Ares, are
> as dangerous to us all as the followers of Ouranian
> Aphrodite. . . . Our problem, as it has always been, is to
> require the gods to take their proper place.[14]

Ares and Aphrodite are the most hated of the Olympians because both can ruin our lives:

> Ares . . . is not just a devil, any more than Aphrodite: our
> fear of him is not unlike the terror that in other ages made
> Aphrodite into the great Temptress; our professions of
> pacific virtue are as hypocritical as the double standards of
> past sexual morality; our good liberal contempt for fighting
> men is as understandable, and as damaging to all, as older
> contempt for women. . . . Perhaps we should ask ourselves
> why we are so ready to assume the worst of those who would
> die for us?[15]

As a pacifist I am not entirely convinced by Clark's or Kazantzakis's case in favor of reverence due to Ares, but it must be admitted that *if* Aphrodite stands for a syrupy sentimentalism or an unpragmatic anesthesia then *some* other god is needed to counteract her influence.[16]

Apollo, conceived as methodical reason, also has his place in Kazantzakian religion, but he is not absolute in the cosmos, not even when he appears in the guise of a manipulative type of science:

> What is lacking in this age of the world is the sense that
> there is some existing pattern in which each proper impulse
> finds its place. . . . Those who have lost their memory of the
> one comprehensive order are at the mercy of whatever
> passion, mood, or fairy chances to drink them up.[17]

The Greek symbol for this comprehensive order was Zeus, who stood for the intelligibility that needed preservation if human life was not to revert to fratricidal chaos in that the service of one god at the expense of another was quintessential blasphemy in the Olympian religion.[18] But how much order or continuity can we expect?

There is something to be learned from the ancient Greek view that only the gods are single-minded, hence human life, as Kazantzakis knew, tends to be unsystematic. Even if one organizes the major deities into a pantheon there are still *kers* (the spirits of spite and reprisal) and the furies to contend with. That is, as Kazantzakis emphasizes, Abrahamic believers might be premature in assuming that the almighty God of the bible necessarily possesses the philosophical attribute "omnipotence." Although Zeus required that gods and mortals know their respective places, and that they not revolt against Themis, or what was proper, he did not have *absolute* control, a fact that was best symbolized by the presence of Kazantzakis's and Nietzsche's beloved Dionysus. The trick is now, as it was then, to discover an orderly system without restricting creaturely freedom. Human knowledge itself insures that this will be a difficult project:

> This "discovery," so to call it, of the possibility of an orderly world-system in which each god has a part to play, and which the demands of different roles were not settled simply by resort to force. . . . This "knowledge of good and evil" was what, in Greek thought, prevented human beings from becoming gods: precisely because they could look before and after, and discriminate, they could not be unselfconsciously absorbed in any single role or mood.[19]

It is part of ancient Greek *and* Kazantzakian genius at moderation to fail to conclude that Dionysus was "the natural man," human nature as it would be if the hegemony of Apollo were broken. Dionysus is not "the natural man" so much as he is a natural possibility. The temporary destruction of Zeus's or Apollo's Olympian order, a destruction symbolized by Dionysus, should be accepted as a moment in life rather than as a defeat.[20] That is, along with W. F. Otto, we should oppose the view that the Olympian deities are a band of brigands: polytheism in its Olympian variety is an attempt to provide a structure for the moods and roles of social humanity and an attempt to convince us that we are vulnerable fragments of a cosmos with its own beauty.

Despite the fact that Christianity is a protest against Olympian religion it is also, as is well known, a type of Dionysian revivalism. It is important from a Kazantzakian perspective that mysticism and/or enthusiasm remain parts of religion so as to prevent a deleterious reification of established order. It is worth remembering that it was not only Jesus who was seen by Hellenized Jews and Christians as similar to Dionysus, but also Yahweh. Eventually, however, Yahweh, God the Father, and Allah were seen as strictly Apollonian and transcendent. Clark is instructive in the Kazantzakian way he points out the need for balance in Olympian religion, the Abrahamic religions, and Buddhism alike:

> Charismatic revivalists . . . succeed only in establishing new patterns of worship and hymnody, so that bourgeois congregations sing words that take their meaning from the last revival. "Come Holy Ghost . . ." how many in the congregation really intend to speak in tongues? . . . How many Buddhists, for that matter, really test themselves upon the nonexistence of the self, and seek to realize the Unborn?

> Like the Olympians, Christians and Buddhists have (to
> some extent) achieved a synthesis: their ceremonial order
> does contain a reference to That beyond all orders, and a
> vocabulary that stands ready for the next revivalist.[21]

This is very much like Kazantzakis's dialectic between Western moderation and Eastern restlessness. A phenomenological account of religious identity,
I allege, can at best recognize *patterns* among the very real Olympians that
influence us. Each god may be a strict actuality with no unrealized possibilities,
but the whole system of gods and mortals must contain a great deal of contingency as the latter confront the former in the course of time. In any event, it
is perhaps more accurate to say that birds court each other *because* of Aphrodite
than it is to say that the obsessional desire of birds *is* Aphrodite. The danger is
that if we do not refer to the gods to explain phenomena then they will too
easily be viewed merely as poetic fictions.

Olympian religion is also very helpful in distinguishing pollution from sin.
One may inadvertently be polluted, as in the case of Oedipus, when one does
something that conflicts with impersonal (usually cosmic) law. By way of contrast, the Abrahamic religions tend to treat the penalties of sin as the response
of a personal God. But when the innocent suffer we are led to take Olym-
pianism especially seriously, as does Kazantzakis, in that some events appear to
be the case independent of any decision made by an omnipotent divine person.
Pollution plays *some* role in Judaism and Christianity, as in the people with
whom Jesus consorted, who had not so much committed moral errors as they
had been outcasts from Israel, that is, they had incurred pollution. One of the
general goals of religion is something like Hindu *mokṣa*, deliverance from both
pollution and sin, even if such deliverance is by proxy, as is the case with Jesus
or Manolios in *The Greek Passion*. According to Clark:

> In morality no one is to be blamed or punished who is not
> personally responsible for a crime. . . . Pollution, on the
> other hand, is only partly deserved, and may be removed by
> another's action. . . . In our own, partly secular, tradition the
> usual conjunction of "holiness" and dirt was cancelled by the
> aphorism that "Cleanliness is next to godliness," which has
> in its turn gone so far toward idealizing the ritual anti-
> septicism of the world of white-coated doctors, plastic-
> wrapped meat, and vaginal deodorants as to elicit a youthful
> rebellion in favour of "naturalness," a largely romantic effort
> to be at one with the usual processes of nature.[22]

The gods constantly pass through our mind's eye for us to accept or reject
or ignore: "To know them is to share experience with them, to live with their

life."[23] One of the gods who might pass before us appears as the thought that we are being, or might deservedly be, punished for our wrongs. And this god may well be an obsessional demon. Polytheism teaches that there are, for lack of better words, angels as well as devils. The plurality of these beings runs counterpoint to belief in divine unity; or better, divine unity and the multiplicity of gods (Kazantzakian moods, pulls, temptations, desires) are like centripetal and centrifugal forces in equilibrium, as Clark notes:

> Faith in Divine Unity amounts to faith in the intelligibility of things, that there is a single pattern, the Logos. . . . That faith was represented for Hellenes, especially the neo-Platonists, in the figure of Zeus. . . . [T]he Logos is not now evident to us. Rational polytheists [like Kazantzakis] deplore the tendency of monotheists to imagine unity too soon. . . . Every mode and mood of our being, of the world's being, should be acknowledged as a fact, and as something to be "welcomed."[24]

But in our age the problem, from Clark's conservative point of view, is not so much that God (the One or *Nous*-Zeus) has been forgotten altogether as that there has been a triumphant, hegemonic return of the ancient deities. The problem is not so much that we do not take polytheism seriously as that we take it too seriously. Does Kazantzakis do this?

The process theism that I have argued Kazantzakis represents can also be designated a dipolar theism, as we have seen: God necessarily exists and remains steadfastly good in the midst of all of the divine and creaturely changes. Hence there is no necessary conflict between this view and the Clarkian one wherein a qualified polytheism is used as a device to criticize the contemporary denigration of divine endurance *simpliciter*. Or again, there is a sense in which those who see spiritual matters the way Kazantzakis does can agree with Clark that the radical desacralizing and deconstruction of all received order is merely fashionable chatter. Kazantzakis also believes that God endures and that in the midst of all of the changes in my life it is still, in a sense, *my* life.

Pure polytheism would consist in the radical plurality and incommensurability of value preferred by some nonbelievers and by deconstructive postmodernists. In this light, polytheism is largely propaedeutic to an appreciation of the whole; it is a prelude to an exposition of belief in a modified Abrahamic or Neoplatonic One (that is, neoclassical theism) that in some sense includes the lives of the many. To take polytheism seriously, rather than to take it too seriously, is to refuse to see any huge gap between it and the perennial Greek predicament. For example, the God-man or the Logos is not *sui generis* in Christianity:

Plotinus, who was certainly as great a philosopher and spiritual leader as Hellenic civilization ever produced, remarked that Pheidias' statue of Olympian Zeus was what Zeus would look like if He did indeed "take flesh and dwell among us."[25]

Nonbelieving, strictly Nietzschean theorists of human identity have unwittingly become polytheistic in their acceptance of multiple and often contradictory ideals and in their moral claim that it is not always possible to do right without at the same time doing dreadful wrong. It is difficult to criticize contemporary polytheism, however, because its defenders do not think of themselves as polytheists. But the invisible world of the gods is not so ethereal that it is trivial. There are undeniable forces in the world, half-glimpsed visions or absent-minded absorptions in memory or fable, that constitute a sort of divine immanence. But it is precisely the "once-upon-a-time" character of these forces that should lead us to consider, by way of contrast, the reality of divine unity. The gods may be evoked by music, poetry, and Zorbatic dance; and to disprove their existence one needs to do more than dredge Loch Ness. The weird mix of matter and spirit mentioned below by Clark is close to Kazantzakis's view:

The argument is a metaphysical one, about the proper description of our experience and the correct metaphysical guess about the ground of that experience . . . an appropriate metaphorical description of certain states of spiritual being. If a broadly spiritist metaphysics is ultimately found to be false, then there have never really been any [gods]; but in that case there have never "really" been any human persons either. If there are persons, then there are at least some spirits weirdly mingled with the material. And if there are some, what reason is there to deny that there are also others, perhaps of a larger and more alien kind?[26]

In sum, my exploration of polytheism in this section of the chapter has consisted in the following steps:

1. The asymmetrical view of time, which is a moderate view between two extremes, leaves human identity in a fragile state, as Kazantzakis well knew.
2. But it does not leave it in a more fragile state than it is in reality, contra the substantialist (traditional theistic) thesis.
3. Any adequate theory of human identity must account for both continuity and change.

4. To the extent that change is a necessary feature of human identity polytheism must be taken seriously.
5. But Clark may be correct that polytheism is taken *too* seriously in contemporary culture.
6. Hence the effort to discover the underlying unity to one's life, an effort integrally connected in Kazantzakis to the effort to understand divine unity, is crucial.
7. But a phenomenology of one's personal experience indicates that this unity can only be partial in that Aphrodite and Ares, Apollo and Dionysus, the furies, and various spirits of spite and reprisal and memory still pull us in different directions, as Kazantzakis's appropriation of ancient religion makes clear.
8. And the theodicy problem, among others in the philosophy of religion, insures that the sort of stability that would be provided by an omnipotent deity—rejected by Kazantzakis—will continue to be difficult to defend.
9. Hence we will have to rest content with only a partial refutation of polytheism. (Even Jesus was on several occasions tempted, as Kazantzakis well illustrates.)
10. And this is exactly what we should expect: neither the "one" nor the "many" in the problem of the one and the many can be wished away.

Mystical Experience and Divine Mutability

In this section I would once again like to support the case in a Kazantzakian way for at least the partial autonomy of mystical experiences against the possible hegemony of the intellect; in fact, I will argue that the experiences of the mystics should help to shape how we think. The possible hegemony of the intellect I will be criticizing comes from two different directions. First, I will consider the view that the phenomenological content of all experience, including mystical experience, is shaped by (indeed, it is in part caused by) a complex, culturally acquired, sociopsychological mold consisting of concepts and beliefs that the experiencing subject brings to the mystical experience. I will attempt to limit this hegemony of intellect, as well as of a second sort to be explained momentarily, through a consideration of one particular concept and its "opposite" (divine immutability/divine mutability) as it is found in mystical literature, in general, and Kazantzakis's in particular.[27]

Steven Katz's view seems to be that there are no purely immediate experiences, that experience is always preformed or preconditioned; or better, that if we do have "immediate" experiences they are heavily affected by the cultural background of the experiencer. Hence mystical experiences largely have the content they have because mystics come to their experiences with traditional religious concepts as a background. Hindus have experiences that phenomenologically are of Brahmin and Christians have experiences that phenomenologically are of God. In fact, there are as many kinds of mystical experience as there are significant religious contexts. Katz's "forms of intuition" theory is explicitly Kantian, as is Kazantzakis's theory at one point in *Spiritual Exercises*; or better, it is a sociopsychological version of Kant's mind-construction theory of human experience applied to the special case of mystical experience.

The strongest case made by Katz is when he talks about Jewish mysticism, wherein the conceptual background of a God who is ontologically distinct from human beings defines in advance what the experience is that the Jewish mystic wants to have. The ultimate goal of Jewish mystics is *devekuth*, a loving intimacy with God, but not identity with God or absorption into God. By way of contrast, in Christian and Kazantzakian mysticism there are reported experiences of both a nonabsorptive type, which are reminiscent of *devekuth*, and of an absorptive or unitive type in which the self is absorbed in God in an all-embracing unity (*theosis*). The latter, Katz seems to say, are due to Christianity's and Kazantzakis's incarnational theology wherein it is more difficult than in Judaism to think of God as *totaliter aliter*.

I would like to make it clear that in criticizing Katz in a Kazantzakian way one does not have to move to the other extreme, say to the position of Walter Stace, where something like a presuppositionless experience occurs that is later interpreted and described and expanded in terms of a subject-object structure and in terms of the traditional attributes given to God by theistic thinkers. That is, a Kantian approach to the problem may in fact be the best one *if* what it means to be a Kantian is to insist that in any experience something is contributed by the experiencing subject and something is contributed by something or someone outside the subject. The problem with Katz's Kantianism lies in his overemphasis of the subject's contribution to the mystical experience. The inadequacy of Katz's account, however, does not justify Stace's claim that the mystic does not really experience a personal God in that this descriptive content (of God as personal) of the experience is added at a later interpretive moment. Kazantzakis was wise in *Spiritual Exercises* to affirm both the Kantian view *and* the attempt to move beyond such a view (systole and diastole).

On Stace's account the theistic interpretation of mystical experience as union with God is like John Stuart Mill's example of someone seeing a colored surface of a certain shape and concluding that he was seeing his brother.[28] Regarding the question as to how we can determine where the report of the mystic is accurate and where it includes a later interpretive element, Ninian Smart offers the following (Stacean) response: a mystic's writing is interpretive rather than descriptive to the extent that it contains doctrinal ramifications or propositions that are presupposed as true by the description in question.[29] In sum, Katz is on the right track with his Kantianism until he overemphasizes the role of the experiencing subject; and Stace and Smart are on the right track in claiming that we should not accept at face value the *ex post facto* interpretations mystics give of their experiences, but there are good reasons, as we will see, not to go so far as to rule out, as Stace does, and as some interpreters of Kazantzakis do, the possibility that mystics experience a personal God.

Nelson Pike emphasizes that part of the conceptual inheritance of traditional Christianity that is alleged to either precondition mystical experience (Katz) or be read into mystical experience after the fact (Stace) is the belief that God is immutable, a view that Kazantzakis rejects, as we have seen throughout this book. But if the soul of the mystic were to become one with God, then something would have been added to God. Even if mystical union refers to a phenomenological reality rather than a metaphysical one, as Pike and some interpreters of Kazantzakis wish to argue, it is nonetheless undeniable that the pervasive use of the bridegroom metaphor in the literature of Christian mysticism indicates that in mystical union God is the receiver of a definite benefit. Relying on stanzas 30–35 of John of the Cross's *Spiritual Canticle*, Pike says the following:

> God is also the receiver of a definite benefit. He, too, is embraced and loved by his submissive and adoring Bride [the soul]. God benefits too!? Of course. . . . John says, God too is "wounded" and "captivated"—that is, made "prisoner"—by the love received from the soul. Appropriately enough, God also gives thanks to the soul for the gift he receives. . . . The mutual embrace of union is, indeed, *mutual* embrace and . . . the bridal metaphor carries the pictorial implication of *equal* partners sharing *equally* the benefits of the love embrace. . . . Not surprisingly, John covers the seemingly inappropriate overtones of this analysis by insisting that it is God who is ultimately responsible for the fact that the soul is his equal . . . a symmetrical exchange of delights.[30]

Of course, Kazantzakis's metaphors used to describe God are often a bit more brutal than the bridal one, but both John of the Cross's and Kazantzakis's point is that we must take divine mutability seriously in the systole-diastole of the religious life.

Both sorts of metaphor—those that indicate an asymmetrical relationship between God and the mystic and those that indicate a symmetrical relationship—are essential parts of the literature of mysticism. Pike's key contribution to the topic of the present section of the chapter consists in the way he alerts us to the fact that symmetrical metaphors, and the partial divine mutability that is their implication (the *constancy* of the divine impulse indicates that divine mutability is only part of the story), conflict in important ways with traditional theological expectations. Kazantzakian mysticism in particular provides a locus for both divine steadfastness and persistence, on the one hand, and passionate-sensuous mutability, on the other. God is unique in being *always* mutable, whereas we mortal beings can be changed by those with whom we are related for only a short while.

The doctrine of divine immutability has been taken as the orthodox standard when determining theological or metaphysical truth, but not when determining the phenomenological truth in mystical experience. Some thinkers may, even after considering the evidence of mystics, continue to insist on divine immutability when the metaphysical status of mystical experience is *assessed* (but even here there are problems), but one cannot insist on divine immutability when the phenomenological content of the experience is being *described*. It is true that phenomenological *context* in part determines phenomenological *content*, as when the silence before the last measure of the Hallelujah chorus is part of the auditory experience, or as when Teresa of Avila compares Christ as present near her to the awareness one might have of someone present in the dark whom one cannot see. But even if context in part determines content, there is an insistency to the phenomenological content of mystical experience that neither Katz's Promethean forethought nor Stace's Epimethean hindsight can explain away.

We saw in chapter 5 that neoclassical (or more loosely, process) theists like Hartshorne have been saying for years that on independent metaphysical grounds there are good reasons for believing that there are problems with seeing divine permanence and divine change as opposites. Rather, Hartshorne claims, they are mutually reinforcing correlatives. God is immutably mutable, the being who is *always* affected by the creatures loved. Mystics like Kazantzakis come to know this.

My point throughout this section of the chapter has been to suggest that we cannot explain away the mystic's experience of divine mutability. And my proposal here at the end of this section is to have us take seriously the mystic's experience of divine mutability such that divine mutability might gain intellectual respectability as a metaphysical, not just phenomenological, reality. We saw in chapter 5 that there are good and bad varieties of permanence (for example, steadfastness and mulish stubbornness, respectively) and good and bad varieties of change (for example, responsive love and fickleness, respectively). The greatest being embodies the good aspects of *both* categories; indeed God embodies them in a supreme way.

In guarding against the hegemony of intellect I am not necessarily committed to the hegemony of religious experience. Rather, religious truth is developed when *both* our attentiveness to experience and our intellectual operations (for Kazantzakis, the fight in the skull) are at their highest pitch of discipline. Religions die, as Kazantzakis well realized during his travels to Russia, when they find their inspiration in their dogmas, say, in the dogma regarding divine immutability. The bases of religious belief lie in the experiences of and in the thoughts of the finest types of religious lives. These bases are always growing, even though some supreme expressions lie in the past (think of Kazantzakis's fascination with Saints Francis and Teresa of Avila, Jesus, Buddha, etc.). Records of these sources are not formulae, but spurs to elicit in us affective and intellectual responses that pierce beyond dogma, in this case the dogma that God is immutable.

Buddha

Thus far in this chapter I have examined Kazantzakis's method in terms of:

1. Its location within the perennial Greek predicament of trying to find some sort of raprochement between the Asian East (including mystical experience) and West (including intellect);
2. The effort to understand the relationship between human identity and divine identity in light of the fact that both of these are temporal; and
3. The effort to secure a defense of divine mutability.

Now I would like to consider in some detail texts from Kazantzakis that illustrate his method and indicate how he deals with (1), (2), and (3).

One of the most interesting features of Kazantzakis's play *Buddha* is how much it deals with the perennial Greek predicament. That is, it is as much about China as Gilbert and Sullivan's *Mikado* is about Japan. It *is* "Oriental" to the extent that Eastern sensibilities enter into the perennial Greek predicament, but only to this extent. The Poet in this play speaks of the "holy communion of wine and flame," for example, that consumes human beings in the "game" of life. And it becomes apparent in this work that when facing the "precipice of God" it is human beings who bear the responsibility of saving God, in typical Kazantzakian fashion. (As before, it is not the *existence* of God that is saved because God is deathless for Kazantzakis, but the particular *mode* of God's existence that is saved; God's *actuality* is saved.) This effort to save God is prevented if we are weighed down in a gluttonous way with too much food. It is true that the communion or transubstantiation that Kazantzakis has in mind is symbolized in terms of the silkworm who eats all of the leaves of the earth's mulberry tree so as to turn them into silk (air or spirit), but we have seen in chapter 4 that there is good reason to believe that Kazantzakis originally adopted this metaphor from Teresa of Avila.[31]

Consider the words of Young Koag, a Buddhist monk who sounds very much like a Carmelite friar under the influence of Teresa of Avila or John of the Cross:

When will this sack, my body, become exhausted,
when will the tears that choke me flow away,
when will this earth sprout wings and be entrusted,
O Buddha, to fly away?[32]

One of the distinctive features of patient Asia that surfaces in this play, and
that informs Kazantzakis's method, is that the transubstantiation of matter into
spirit or air passes through thousands of bodies and takes an immense length of
time. And in this play Kazantzakis refers to the familiar transubstantiation of
matter into spirit as a liberating Buddha. Various characters in the play hear the
divine Cry yet they cannot, not even through fasting and great thoughts, fully
transform themselves into spirit through their own individual efforts. Their
predicament is, strange as it seems in that they are Chinese, the perennial
Greek predicament.[33]

Suffering itself is a mode of transubstantiation for both Buddhists and
those influenced by "Western" religions; as Mogalana puts the point in the play,
"liberation begins from the summit of pain." It is true that this suffering is
transformed in Buddhist fashion into "nothingness," but, as we have seen, this
term can be variously interpreted. It is by no means clear that it should be seen
as indicative of nihilism if the experience of nothingness (of suffering transubstantiated into air) is not a consummatory moment in the spiritual life but an
instrumental one in the ongoing dialectic of *gnōsis* and *agnōsis*. Even in *Buddha*
we find the wise Old Man declaring that God is at the center of things, and it is
appropriate that this Old Man is depicted as a Christlike figure who takes on his
shoulders all of the sufferings of a village about to be swept up in a flood.
Buddhist nothingness at least in part consists in an attitude very similar to the
ancient Stoic one: to watch the Yangtze come and not cry out. God is in no
hurry, "that's why he is God."[34]

I will discuss Kazantzakis's view of death in the following chapter, but here
it should be noted that Kazantzakis is like Buddhists in thinking that we come
from a somewhat undifferentiated unity and we will return to one as well. In the
middle we struggle, yet we are, perhaps, somewhat consoled by the fact that God
is incurably miserable by our sufferings, as the character Vishnu claims in this
play. Kazantzakis's method, I have alleged, is paradoxically moderate, despite his
frequent panegyrics in favor of immoderation. For example, in *Buddha* we find
him wavering between sheer nihilism (as opposed to the positive nihilism found
at one moment in Kazantzakis's systole-diastole method) in the face of human
suffering, on the one hand, and the view of a Greek visitor to the Yangtze flood-
plain who thinks that Buddhist (or Stoic) nothingness is no better than the
attitude of those in the Land of the Lotus-Eaters, on the other.[35]

To understand Buddha is to dance with exuberance and yet to be willing
to allow this exuberance to vanish in air. Or again, it is to allow the phantasmagoria of our minds to pass over into eternity (or everlastingness), as the

Magician puts the point. We live only a short while, but the everlasting whole of things continues without us. The trick is to retain equanimity in the face of the fact that it is necessary that we die, a feat that is easier talked about than actually accomplished.[36]

Russia

We have seen in the previous section that Kazantzakis identifies Buddha with God, an identification that Kazantzakis makes as well in his novel about his travels in Russia, *Toda Raba*. In a peculiar sense even Lenin was divine in the way he unleashed barbaric forces that cleansed the earth so as to prepare the way for a new Middle Ages and eventually a new (constructive postmodern) civilization. Kazantzakis is to a limited degree like the communists in thinking that bread is needed to keep the spirit alive, but it is the spirit of Jehovah, Jesus, Mohammed, and Buddha that he is most interested in preserving, even here in his writings on Russia. He is scandalized by the famine in Russia and notes the Zorbalike gusto with which citizens fulfilled the "high physical need" for food. But the point to these Russian citizens eating, for Kazantzakis, is to develop the strength to sweep away the old God who protected priests, rabbis, thieves, kings, and prostitutes so as to prepare the way for a new God, a God who nonetheless preserves the best in figures like, ironically, Jehovah, Jesus, Mohammed, and Buddha. In this preparation for an improved religious belief Kazantzakis makes it explicit that Russia plays a role in bringing "the fine Asiatic madness under the control of the rigorous logic of the West."[37] Russia is very much like Greece in symbolizing the problem that Kazantzakis's method is meant to solve.

Unfortunately, Kazantzakis succumbed at least at some points in his career to the Marxist and fascist belief that the individual is solely for the sake of the whole (we are thinking insects, he said), rather than to the more defensible view that balances the legitimate claims of both the individual and society. At one point in *Toda Raba* he seems to endorse the view that we should not love individual human beings but the inhuman flame that devours them. Perhaps he is speaking metaphorically here. But in hindsight one cannot help but notice the danger in being as unclear as Kazantzakis was regarding the extent to which one would be willing to endorse the actions of left- or right-wing totalitarian governments. Bien does the best job possible in making Kazantzakis's view palatable here; Kazantzakis is primarily interested in the extent to which politics aids in the *spiritual* development of human beings. In the following remarkable quotation we can see that: (1) even in his works about Russia Kazantzakis is primarily interested in spiritual concerns; (2) that his "materialism" can perhaps better be termed an incarnational theology; and (3) that Kazantzakis is very much concerned with his method of reconciling East and West:

> Every man is an ephemeral Son who contains the eternal
> Father within himself. The purpose of art is to discover the
> invisible spirit of the Father and to express it through the
> visible body of the Son. If man can grasp and express
> nothing but the Son, he creates a merely superficial work of
> art; if he expresses nothing but abstract ideas, nothing but
> the Father, he produces not art but metaphysics. The Effort
> to find the Word able to capture the immortal essence alive
> in us: this is magic. That's why art is a mysterious science, a
> veritable theurgy. Words attract and imprison the invisible
> spirit, force it to become incarnated and to exhibit itself to
> man. *Sitka*, meaning Utterance, the Word, in Georgian
> means also seizure and sexual intercourse. The Word must
> seize, subjugate and fecundate matter. Just as Adam knew
> woman, so must the Word know Matter. . . . The conscious-
> ness of the West . . . is dominated by appreciation of the
> individual; that of the East by a profound sense of union
> with the Universe. The Westerner has been liberated from
> the great Whole; the umbilical cord binding him to the
> Universe has been cut. . . . turned him into a monad. . . .
> The Oriental on the other hand is a hybrid. . . . The Father
> predominates in the Oriental, the Son in the Westerner. But
> holy wedlock has already been announced between Asia
> with her abandonment to the Whole and Europe with its
> individualistic logicality.[38]

This wedlock was taking place, he thought, in Russia. Lenin's revolu-
tionary ideas are like Jesus' in that the latter's command to "Love one another"
was initially incomprehensible to many such that it was only after an ardent
drive that it gained some degree of acceptance. It is precisely this forcefulness,
Kazantzakis suggests, that God the creator also exhibits. Marxism was doomed
to failure, he thought, if it was not driven by *souls* on fire. The First World War
intensified the process of decomposition and made it possible for a type of
Marxism to come to power, but to truly take advantage of this situation *spiritual*
maturity is needed. Just as Simeon in the Bible held an infant in his hands
whom he hoped would be the Messiah, the birth of the Soviet Union signaled
for Kazantzakis a messianic "mysterious force." But Kazantzakis thought himself
saddled with the "thankless" task of defending the Soviet Union despite the fact
that it, like all institutions at the end of a civilization, stood for the view that
materialism is the key to all mysteries, even if a commitment to materialism can
lead to ruthlessness.[39]

The character Geranos in *Toda Raba*, who presumably presents Kazantzakis's own views, says the following:

> Like Loyola . . . I, too, have my spiritual exercises. First step:
> contemplate the whole circle, the waves of human beings
> undulating up and down. Second step: train every beam of
> light on the precise point marked by my own epoch. Third
> step: burn it up.[40]

Once again, to what extent is Kazantzakis speaking here of a metaphysical or spiritual effort to transubstantiate (or "burn up") matter into spirit and to what extent is he making a political point regarding the expendability of individual human beings? I do not know, but I am very much bothered by the possibility that Kazantzakis may well have in mind the latter. Yet the evidence in favor of the former alternative is nonetheless considerable. Marxism is like a John the Precursor for Kazantzakis, a divine voice standing on the edge of the abyss, that is, *leading us to* a more refined and higher spiritual level. At one point Kazantzakis describes God abandoning the tortoise-shell carapace of the Russian Orthodox Church and moving to the new Soviet Radio Institute where divine antennae appeared; but he is also clear that this is only a temporary resting place.[41]

There can be no doubt that in the short run Kazantzakis favors the Eastern constituent of the perennial Greek (and Russian) predicament, but whether he does so in the long run is a debatable question:

> [I]f we allow ourselves to be too much enchanted by Greek
> harmony, we are in danger of missing the first step of
> Creation—destruction and Chaos—and we run the risk of
> moving on prematurely toward our second duty: the
> establishment of a balance, which is certainly not the mis-
> sion of our generation on this earth. . . . For art and beauty, I
> often have the same feeling of hatred that the primitive
> Christians used to have. The first adherents of a faith always
> have a similar hatred for the lovely balanced form of the
> universe they are called on to destroy. For in truth this
> beauty is the great temptation; it gives the mystical enchant-
> ment to the idols—those "false" manifestations of God.[42]

Kazantzakis makes it clear, however, that the "violent excitement" of the current transitional age does not eliminate the "overwhelmingly significant" character of the "normal balance" in human affairs:

> My deepest joy is to see how the mysterious force takes hold
> of man and shakes him like a lover, an epileptic or a creator.
> Because, as you know, I'm not interested in man but in the
> being that I so imperfectly designate as God.[43]

This divine seizure is, for Kazantzakis as for Christian and other mystics, followed by a divine silence that floods and nourishes the soul like the Nile.[44]

In Kazantzakis's travel book *Russia* it becomes obvious that he was pained by the relentless antireligious campaign of the Soviets. This was especially bothersome to Kazantzakis because the Russians were, he thought, like the Greeks and especially the Cretans, only half-European; their half-Asian nature gave them the paradoxical blend necessary for mysticism.[45] Regarding the people in Moscow, he notes the following:

> [T]hey are striving to subdue all of the Eastern chaos within
> and without them with an austere, logically assembled Idea.
> You see you have entered a city of fanatic believers. In no
> other city in the world can you find these stern and resolute
> aspects on people's faces: the burning eyes, the tight,
> stubborn lips, this intensity and this religious fever for work.
> It is as if you have transported yourself into a sullen medieval
> city that is all castles and battlements.[46]

It seemed to him that God, the great Combatant, had centered all of the divine energy, including all of the divine agony and hope, on pioneering Russia. There is disagreement, however, as to whether Russia is saddled with what we have referred to in this chapter as (in Bien's words) the perennial Greek predicament. The Slavophiles agree with Kazantzakis that Russia is in a unique world between Europe and Asia. The Francophiles, however, think that Russia will or should follow the evolutionary stages that Europe went through. Both groups historically agreed that Russia was on a mission from God to save the world, a view with which Kazantzakis, in his own peculiar way, agrees.[47]

As was noted earlier, the Jews inherit Asiatic mysticism, hence it follows that Russian Jews have ironically aided in Russian messianism by contributing passion, a searing flame that is invincible in its combative endurance. And he notes that Marx himself was a Jew (albeit apostate), as was the passionate Trotsky. Jews provide Russia with a turbulent air, a Dionysian vertigo that causes an exodus from quotidian reality, a heightened Logos. But Kazantzakis was also aware of antisemitism in Russia and of the possibility of future massacres of the Jews. Despite this awareness and his awareness of the gross materialism of the Soviets, he seems to endorse or at least permit Marx's dictatorship of the proletariat, but with typical Kazantzakian optimism he compares an international conference organized under the sponsorship of this dictatorship to the Ecumenical Councils of the early Christian church. And Lenin is compared to St. George, who killed the beast in order to save the princess, that is, the soul personified as feminine as in John of the Cross. Kazantzakis's ambivalence is nowhere more apparent than in the following moving quotation:

> Here in the Soviet Union, one very often finds the figures of the saints in the streets, in the hollow spaces in walls, or simply hanging on the doors of churches. They are neglected: Their clothes are shabby and dirty; their beards, unvarnished and unkempt. People have stopped nourishing them with prayers and offerings. I know a wooden angel who came unscrewed from the door of a church in a main street in Moscow. Someone had nailed him there to guard the entrance. Now he hangs there, with one wing down like a wounded bird. And a tin Saint Nicholas at a certain crossroads in Moscow has also become unhinged and now hangs precariously above the frozen sidewalk. When the wind blows, he squeaks and yells like a loose shop sign. No one cares enough to hold him by the legs and steady him or at least take him down altogether so that he will not continue to be tormented. The saints are hungry in Russia. The angels suffer pain as they hang between sky and earth. God wanders through the streets—homeless, unemployed, persecuted—like a bourgeois.[48]

Unlike Nietzsche, Kazantzakis does not see Jesus as cold and Apollonian, but he perhaps appears cold because *our* hearts have turned to ice in the decline of our modern civilization. Russia signaled both the decline of Western civilization and its renewal, for Kazantzakis. The former was in evidence when Kazantzakis was unnerved by the heavy-handed answers given with naive certainty by Soviet officials to eternal, theological questions; the new antireligion religion in the Soviet Union was tolerated by Kazantzakis only because he knew it to be temporary. Kazantzakis's Jesus is warm and Dionysian perhaps because of Kazantzakis's own supposed African (elsewhere he says Bedouin) blood. This warmth and this Dionysian passion led Kazantzakis to appreciate Russian literature to a greater degree than any other, even more perhaps than that of ancient Greece itself. There are several reasons for this attraction. One is that Russian literature generally pushes beyond merely aesthetic considerations toward ethical and metaphysical goals, as does Kazantzakis's own literature. Further, because Russian literature is not bound by a long and burdensome tradition, it can throw itself uncompromisingly into theories, leading to the sort of boldness that is needed in the present age; it can learn to be moderate later. The two greatest Russian writers in different ways were religious writers whom Kazantzakis admired. These writers corroborate in a complementary way Kazantzakis's method: Tolstoy was a prophet of divine harmony and Dostoevsky pushed toward a God who lies beyond such a harmony.[49]

Once the word became flesh at the time of the Bolshevik Revolution, writers and intellectuals were no longer at the spiritual vanguard. Rather, practical men of detail came to the fore, and details struck Kazantzakis as frightful. His fear was that the spiritual task with which Russia was entrusted would fail due to a grinding materialism; luckily the populace was, he thought, hungry for books such that the best results of the revolution could be preserved. Kazantzakis hated both materialists and intellectuals, yet he nonetheless hoped that a mystic unity of matter and spirit, of bread and books, of East and West, respectively, could be forged in the Russian experiment.[50]

In Bergsonian fashion Kazantzakis traces evolutionary history in the following way:

> But fortunately life does not heed the sensible bourgeois mind, and that is why it can forge ahead; that is why we have surged beyond the plant to the animal, and from the animal to the human being. And now from the enslaved human being, we are evolving into the free one. A new world is being begotten again with all the blood of birth.[51]

It was Kazantzakis's hope that this bloody birth would eventually lead to real spiritual progress, a progress that Orthodox believers, in fact believers in the Abrahamic religions in general, for the most part think unnecessary. He recounts a sad story of a Russian Orthodox priest who, when asked by Kazantzakis about the need to make the Church compatible with contemporary realities, could only think in terms of updating his particular church's clubs. In fact, the priest was offended by Kazantzakis's suggestion that religious truth itself needs to be updated, indeed the suggestion that one's view of God needs to be rethought.

Kazantzakis agrees with this priest and with Abrahamic believers in general that there are limits to the human intellect and that science should not be treated with reverential awe. But his Bergsonism puts him equally at odds with Orthodox religious belief and with positivistic Marxist belief. The following position by Kazantzakis serves to refute any traditional belief in divine omniscience in the present regarding the outcome to future contingencies:

> Time is an ever-evolving creative force—a perpetual maturation. That is its essence. It is not a composite of elements, all of which pre-exist and, with the passage of time, simply merge mechanically into predictable new combinations. Time is a continuous emergence of unexpected elements—in one word, creation. . . . And the essence of life, its qualitative difference from matter, is precisely the creative act. . . . Never, in any circumstances, can the same identical causes recur. . . . A system of laws, cannot by nature exist for social phenomena.[52]

Historical events do not occur necessarily. If Napoleon had drowned as a child, rather than a neighbor child with whom he was swimming, would history, even religious history, have been the same? Probably not, according to Kazantzakis. One is reminded here of Voltaire's remark that if Cleopatra's nose had been an inch longer history would have been radically different. In social science's effort to replace religion it is crucial to remind the former that what it does best is dissect the past. Concerning strict predictability regarding the future, Kazantzakis makes the following accurate observation: "this doesn't happen with absolute accuracy even in the physical world, since a small coincidence, a minor event that has depended on unimaginably complicated details, can give a new, unforeseen turn to history."[53]

Kazantzakis was a heterodox religious believer and a heterodox Marxist for the same reason; he saw history as a play of many factors: economic, racial, and religious. For example, he asks how one can account for the sudden triumph in the seventh century of an insignificant Arab tribe on economic factors alone? Rather, it was largely because of a religious idea (monotheism) that such a triumph occurred. On this basis, an unimaginable civilization from West Africa to Indonesia was established. Economic factors are in fact among the most powerful motivations in human life because, quite simply, human beings must eat. Sometimes one factor dominates history, sometimes another, sometimes they are in unison. Kazantzakis makes at least this much of a concession to the Marxists: "In normal times, when the masses are not inflamed by a religious faith, the primary role is, I think, played by economic factors."[54] But even in normal times there is behind the economic banners a hidden force. Kazantzakis holds this view here in *Russia* as well as in *Spiritual Exercises*. Economic changes may manifest themselves before the religious ones and still ultimately be the result of some Eastern, harmony-breaking religious idea:

> Even the most fanatic Marxists agree that the economic liberation of mankind is not a goal but a means. What does this mean? That there is in man a need more powerful, more profound, and it is for this need that man struggles.[55]

The interplay of economic and religious factors in history is like the interplay of Western and Eastern factors within religion itself: both pairs operate in cyclic, or better spiral, fashion.

Throughout this section of the chapter I have emphasized that even when most under the spell of Marxism while in Russia, Kazantzakis maintained the method at work in his thought on God. No doubt this struck some as odd, as when Panait Istrati said that he was told that Kazantzakis was a mystic, but upon meeting him in Russia found out that Kazantzakis's head was on straight. Of course Istrati has assumed here, as Kazantzakis would not assume, that there is something wrongheaded about mysticism. In fact, Kazantzakis implies that Istrati was *too* Dionysian. In that he was insufficiently Western and rational he lacked the "superior balance" for which Kazantzakis hoped, and he lacked a stable enough foundation on which to leap into the future. Nonetheless, Kazantzakis obviously recognized genius in Istrati's approach. He says the following, where we can notice a concentration on the individual that would be anathema to most Marxists:

> Each human being is a solitary animal of the desert, the abyss all around each one, and there is no bridge. . . . "I know it," he said, "but I always forget." "This is your great value, Panait. If you didn't know it, alas, you would be stupid. If you knew it and didn't forget it, alas, you would be cold and insensitive. While now you're a true human being, warm, contradictory, a bundle of hopes and disappointments and later again new hopes. And so on until death."[56]

Kazantzakis was not so estranged from Istrati's approach at the time *Russia* was written that he would disassociate him from the perennial Greek predicament. Both of them were caught between the Western intellectuals they met in Russia and the *"excessively silent and incomprehensible"* Asians they met there (emphasis added).[57]

An abyss separates the Western and the Eastern soul, according to Kazantzakis, an abyss that can be crossed, perhaps, if Westerners simplify their material wants and discipline their inner lives. It is for this reason that Kazantzakis worried that starved Russians might not transubstantiate the food they ate into spirit, but would instead develop a fetish for the food in itself and for its own sake. Workers who are historically deprived dream of roasting meat and undressing women. By way of contrast, Kazantzakis admires those individuals who can take advantage of the inherent instability in life, and especially in life at the current stage of history, so as to surge forward. He puts his point in explicitly Christian terms:

> An apocryphal story in the Bible states that the beloved disciple John, as he was weeping in front of his crucified teacher, saw an astonishing vision: The cross was not of wood but of light; and on the cross, not one man but thousands of men, women, and children were groaning and dying. . . . The innumerable faces kept changing and flowing. Slowly the faces were blurred and all that remained was a great crucified cry.[58]

Both capitalist and Marxist materialism tend to block the way of the spirit, but the latter seems to offer an aperture to Kazantzakis, however small, to stagger through with holy terror.[59]

The face of the Combatant who has ascended from inorganic matter to plants, to animals, to human beings, now appears as the global proletariat, according to Kazantzakis. It decidedly does *not* appear in the guise of any one of a number of romantic superficialities that would have us return to the old Middle Ages, or to the love of the early Christians, or to the Presocratics (Nietzsche? Heidegger?): "[A]ll these are dreams of impotent men. Life does not turn backward; it advances."[60] That is, Kazantzakis has no hope that contemporary workers will love their work, as they did in the Middle Ages; paradise is on this earth, he thinks, but so is hell. In the interregnum of the current Middle Ages the primary work to be done, however, is to accept the divine, transubstantiating idea in a dynamic fashion. Human passivity is dangerous precisely because it turns us into plantlike beings.

In sum, Kazantzakis's Russian experiment not only exhibits his overall method, but also his Bergsonism, as scholars such as Bien, Poulakidas, and N. Georgopoulos emphasize. As early as letters written in 1908, and in his lengthy 1913 article on Bergson that appeared in the *Bulletin of the Educational Society*, we find Kazantzakis stressing that his individual concept of life and his world theory are thoroughly Bergsonian. Marxist humanism must be grounded in something transhuman, he thought, if it was to avoid those phenomena that Bergson revolted against: scientism, intellectualism, materialism. And whereas Kazantzakis initially thought the Russian experiment to be the daylight marking the end of the transitional age, in short order he realized that it was very much a part of the transition itself.[61]

Some Plays

In the play *Sodom and Gomorrah* we can see why Kazantzakis, despite his enormous literary output, did not consider himself a writer or an intellectual, but a prophet or a visionary. All of his works, as Friar notes, consist in a battle between the human and God:

> One is moved not so much by technical sophistication as by pyrotechnical apocalypse, not so much by measured effect as by shattering impact. . . . But the word "God" as used by Kazantzakis is laden with ambiguous and shifting meaning. At times he will erect it like an idol of Christendom, but simply in order to smash it better. At times he will weigh it down with his own evolutionary concept of God as the *élan vital* in Nature itself.[62]

This quotation exhibits both Kazantzakis's dipolar theism and the systole-diastole nature of his method.

In this play even the character "Abraham" has the courage to state what is obvious in the face of evil, that God is not omnipotent; or at least initially he had such courage. He changes his mind after the character "God" intimidates him, as did the voice from the whirlwind in the Bible with Job. Kazantzakis captures well the ability of the Old Testament God to burn people up and leave them like cinders. In fact, although Kazantzakis's God is not omnipotent, his God *does* retain this burning character, referred to by John of the Cross as the "living flame of love," a flame that is so intense that the uninitiated have a difficult time appreciating it as loving. Nonetheless, Abraham as well as Lot want to purify themselves and unite with God. The tension in the play is exactly that found in the traditional theism found in the Abrahamic religions in general: if God is omnipotent and is responsible for (or at least permits) everything that happens, then God is responsible for some morally reprehensible things.[63]

Theism has survived despite the inaccurate things said about God for centuries by traditional theists largely because in every age there have been those like Lot who feel the "Great Spirit" riding the wind—those who experience the inwardness of religious tradition. But Lot, identifying God's consuming fire with God's salvific power, has, like Kazantzakis himself, a hard-nosed view of God. In moments of silence Abraham and Lot come to appreciate this identification, but for the most part they are like most human beings in seeing only one of God's many faces and being struck with terror at that. Yet Abraham, Lot, and Kazantzakis alike see God as deathless, and despite the fact that we are not deathless our goal should be to merge with what Kazantzakis refers to as the "Great Conflagration."[64]

Kazantzakis's method, as I have summarized it at the beginning of this chapter, is in evidence throughout his corpus, even in lesser-known works. In *Christopher Columbus* we find the Kazantzakian commonplace that God listens only to the prayer of the hungry. And there is an obvious tension in the play between those (for example, the abbot) who wish to transubstantiate this hunger into prayer and those (for example, Fr. Juan) who, perhaps disingenuously, wish to transubstantiate the anticipated gold to be found in the new world into prayer. Columbus himself embodies the former tendency; indeed he, like St. Christopher, carries Christlike suffering across the ocean in the effort to advance the divine cause. That is, Columbus sets sail in order to transcend the boundaries of established belief. This Eastern leap, albeit accomplished by sailing West, is taken by him to avoid what he takes to be the greatest sin: humility (contra the ancient Greek belief that *hybris* was the greatest sin).[65]

As in his critique of Marxism in his books on Russia, here Kazantzakis makes it clear that it was because the new world was first born in Columbus' heart that he was able to physically see it rise from the sea. And after frantic activity—whether intellectual or nautical—a period of silence is needed to hear God's voice. Columbus is a hero for Kazantzakis because he was able to pierce harmonious order due to his talent at dreaming with his eyes open, the only eyes able to see. The fact that his eyes *were* open, however, indicates Kazantzakis's desire to preserve the best in rationality and common sense in his simultaneous glorification of visionary thinking. In the following words to Queen Isabella, Columbus in effect chastises those who would reduce Kazantzakis's theology to a mere anthropocentrism:

> The strength of true man is as immeasurable as the breath of God. Who could possibly calculate how far the daughter of God—our soul—can reach? It is a great sin, my Queen, to place boundaries on the soul, or humble it by saying, "You cannot go any further." It is like humbling God.[66]

Neither God nor a great human soul that has passed through the desert can have boundaries. But on the far side of the divine abyss, symbolized in this play by what was assumed to be the end of the earth, is *terra firma* and a new, higher order harmony. For Columbus, however, merely striving for this higher harmony was a reward in its own right; like Moses he could see the promised land if he wished, but he realized that it would be fraudulent to think that this promised land was anything other than a temporary resting point.

In the play *Melissa* Kazantzakis develops a powerful image of his goal regarding the traditional view of God in the Abrahamic religions. He speaks of a god who was the protector of an ancient Greek city. The citizens reified the god by erecting a bronze statue in his honor, but the god-statue stirred, stretched its legs, and silently descended the stairs of his temple and fled.[67] We have seen earlier in this book, however, that this reification of God cannot in an unqualified way be blamed on Greek philosophy, some commentators to the contrary. The Platonic distinction between the visible and the invisible does not condemn us to a view of God as eternal and completely removed from the visible, natural world. In fact, as I have alleged before, Kazantzakis's view is very close to Plato's that *the* mark of soul and of divinity is self-motion, and that not even divine self-motion has sufficient power to overcome necessity (*anangkē*), the recalcitrant element in the universe that eludes control by besouled beings. That is, life is, for Kazantzakis as well as for Plato, tragic.[68]

Despite the fact that life is tragic, Kazantzakis has confidence that many human problems can be ameliorated, and such progress is concomitant with the degree to which God can be liberated from matter. In the play *Kouros* Kazantzakis compares this progress with the stages by which the ancient Minoan civilization, in seeking to liberate the divine body from the beast, succeeded only from the feet to the neck, leaving the Minotaur as a result. It should not surprise us that transubstantiation (including "mystic wine") should be read back into ancient Minoan civilization as it was read back into Chinese civilization by Kazantzakis. And Kazantzakis also has the Minoans concerned with the tension between kataphatic discourse about God and apophatic silence. But here we learn that such silence can be of three sorts: (1) the silence that comes after reconciliation of apparent opposites; (2) the silence that follows death; and (3) the silence that follows victory, say if the Minotaur is killed. Only (2) is final; (1) and (3) are symbolic of the positive function of silence in that apophatic considerations are momentary affairs that prepare the way for the renewed efforts of the "Great Fighter."[69]

In the deepest recesses of the labyrinth, Theseus is described by Kazantzakis as entering into "holy silence" with the Minotaur, who, as before, symbolizes God as half-liberated. Theseus had passed through the three doors necessary to bring about spiritual progress: blood, tears, and silence. Killing the Minotaur itself brings a sort of silence and is propaedeutic to the further refinement of the divine idea by some later "Theseus," and so on, apparently *ad infinitum*. The "liberated" Minotaur (that is, Kouros) establishes a higher-order harmonious balance that, in turn, brings to light the need for further courage and flights of the imagination.[70] Kazantzakis's antimethod method, which is usually just beneath the surface of his writings, is sometimes *on* the surface.

PANEXPERIENTIALISM

AND DEATH

Thus far in the book a great deal of evidence has been cited in favor of the claim that Kazantzakis is a panexperientialist. But this evidence has been scattered about in different chapters and used for purposes other than a defense of this claim. In this chapter I will both defend this claim and argue for the claim's significance; then I will examine some texts from Kazantzakis in support of this claim; and finally I will end the book with a treatment of the relationship between Kazantzakis's panexperientialism and his view of time as asymmetrical, on the one hand, and his view of death, on the other.

The evidence mentioned earlier in the book in favor of the claim that Kazantzakis is a panexperientialist includes the following:

1. Kazantzakis sees God as an explosive power who breaks out in the smallest particle of matter.[1]
2. Even bats and manure have the potential to be transubstantiated, that is, deified.[2]
3. The transubstantiation of mud into sap and then into the blossoms of a tree is made possible by the presence of God in lightning and rain.[3]
4. That is, God, for Kazantzakis, is not suspended in mid-air but is rooted in earth, water, stone, and fire.[4]
5. Nonetheless the ubiquitous character of deity in Kazantzakis does not preclude an intensification of the process of transubstantiation in

human beings, say when he suggests that God is in the guts of a potent man on his wedding night.

6. But despite Kazantzakis's clarity regarding the point that divinity as found in human beings is at a higher level of dematerialization than that found in the remainder of nature, he is equally clear that the divine struggles in every cell of flesh and is striving for light.[5]

7. Or again, God, for Kazantzakis, is like the Platonic divinity in being the soul for the body of the world, forever in self-motion; transubstantiation is a cosmic process that is as refreshing as cool water or an enchanting woman, he thinks.[6]

8. It is especially the mystics who hear God breathing everywhere,[7] although, presumably, most human beings could perceive God if their lives were appropriately disciplined.

On Panexperientialism

To say that Kazantzakis is a panexperientialist obviously puts his thought in a position to be compared with various tendencies in Eastern religion. But it also puts his thought in a position to be compared with various tendencies in Christianity, most notably with the Franciscan one in Catholicism and with the effort in Eastern Orthodoxy to bring the physical world into conformity with the spiritual.[8] Despite a body-hating tendency within Christianity, there is a more defensible tendency, tapped by Kazantzakis, where the body participates in *theosis*.[9] (Indeed the official view in Catholicism and Eastern Orthodoxy regarding the afterlife—albeit rejected by Kazantzakis—is *bodily* resurrection, not a completely disembodied existence for the soul.) And the somatic Jesus Prayer leading to *theosis*, for example, is similar to the somatic invocation of the names of Allah leading to *wisal* or *tawhid* in Islam; there is a positive role for the body in both.[10] In the thought of Maximus the Confessor, Francis of Assisi, and Kazantzakis alike, however, it is not merely the human body that erotically responds to God in the process of *theosis*, but the whole universe. Matter is not to be suppressed, but rather transposed, molded, and illumined.[11] We will see in this chapter that this interpenetration of matter and spirit not only makes Kazantzakis a panpsychist or a panexperientialist, but also a panentheist.[12]

Regarding the traditional mind-body problem, it is important to notice that three—not merely two!—logical alternatives are open to us: (1) dualism, the view that reality is composed of two quite different sorts of stuff, soul-spirit-mind, on the one hand, and body, on the other; (2) materialism, the view that material reality is all there is; that is, mind or *psychē* is in some way reducible to body; and (3) panexperientialism or panpsychism, the Kazantzakian view that every instance of reality is *psychē*-like or at least exhibits some slight ability to feel the difference between itself and the rest of what is. That is, for a panexperientialist or panpsychist like Kazantzakis there is no completely inert or dead matter. (The ancient Greek word *psyche*, as is well known, originally meant "life" or "breath," and then later referred to "cognition" or "mind.") As we will see, panexperientialism or panpsychism explains abstract material beings in terms of more concrete sentient instances of becoming. Although I have used "panexperientialism" as well as "panpsychism," I will generally use the former term for two reasons. First, the term *psyche* often suggests a very high level of experience, whereas the Kazantzakian view is that all units have experience; and second, the term *psyche* often suggests an enduring individual, whereas the ultimate units of experience are momentary.

We should not assume that we must choose between materialism or dualism, or take an agnostic stand between these two positions, because so much of the world is supposedly inert, as in rocks or tables. It is to Kazantzakis's credit that he gives literary expression to panexperientialism because he notices in a Bergsonian way the following as a mistake: that we only have the tenets of dualism at our disposal to hold aloft their flickering torches against the encompassing darkness of a mechanical and meaningless view of the world fostered by materialistic monism.

A panexperientialist holds that feeling characterizes anything concrete— leaving out of the picture abstractions like "blue" and collections of concrete individuals like "two cats," which may feel individually, but not collectively. Of course, tables do not feel, but that does not mean that there is no feeling *in* them. Although the table is *relatively* concrete, being more concrete that the color blue or the number four, it is really a collection of more concrete singulars: subatomic particles, atoms, molecules. As contemporary physics, chemistry, and biology have made apparent, these concrete singulars do show signs of spontaneous activity and sensitivity to the environment around them; they are always in process. "Mere matter," construed as the "zero of feeling" and process, is an absolute negation whose meaning is wholly parasitic on what it denies. Nothing concrete is obviously devoid of experience; even inert rocks, as Kazantzakis seems to have realized, have active molecules, atoms, or particles. No positive meaning can be given to the negative of "sentient" because all concrete things react to their environments. If all concrete individuals are sentient, it might be asked if "sentient individual" loses its distinctive meaning. Not necessarily, because, as in the cases of tables or trees, many pseudo-individual entities are not really individuals at all. Rocks as swarms are dead. That is, those influenced by Kazantzakis do not have to feel ashamed of the fact that he often notices the striving *in* rocks and trees and mud, as when Zorba learns that rocks are alive when he measures the slope of the mountain he and the boss intend to mine.

Materialism groundlessly attributes the qualities of the apparent singulars (like rocks) to the generally unperceived real singulars. In order to accurately describe these active units of process, we must have recourse to the only active singulars we perceive as such: ourselves or other animals. The principle of change or dynamic unity in the world is soul-like, in that a self-moving character, or appetitive aspect, must be used to explain changes in each monad.

A panexperientialist like Kazantzakis can do justice to the relative difference between life and "lifeless" matter. That is, the word "sentient" does not lose its distinctive meaning in that two contrasts remain: that between active singulars and inactive aggregates, and that between low sentient activity or microscopic sentiency (S1) and high sentient activity or sentiency per se found in the animal or human individual (S2). And a panexperientialist like Kazantzakis is able to show how soul and body are related in animals. Pain is due to damaged cells; we participate in their suffering. Soul is found on both sides of the relation, but on different levels; the gap is crossed by sympathy. Our cells can enjoy themselves or suffer. So it should not be surprising that sympathy can occur in the reverse direction as well, although cells cannot be as much aware of us as we are of them.

The dynamic unity of action in a tree or in a plant is either nonexistent or too slight to justify the attribution of sentiency (S2) to them, although there is obviously striving in plants (S1), even if they do not experience pleasure and pain as wholes. We should not be harsh on those like Kazantzakis who have a panexperientialist view of trees, however, in that the pathetic fallacy is no more dangerous than the "prosaic" or "apathetic" fallacy, its opposite, which assumes that reality is as dull as many sober souls imagine. The admission of contingency and partial disorder into concrete singulars removes the modern materialistic artificialities that precluded appreciation of panexperientialism from the time of Newton to the present.

The actual things in the world are careers, or series of actual occasions. The primary concrete entities are happenings, including divine happenings, unit cases of becoming or activity. Because none of these events in process is completely determined by antecedent conditions, which would end change in all its forms, creativity is a universal principle for panexperientialists like Kazantzakis. A feeling (of a microscopic event or of an animal individual) reacts to prior feelings, but it is also spontaneous, in however slight a way. We should oppose those neat and tidy minds who claim that indeterminacy is our lack of knowledge; in fact, it seems that when quantum physics in its present form is superseded we will move even further away from classical conceptions of substance, determinism, or insentient matter. It is not only human beings, nor only animals, who defy an absolute regularity in their actions (although statistical regularity may be present, distorted as it is by our observation of it). Even the very atoms defy such absolute regularity, as any student of contemporary physics knows. One of the objections a panexperientialist like Kazantzakis can raise with the positions he opposes in *Russia* (materialism, determinism, atheism) is that they are purely negative or derivative (denying, respectively, experience, creativity, and unsurpassable experience and creativity).

Dualism, like materialism, can easily lead to the view that nature is there for us to plunder, in that reality is mostly mindless, except for a few minds scattered about that deserve consideration. The clearest basis of respect for nature consists in a renunciation of two different sorts of dualism: an absolute schism between *psyche* and matter and a near-absolute schism between the human and other forms of *psyche*. The fallacy of composition would be committed in inferring the sentience of stones from that of molecules, and the fallacy of division prohibits us from inferring the insentience or inactivity of molecules from that of stones.[13]

In short, panexperientialism is opposed to materialism, dualism (in its various forms: experience versus nonexperience, mind versus matter, sentience versus insentience) and idealism (in the sense of the doctrine that finite things have no existence apart from their being perceived). A panexperientialist like Kazantzakis is also obviously opposed the the fallacy of misplaced concreteness, that is, taking abstract composites for concrete singulars.

Kazantzakis employs a cautiously positive form of anthropomorphism. We should attribute to other creatures neither the duplication of, nor the total absence of, those properties exhibited in high degree, and in a refined or complex way, in us. Primitive animism is defective in many ways, but it is nonetheless, for Kazantzakis (consider Zorba himself or Toda Raba), more reasonable than a modern view of the world inherited from certain forms of seventeenth-, eighteenth-, and nineteenth-century science (reliant on Newton, even if Newton himself did not hold this view): that the world is a machine whose parts are submachines. Machines only occur when animals, especially human beings, make them. To use Karl Popper's terms, it is probably more accurate to say that clocks (symbols for absolutely determined regularity) are clouds (symbols for indeterminate reality exhibiting only statistical patterns) than it is to say that clouds are clocks. Not even machines are mere machines in their microscopic parts.[14]

We have no alternative to interpreting nonhuman nature by analogy with human nature. Our own natures are for us the basic samples of reality. Dialectic takes us *to* nonhuman nature, even if we can never have *concrete* nonhuman feelings. The riddle is to try to know, or at least imagine, how it feels to be another subject of feeling than one's own present self. This is often difficult even for one's own past selves, as an infant, say. Because of their simplicity, chimpanzees make the project easier, strange as that may seem; but because of their vastly different lifestyles, whales are much harder. Fish and insects are harder still; the hardest of all are paramecia, molecules, atoms, or particles. There is no need even to try for clouds, winds, rocks, oceans, or perhaps even plants when taken as wholes, for these are swarms or colonies of individuals rather than true individuals. A reasonable Kazantzakian anthropomorphism can move cautiously upward to more exalted and universally efficacious *psyche* and downward to lesser souls.

Materialism dies hard, however. There are those who wish to preserve the belief that reality is made of bits of stuff, substances. The panexperientialist's view, on the other hand, is that every singular active agent—there are no singular inactive ones, the seemingly inactive being composites of active agents—resembles an animal in having some initiative in its activity, or spontaneous movement, or feeling. The feelings of cells would include their internal relationships and the stimuli they receive from other cells—or in nerve cells, across synaptic connections. We have direct evidence that cells *do* feel, as Kazantzakis alleges; that is, we feel pain because cellular harm is done. Our suffering is an immediate sharing in, or sympathy with, feeling in our cells. Granted, awareness of our cells is blurred, in that we cannot identify the microindividuals as such, but our experience of pain indicates cellular feeling nonetheless. Notice that pain is localized, as is sexual pleasure. And where there is feeling there is Kazantzakian valuing or mattering, and in more than an instrumental sense. But this is not a night in which all cows are black. Important distinctions among the different sorts of sentient reality can be made. Mountains, trees, vegetables, winds, and rivers have feeling in them, but they are composites of active singulars. Only their invisibly small constituents have a remote analogy to our own inner life and activity.

Although molecules within an animal body exhibit peculiarities not noticed outside an animal body, it is only persons who can have a grasp of universals. Even human persons, however, have many bodily actions that are not completely under unifying control; for example, localized pleasure and pain or a heart beating. Worms, including Kazantzakis's silkworms, and jellyfish are extreme examples of decentralized, democratic societies, but even persons are a little like worms in that their personal dominance is always only partial.

Although it is hard for creatures (even human creatures) to know how much Kazantzakian creativity they have, they most definitely have it. Causal regularities mean not the absence of open possibilities, but their confinement within limits. Just as the banks of a river determine where the water will go (ignoring floods), although leaving open an infinite number of possibilities for each drop of water, so also causal regularities regulate creaturely freedom. The complete determinist would have to reduce the gap between the banks to zero, but he or she would thereby eliminate the river altogether. Likewise, to eliminate creative process altogether is to eliminate Bergsonian/Kazantzakian life.

There is a philosophical difference between the "categories" applicable to all creatures and the "transcendentals" applicable to creatures *and* creator. For panexperientialists like Kazantzakis *the* transcendental is creativity, or, in other words, response to previous instances of response. God is the unsurpassable form of creativity (or better, surpassable only by this very form in a subsequent phase); creatures are surpassable forms of creativity. A reasonable indeterminism holds not that some concrete events have no causes, but that the exact nature of ensuing events is left unspecified by the totality of their causal conditions. Something is left for the momentary self-determination of events.

All will agree that the parts of an animal (Kazantzakis's cells) have their value primarily, if not entirely, in their contribution to the whole animal. But when the inclusive or cosmic whole is considered, we hesitate. Kazantzakis, however, would share agreement with Hartshorne regarding the following four-term, organic analogy: S1:S2::S2:S3, where S1 refers to sentiency at the microscopic level of Kazantzakian cells, atomic particles, and the like. (Contemporary physics has vindicated the panexperientialist position. The nightmare of determinism has faded, as reality in its fundamental constituents itself seems to have at least a partially indeterminate character of self-motion. That is, the sum total of efficient causes from the past does not supply the sufficient cause to explain the behavior of the smallest units of becoming in the world. Kazantzakis was wiser than he knew: in twentieth-century physics near universal mechanism has given way to a cosmic, Zorba-like dance.) S2 is sentiency per se, sentiency in the sense of feeling of feeling, found in animals and human beings, whereby beings with central nervous systems or something like them can feel as wholes, just as their constituent parts show prefigurements of feeling on a local level. (And, once again, feeling *is* localized; think of a knife stuck in the gut of any vertebrate. S2 consists in taking these local feelings and collecting them so that an individual as a whole can feel what happens to its parts, even if the individual partially transcends the parts. Hurt my cells and you hurt *me*.) S3 is divine sentiency. The universe for Kazantzakis is a society or an organism (a Platonic World-Soul) of which one member (God) is preeminent, just as human beings are societies of cells of which the spiritual part is preeminent.

Neither Kazantzakis nor Hartshorne could find the following four-term analogy an adequate tool in describing the cosmos: S1:a table::S2:the "uni"verse as a concatenation of parts. Intrinsic value gives power: I can only feel because my cells feel; my sense of goodness must intuitively take the goodness of cells into account. Give my cells a healthy life, and they give me a feeling of vitality, of *élan vital*. Feeling applies to all concrete singulars; consciousness or knowledge only to higher levels of reality, including animals. Or better, there are physical aspects of feeling that give one a sense of the past, and mental aspects of feeling that give one a sense of the future and the ability to think. So whatever is conscious and can think can also feel, but not vice versa.

Recent physics has made materialism and dualism problematic, thereby making Kazantzakis's view of nature more plausible than ever. It is true that quantum mechanics has been variously interpreted. All will agree, however, that the view that physical processes are spatially and temporally continuous must be dropped, even if macroscopic objects do conform to the thesis of continuity. Atoms do not travel from one energy state to another in a smooth motion; they do so in discrete, quantum jumps. Atoms "jump" because they are subject to forces from other particles. The "free" particle (even in quantum mechanics) has a continuous spectrum of *possibilities* of motion, but there are no *completely* free particles. Every particle has an existence defined by its relations with others. "What *are* the 'things' that jump?," one might ask. Some physicists have argued that we are dealing merely with numbers or mathematical entities; others defend a pragmatic stance in which quantum formalism does not reveal the essence of the physical world, but it does *work* in experimental situations.

Hartshorne is obviously more interested than Kazantzakis in science, but both are very much interested in how we *experience* nature, or speaking crudely, in what *works* for us when we try to explain the world. The principle of indeterminacy led some to speculate that hidden variables would be found to save absolute determinism—these hidden variables have never been brought to light. At the very least, this much must be said about the effort to speculate metaphysically on the basis of discoveries in contemporary physics: we cannot understand microscopic (or submicroscopic) events on the analogy of macroscopic objects like billiard balls, yet it is precisely these objects that give us our modern notions of inertness and determinism. What is not discussed in physics is not denied.

This fact does not give us a carte blanche, but it does give us the freedom to take Kazantzakis's view of nature seriously. Kazantzakis's view includes the following features: throughout animate nature, even plant life, there is feeling; so-called "inanimate" nature is not really inanimate; nature as a whole expresses a unified soul-like reality, of which lesser lives are participants; in our perceptions of nature we at least indirectly experience the above features; but most civilized people are not aware of the above truths because after childhood they lose the message of experience of nature, being preoccupied with supposedly more practical concerns; these ignorant or forgetful people claim to know most of the universe is "dead matter," whatever that means.

The view of nature of Kazantzakis, primitive animists, children, and at least some who are familiar with contemporary science, may win out yet. Life and feeling, in many forms, pervade and constitute nature. As before, the cosmic machine of the eighteenth century has become the Zorbatic "cosmic dance" of the twentieth. Although contemporary science does not exactly prove Kazantzakis right, it cannot prove him wrong, and it does provide him with some support.

Each of three views has a price: (1) Dualism admits feelings or experiences to persons, at least, but it strikes many as an admission of defeat in the attempt to explain animate creatures; that is, dualism leaves the *psychē* unintelligible or insufficiently related to body. (2) Mere materialism or behaviorism not only fails to explain mind, but it also leaves matter as an empty abstraction. And (3), panexperientialism's more reasonable price is that it makes us aware of our human or animal incapacity to share in feelings radically different from those produced for us by our nervous systems. This price is even easier to pay because of Kazantzakis, whose glory is that he gives literary expression to one of the three options for thought, an option to which disciplined speculation now imposes fewer obstacles than it did two centuries ago.

The key issue is: are we, in part, creators of the world, further determiners of a partly indeterminate reality? The dignity of the individual is in the power to settle, here and now, what all the past, and divine power, have left unsettled. For Kazantzakis, divine creativity does not settle the details of cosmic history. It is only human beings, when imitating God as tyrant, who try to do this. Creative freedom even in animals means a pervasive element of real chance in the world. Thus, some conflict and frustration are to be expected, hence Kazantzakis's hard-nosed view of life.

When panexperientialists refer to "body," they mean the causal inheritances that concrete singulars receive from the past, making rather routine or reiterated responses prevalent, say, in an "inorganic" rock, but less prevalent in human beings. Dualism is avoided by claiming that soul or mind includes body; as before, body is an abstraction that refers to an aggregate of sentient units in process. If what I apprehend most intimately is my soul-body, and if God apprehends in a supreme way on the analogy of human apprehending, then it makes sense to talk about the world as constituting God's body.

Because animal individuals must, to maintain their integrity, adapt to their environment, mortality is implied. But if we imagine the World-Soul we must not consider an environment external to deity, but, in Kazantzakian fashion, an internal one: the world-body of the World-Soul, where, as we have seen Kazantzakis put the point, God is struggling for liberation in every cell. This cosmic, divine animal has such an intimate relation to its body that it must also have ideal ways of perceiving and remembering its body.

Belief in a World-Soul is connected with a belief in a world-body that is superior to our bodies because there is nothing internal to it (for example, cancer cells) that could threaten its continued existence. Further, our bodies are fragmentary, as in a human infant's coming into the world as a secondary lifestyle expressing its feelings upon the mother's system, which already had a basic order in its cells; whereas the divine body does not begin to exist on a foundation previously established. Kazantzakis is quite clear, as we have seen, that God is deathless and, presumably, birthless. When a human being or another animal dies, its individual lifestyle no longer controls its members, yet the result is not chaos, but simply a return to the more pervasive types of order expressive of the cosmic soul-body. The World-Soul is aware of the divine body, and can vicariously suffer with its suffering members, but it cannot suffer in the sense of ceasing to exist due to an alien force. An individual can influence it, none can threaten it. This is the source of the sublimity of God often found in Kazantzakis's writings; as before, human beings save God only in the sense that they prevent the divine advance from stagnating, they protect the *mode* of divine existence from inertia, not the divine existence itself. Not even brain death can threaten God because the soul-body analogy cannot be pushed to the point where a divine brain is posited. The contrast between the brain and a less essential bodily part only makes sense because an animal has an external environment. Consider that the divine body does not need limbs to move about, for it is its own place: space being merely the order among its parts. It does not need a digestive system or lungs to take in food or air from without in that there is no "without." So it is with all organs outside the central nervous system, which is the organ that adapts internal activities to external stimuli, a function that is not needed in the inclusive organism. The only function of the divine body is to furnish the World-Soul with awareness of, and some power over, its bodily members. So although there is no special part of the cosmos recognizable as a nervous system, every individual becomes, as it were, a brain cell directly communicating to the World-Soul, and likewise receiving influences from divine feeling or thought, as Kazantzakis often attests.

Kazantzakis's panexperientialism in *Spiritual Exercises* and elsewhere includes an insistence that the notion of being cannot be separated from that of experience; experience is not merely a bridge to reality, it is the paradigm case of reality. The ultimate structure of experience is social in that experience is united either in animal bodies or in the divine body. This metaphysics of social structure can be cited along with other reasons in the attempt to deemphasize a pretentious theory of self-interest that Kazantzakis hated, a theory that suggests that a rational ethics depends upon the possibility of showing that the good person is bound to be benefited in the long run by his own good acts. If there is no *universe*, no World-Soul to bring the world together into a social (animate) structure, then the atheistic virtue of courage, as opposed to love, in the face of the distant doom of humanity seems childish. If love is the heightening of internal relations among beings that care for each other, then love (the tough love Kazantzakis defends, not any syrupy sentimentalism) must ultimately be grounded in God, who is internally related to all beings: this is why God, for Kazantzakis, is the proper object of worship.

There is a close connection between Kazantzakis's mysticism and his panexperientialism. Wordsworth's description in "Tintern Abbey" could apply as well to Kazantzakis: "With an eye made quiet by the power of harmony and the deep power of joy," the mystic sees "into the life of things." The first human beings who emerged on earth inherited a magnificent environment, and they appreciated this fact. However, their appreciation (or better, their reverential awe) was clouded by fear. Events in nature, especially animals, were themselves deified. Civilization has stripped, in a commendable way, human beings of this fear of nature, and of the deification of animals. But for Kazantzakis it has also stripped human beings of their sense of the inexhaustible beauty and glory of the web of life. Paradoxically, it is only now that beauty and glory, in their planetary totality, are being made accessible by the very industrialism that tends to destroy them. Our machines have not enabled us to find our place among the natural kinds. Only art or philosophy or religion can help us to do this. The trick is to avoid primitive fear while still respecting nature. Kazantzakian panexperientialism enables us to do this.

Panexperientialism and Divine Embodiment

The background to Kazantzakis's panexperientialism is to be found in his fascination with ancient Greek animism and perhaps as well with the Platonic belief in the *Sophist* that being is dynamic power (*dynamis*) rather than something static or inert; and definitely with his appropriation of Bergsonian *élan vital*. And his panexperientialism is connected with his denigration of divine omnipotence. To have the greatest possible power over individuals cannot leave them powerless if being *is* dynamic power or *élan vital*. Even the greatest possible power must leave something for others to decide. Hartshorne puts the Kazantzakian and Bergsonian point in the following way:

> [P]ower must be exercised upon something, at least if by power we mean influence, control; but the something controlled cannot be absolutely inert, since the merely passive, that which has no active tendency of its own, is nothing; yet if the something acted upon is itself partly active, then there must be some resistance, however slight, to the "absolute" power, and how can power which is resisted be absolute?[15]

Hence God creates *ex hule* (from beings already in existence) rather than *ex nihilo*. We can utter the words "God is omnipotent" or "God has all power," but we cannot really conceive what these words mean if there are other dynamic beings in existence:

> That God cannot "make us do" certain things does not "limit" his power, for there is no such thing as power to make nonsense true, and "power over us" would not be power over *us* if our natures and actions counted for nothing. No conceivable being could do more with us than God can . . . and so by definition his power is perfect, unsurpassable. But it is a power unique in its ability to adjust to others.[16]

Note that this divine adjustment is part of what Kazantzakis means by our saving God.

Creation *ex nihilo*, a convenient fiction invented in the first centuries B.C. and A.D. in order to exalt divine power, is not the only sort of creation that religious believers have defended, nor is it defensible if being *is* power; that is, the power to affect or be affected by others. Bergson's own argument regarding the unintelligibility of the "absolutely nothing" in creation *ex nihilo* is a complicated one, but, in simplified form, it looks something like this: one can in fact imagine the nonexistence of this or that, or even of this or that class of things, a fact that gives some the confidence to (erroneously) think that this process could go on infinitely such that one could imagine a state in which there was "absolutely nothing." However, not every verbally possible statement is made conceptually cogent by even the most generous notion of "conceptual." At the specific, ordinary, empirical level negative instances are possible, but at the generic, metaphysical level only positive instances are possible: the sheer absence of reality cannot conceivably be experienced, for it it were experienced an existing experiencer would be presupposed. "Exist" and "exist contingently" do not, as defenders of creation *ex nihilo* and divine omnipotence imply, say the same thing. Or again, one cannot predicate "being" of a thing, even if one can predicate "necessary being" of a thing, for unless one has already in thinking the thing, unless one has thought its being, one has thought nothing. Once again, Kazantzakis is wise to deny divine omnipotence (and hence to deny creation *ex nihilo*).

None of the above commits one to the view that Kazantzakis is a pantheist. There are at least three logically distinct views regarding God, a consideration of which should help one to respond to those who are confused regarding divine embodiment:

1. God is merely the cosmos, in all aspects inseparable from the sum or system of dependent things or effects (pantheism).
2. God is both this system and in some way independent of it (panentheism, literally all is in God).
3. God is not the system, but is in all aspects independent (traditional theism).

(1) and (3) are simple views, (2) is complex. (1) and (2) refer to God as "the inclusive reality," but much depends on what one means by this phrase. That (1) and (2) are not identical can be seen by the fact that for *both* (2) and (3) the error of pantheism is to deny the externality of concrete existence to the essence of deity, as is obviously the case in *Spiritual Exercises*, as we have seen in chapter 5. Note that "God is all things" is not equivalent to "God includes all things," for example through *élan vital* spread throughout nature.

God, for panentheists like Kazantzakis, is necessary or absolute or self-sufficient only in bare essence or existence, but is contingent and embodied in actuality because how God exists at least partially depends on the other embodied things that exist, which enrich the divine life, in fact "save" it, according to Kazantzakis. The actual state of deity is partly determined by bodily creatures as a consequence of the social character of the divine self-decision. Hence the divine soul is not in the body of the world the way a bean is in a box any more than the human *psychē* is in the body in such fashion. Rather, it is in *psychē* that a bodily cell lives and moves and has its being, just as St. Paul suggests that we, as members one of another, are in the mystical body of Christ, and as Kazantzakis suggests in *Spiritual Exercises*, where we are related not only to members of our own race, but to all human beings, indeed to all of nature.

Some Texts

Almost any major work, and many minor ones, will reveal evidence of Kazantzakis's panexperientialism. In addition to the evidence cited at the beginning of this chapter, one should also note at least the following texts.

In *Buddha* it is claimed that *every* small insect (not only silkworms who produce magnificent thread) is a miniature intact Buddha who thrusts itself into the earth and works at liberation night and day. Both the insect and the earth are parts of the process whereby matter can "sprout wings" and "fly away."[17] The same point is made in *Toda Raba* regarding the need for God to work through human beings, children, oxen, and earth. In fact, God's strategy to win human beings over to the divine cause relies on the ubiquitous striving found in nature, exhibited most forcefully in human hunger. An example is cited of a Russian man 110 years old who, upon being asked what made the biggest impression on him in his life, responded in terms of the desire to eat. Speaking of Toda Raba himself, however, Kazantzakis makes it clear that desire and hunger, broadly construed, are not restricted to human beings or even to animals:

> The earth drank . . . the stones laughed. . . . He felt the grains of wheat vibrating under the earth in secret joy, entwining themselves together like brothers, gradually modeling under the earth's hard crust a huge, vigorous body with hands folded, eyes closed, and a forehead sparkling and solid.[18]

To suggest that God is diffused throughout nature is not to suggest that every natural event is sent by an omnipotent God (even if Kazantzakis offers some passages in which he might be interpreted in these terms; for example, when he says that when God raises a storm one can pity the man who pours oil into the sea). Rather, when Kazantzakis refers to "God" or to the "Invisible" he has in mind a quite different relationship with nature from that which would occur (*per impossibile*) if God were omnipotent. Note the words "as if" in the following quotation:

When I say "Invisible," I do not mean a priest's God or a
certain metaphysical consciousness or a poetic reflection of
wish fulfillment. I mean the cosmogonic Force, which uses
men as its carriers and beasts of burden—and before us the
animals, plants, matter—in its forward surge, as if it had a
purpose and had to follow a certain road.[19]

Even manure has a purpose, it seems: to fertilize (indirectly) the fruit so as to
become honey and sweetness. (Blessed is the manure, according to Kazantzakis.[20]) As before, Kazantzakis articulates his position in explicitly Christian
terms even in his travel book on Russia. The progress of the universe consists in
the process whereby the Word becomes flesh and marches again and again *on
earth*. Or again, spiritual progress is painful, as painful as being a woman in
childbirth, because (if the mixed metaphor be permitted) the *whole earth* is
mobilized.[21]

Kazantzakis does a better (Bergsonian) job of making believable the claim
that "God is everywhere" (he explicitly uses this phrase[22]) than did the
catechisms. To the extent that there is striving in nature (say an acorn struggling
to become an oak tree) God is at home everywhere, but especially in the hearts
of human beings. And, as before, even if stones as composites do not strive, this
does not preclude striving *in* them, hence it does not preclude the presence of
God in them, as Kazantzakis has Christopher Columbus attest. The worldly and
the heavenly kingdoms, in Kazantzakis's panexperientialist scheme, interpenetrate, as we have seen regarding his view of transubstantiation.[23] In Israel
especially the blood-soaked stones cry out as they come to life.[24] In (mystical)
lightning flashes of intuition, the perceptive viewer can see the greatest, divine
wealth displayed in a not so quotidian nature. As we saw in chapter 6 on
mysticism in Kazantzakis, the key to understanding his transubstantiation of
matter into spirit is to (re)develop the ability to see soil and water, earth and sky,
everything, for the first time, specifically to see the "Great Fighter" in these
phenomena.[25]

Panexperientialism, Asymmetrical Time, and Death

Kazantzakis was obviously interested in the topic of death, and such an
interest is perfectly compatible with his panexperientialism and his process,
asymmetrical view of time. As Thomas Nagel puts the point in Kazantzakian
fashion, death is an evil because it deprives us of something:

There are elements which, if added to one's experience,
make life better; there are other elements which, if added to
one's experience, make life worse. But what remains when

these are set aside is not merely *neutral*: it is emphatically
positive. Therefore life is worth living even when the bad
elements of experience are plentiful.[26]

It is *be-ing* alive and *do-ing* certain things that is good. That is, it is not the
static state of death that is evil, but the loss of the process of living. This is why
Zorba thought he should live a thousand years and why Kazantzakis indicates in
Freedom or Death that some great human beings should *never* die.[27]

Nor is death evil merely because it implies one's nonexistence. The asym-
metricality of time is most apparent in the fact that we do not regret the period
before birth even if we are bothered by the period after death. Obviously there
are evils besides death, but to know these as evil also very often requires a
knowledge of the asymmetrical history of the person in question, a knowledge
of what has occurred thus far and what the possibilities or probabilities are for
the future. It is very often not the categorical or the temporally isolated state
one occupies in the present that determines evil: we do not mind that an infant
drools like an idiot, indeed at times it is cute that it does so, but we do mind a
great deal that an intelligent woman with brain damage from a car wreck drools
like an idiot. In the latter case our concern is due to our knowledge of the
person she was as opposed to the person she is now. "Success" or "failure" in
general are process or relational terms. Obviously a corpse is not to be pitied (it
is merely an instance of the sort of dynamism found in "inorganic" matter
characteristic of nature in general), but a person who seems most likely to
become one soon generally *is* to be pitied.

Process thinkers like Kazantzakis would agree with Nagel's claim that
Lucretius misunderstood temporal asymmetry: we should not mind, Lucretius
thought, posthumous nonexistence any more than prenatal nonexistence. But
in between these two existences is life itself and awareness and hope. Nagel puts
his Kazantzakian view as follows:

> The direction of time is crucial in assigning possibilities to
> people or other individuals. Distinct possible lives of a single
> person can diverge from a common beginning, but they
> cannot converge to a common conclusion from diverse
> beginnings. (The latter would represent not a set of different
> possible lives of one individual, but a set of distinct possible
> individuals, whose lives have identical conclusions.)[28]

The key question regarding the degree to which death is an evil is, *how* possible
are our possibilities? The death of Keats at twenty-four or of Captain Mihalis in
middle age is a monumental loss, but the death of Tolstoy at eighty-two or of
Zorba in old age is still a loss. Blindness is not a nightmare for a mole because it
is not the sort of being one would ever expect to have vision. Yet:

> The trouble is that life familiarizes us with the goods of which
> death deprives us. We are already able to appreciate them, as
> a mole is not able to appreciate vision. . . . Observed from
> without, human beings obviously have a natural lifespan. . . .
> A man's sense of his own experience, on the other hand,
> does not embody this idea of a natural limit. His existence
> defines for him an essentially open-ended possible future,
> containing the usual mixture of goods and evils that he has
> found so tolerable in the past. Having been gratuitously
> introduced to the world by a collection of natural, historical,
> and social accidents, he finds himself the subject of a *life*,
> with an indeterminate and not essentially limited future.
> Viewed in this way, death, no matter how inevitable, is an
> abrupt cancellation of indefinitely extensive possible goods.[29]

Some, including some process thinkers like Hartshorne, might object that the
inevitability of death should make it tolerable; otherwise we simply fail to understand ourselves as biological animals. But Nagel's Kazantzakian view is as follows:

> Suppose that we were all inevitably going to die in *agony*. . . .
> Would inevitability make *that* prospect any less unpleasant?
> . . . If the normal lifespan were a thousand years, death at 80
> would be a tragedy. As things are, it may just be a more
> widespread tragedy. If there is no limit to the amount of life
> that it would be good to have, then it may be that a bad end
> is in store for us all.[30]

It should be emphasized that Nagel is dealing here with the topic of death
by itself apart from considerations of immortality, considerations that do not
concern Kazantzakis, either. It is Nagel's and Kazantzakis's belief that death
provides the background against which we can come to see our lives as ironic
while we are still alive. One can legitimately wonder if our lives are leading
nowhere because we die and because those that we have an effect on die as well.
Perhaps we can contribute something to our people or to God (Hartshorne's
objective immortality), but we can always doubt that this is the case.

A consideration of death, however, only starts us on our way to a coming
to grips with life as ironic. Even if we lived forever our lives might be ironic if
this word refers to

> a conspicuous discrepancy between pretension or aspiration
> and reality: someone gives a complicated speech in support
> of a motion that has already passed . . . you declare your love
> over the telephone to a recorded announcement.[31]

There is an inevitable clash in the lives of rational beings because they can engage in (Cartesian) doubt. On the one hand, there is a pragmatic necessity to be serious and, on the other, we can always step back from this pragmatic seriousness so as to survey our lifespan—however long—from the outside. It is crucial to notice, however, that the ironic character of life, according to Nagel, depends on what he calls a view of ourselves *sub specie aeternitatis*, from a fixed point outside of time and outside the bounds of temporal asymmetry.

Nagel's fascination with a view *sub specie aeternitatis* is odd in that it presupposes the divine point of view outside of time found in traditional theism, a point of view rejected by Kazantzakis. It is unfortunate that Nagel does not engage himself with process thought here. The view of time as asymmetrical conflicts with the view *sub specie aeternitatis* because in the latter there is no lesser degree of determination with respect to the "future" than there is with respect to the "past."

In any event, Nagel is intent on distinguishing his Kazantzakian view of life as ironic from the view of Camus that life is absurd. (Actually, Nagel prefers the word "absurd" to "ironic," but I have used the latter word in reference to Nagel's position to avoid confusion with Camus's quite different position.) Camus's view consists in a histrionic and heroic collision between the self and a recalcitrant world. But for Nagel and Kazantzakis, life is ironic because it consists in a collision within ourselves. When we step back from temporal pursuits so as to see our lives from the perspective of "eternity" (or from the perspective of divine everlastingness, in Kazantzakis's case), we need not abandon our pursuits because of their futility, but we will return to them with at least a grain of salt. After we see the ironic character of our beliefs:

> we take them back, like a spouse who has run off with someone else and then decided to return; but we regard them differently. . . . It is useless to mutter: "Life is meaningless; life is meaningless . . ." as an accompaniment to everything we do. . . . What sustains us, in belief as in action, is not reason or justification, but something more basic than these.[32]

This more basic element, if I understand Nagel correctly, is Zorbatic verve or Bergsonian intuition or Jamesian-Santayanian animal faith. We pursue our everyday, pragmatic affairs with intuition and *élan vital* on our side until we take the backward step and are then confronted with the irony of our lives. The nonhistrionic response to life as ironic that is Kazantzakis's and Nagel's hallmark is, perhaps, punctuated by periods of alarm. These can be ameliorated either by not taking the backward step and living our lives somewhat unreflectively, as is the case in the lives of animals, or by reducing our beliefs and our pursuit of things, as in certain forms of religious asceticism, including

Kazantzakis's. But the ironic tension between our taking our lives with intense seriousness and our realization that at the end of our lives comes death is one of the most normal things about human beings in general.

The irony of life makes it possible to view it as a game, but games, it should be emphasized, are serious things. Two extremes are to be avoided. On the one hand, we should not view games so seriously that they become preparations for war, as does Periander regarding the athletic games in the play *Melissa*.[33] On the other hand, games—including the game of life—should not be viewed frivolously. The trick is to compete in the game of life strenuously while maintaining a sense of humor and a sense of lightheartedness. Consider the following anecdote by Kazantzakis:

> The young professor of sociology at the Communist University of Moscow analyzes in a clear and confident manner all the economic factors present in ancient Greek society and proves that the smile of the caryatids on the Acropolis of Athens has its origins in economic causes. The audience, orthodox Marxists, accepts this wise explanation without hesitation and bursts into applause. I smile, and the young professor, unnerved, turns to me: "Why are you smiling?" "I assure you, comrade Professor," I reply, "my smile is not the result of economic causes."[34]

It is this serious-lightheartedness that characterizes Kazantzakis's entire corpus and that enables him to say that attainment of spiritual perfection is inferior to the struggle for it. Kazantzakis is in earnest when he says that some people should not die, and he at least flirts with the idea of immortality of the soul, say when the old grandfather in *Freedom or Death* washes his blood off from war, goes to church to communion, then feels his body to be a lightly flying cloud. At death the same grandfather had a similar experience that was supplemented by a magical voice, perhaps from "God Himself," that came from *beyond* life. At the moment of death his body lightened as it was softly transformed into a cloud. But this cloudlike body does not completely evaporate or fly off into the heights; rather it condenses and falls as rain to the ground so as to nourish the young shoots.[35] In the final analysis it is in *this* world that we must find God and, hence, find meaning in our lives. In a peculiar way it makes sense to say that for Kazantzakis transubstantiation is from spirit into flesh; our project is to redeem the bodies we have. For example, despite all of his accomplishments in life, Zorba did not think on his deathbed that he had done enough, thus his claim that men like him *ought* to live a thousand years.

Further, the Cry passage from *Report to Greco*, quoted at length at the end of chapter 1, captures many of the features of Kazantzakis's thought as they bear on both panexperientialism and death, the topics of the present chapter. In this passage Kazantzakis makes it clear that he thinks of Jesus not as a disembodied cogito or as an overly Apollonian character, but as a model of *élan vital*, transubstantiation, and ascension. Like Jesus and the rest of creation—wood, rocks, birds, everything—we struggle to liberate a God who is incessantly defeated only to rise again, full of blood and earth, so as to be thrown into the battle once more.[36] Blowing through all things is a great Cry that prevents plants and animals from stagnating, and that acts as a lure for centaurlike humanity, which has been struggling for thousands of years to draw itself out of its human scabbard. When the locus of this struggle is the human confrontation with death, human beings are often tempted to despair. The Cry answers, "I am beyond. Stand up!"

The meaning of our lives is obviously not found, for Kazantzakis, in any sort of personal or subjective immortality. As the famous epitaph on Kazantzakis's grave has it, "I have ceased to hope, I have ceased to fear, I am free."[37] We and everyone we know will, in fact, die, but in addition to the intrinsic value of our transubstantiating struggles we have the solace that comes from knowing that our efforts will be taken up into the divine life. Some of us do not wish for more than this solace: we die but God is eternal.

Heroic Resistance, Again

This solace should not be overemphasized, however, in that heroic (or saintly) resistance (*levendiá*) is the order of the day for Kazantzakis. It is comfort, not adversity, that is the devil's snare. The sense of peace, or what I have above called solace, in Kazantzakis comes from an awareness that to be religiously inclined is to struggle to transubstantiate matter into spirit.[38] As we have seen, however, a better way to put the point when Zorba's zest for bodily life is considered, and when Kazantzakis's refusal to defend personal immortality is considered, is that Kazantzakis extols "the earthly incarnation of cosmic spirituality in the natural."[39] The goal is not *really* to escape this earthly life but to transubstantiate it, indeed to improve it. Flesh is metamorphosed by infusing it with spirit.

In any event, whether it is more accurate to say that the goal of Kazantzakian theism is the transubstantiation of matter into spirit or the transubstantiation of spirit into matter is not as crucial as the avoidance in religion of what Whitehead calls the fallacy of misplaced concreteness. This is the error whereby we either literalize our religious myths or reify our current religious states or beliefs. Kazantzakis thinks that as long as we are alive we must engage in the process of de-literalization or de-reification. God, for him, is, in a way, the "uncatchable bird."[40] But this does not signal the hegemony of the apophatic. There are some things we can say quite clearly and literally about God. For example, when Fotis in *The Greek Passion* asks, "Who is this God who lets children die?,"[41] the literal Kazantzakian response regarding God's *abstract* properties would be: God is not omnipotent, so we should not think that it is within God's power to prevent all children from dying. Or again, regarding the *metaphorical* description of God in the image of Egyptian, Persian, and Roman imperial rulers we need to de-literalize. Kazantzakis complements, supplements, and refines the process thought of Bergson, Whitehead, and Hartshorne by emphasizing that God's agency in the world is most evident to us in periods of psychic turmoil.[42]

The fact that Kazantzakis does not believe in personal immortality should not get in the way of the realization that at no time in his mature life was he without some form of theistic belief; further, this theistic belief was often a response to the psychic turmoil created by the figure of Christ, who remained for Kazantzakis throughout his life a cyst that he repeatedly removed, only to have it grow back again. It should be remembered that *The Last Temptation of Christ, The Greek Passion*, and *Saint Francis* were all written in the last decade of his life.[43] But even in his most apparently anti-Christian moments, according to Bien, Kazantzakis was trying to transubstantiate the old religion rather than to abandon it altogether. When he rejects Christ in his works, it is invariably the traditional Christ who promises an after-life or who asks us to renounce this one. It is rather a meta-Christian Christ that Kazantzakis defends, to use Bien's language.

One of the most paradoxical features of Kazantzakis's thought on God is that he is both a great defender of (Bergsonian) spiritual progress and a critic of hope, in that, as Frederick Sontag notes, too much hope dulls one's desire to engage *élan vital*.[44] Likewise, Kazantzakis's this-wordly mysticism is of a dynamic sort for no other reason than the fact that for him religious ecstasy is to be understood in its root meaning: out of (*ek*) "stationariness" (*stasis*).[45]

NIETZSCHE

Throughout the present book I have emphasized the Bergsonian background to much of what Kazantzakis says about God, and I have emphasized the fact that his thought on God can be best understood as offering what Darren Middleton calls a "mythopoesis" of process philosophy of religion or process theology. I have not denied that in addition to Bergson the other great philosophical influence on Kazantzakis was Nietzsche. But I have not spent much time on Nietzsche's influence, which is understandable, I think, when it is considered that this book is about Kazantzakis and God. The current revival of interest in Nietzsche by deconstructionist postmodernists, however, makes it necessary to explore in more detail the connection between Nietzsche and Kazantzakis.

Thus far I have claimed that Nietzsche influenced Kazantzakis in at least two ways:

1. Kazantzakis learned from Nietzsche that the traditional view of God is dead, a death that cannot be dismissed lightly in philosophy, literature, politics, or religion. Likewise, Kazantzakis shared Nietzsche's anticlericalism and his distaste for religious ritual and the paraphernalia of organized religion. (It should be reiterated, however, that Bergson was also a critic of traditional, "closed" religion.)
2. Kazantzakis also liked Nietzsche's (and Bergson's!) critique of the hegemony of a particular variety of rationality. Nowhere is this more

apparent than in his adoption of Nietzsche's desire to fuse clashing forces, especially the Dionysian and Apollonian. Kazantzakis was especially enamored of Nietzsche's ability to turn unhappiness into a sort of Dionysian or tragic optimism.

Although Nietzsche's tone is quite different from Bergson's, it is important to note, as did Frederick Copleston some time ago,[1] that Nietzsche and Bergson were both philosophers of organism who had much in common, as the above two points indicate.

I have also alleged that there are at least two notable differences between Nietzsche and Kazantzakis:

1. Jacques Derrida and others are perhaps correct in seeing Nietzsche as a forerunner of deconstructionist postmodernism, whereas Kazantzakis, despite his Nietzschean tragic optimism, is much more of a constructive thinker who repeatedly describes characters driven by the *élan vital* toward ever progressive levels of spiritualized matter.
2. In fact, the progressive nature of Kazantzakis's thought is largely due to his reformulation of some basic Christian phenomena. Kazantzakis did not, as did Nietzsche, see Jesus as a deracinated opponent to Dionysian passion; nor did he think it *necessary* that religion be seen in these terms, as apparently Nietzsche did, as we will see, and unlike Nietzsche, Kazantzakis admired the person of Christ. This constructive approach to the spiritual life can be seen in *The Last Temptation of Christ*, *The Greek Passion*, *Saint Francis*, and many other works. Kazantzakis's positive attempt to revise thought about God, to make it more "open" in a Bergsonian sense, can also be seen in his use of the theme of transubstantiation, his dedication to the writings of the great mystics, his desire to preserve the best in the Middle Ages, etc. All of these activities would have been foreign to Nietzsche.

In the remainder of this appendix I will expand on both the strong influence Nietzsche had on Kazantzakis and on the ways in which Kazantzakis is markedly unNietzschean. Finally, I will respond in a Kazantzakian way to some recent challenges to religious belief made by some deconstructionist postmodernists who have been inspired by Nietzsche.

Nietzsche's Influence

Kazantzakis himself tells us in *Report to Greco* (and *England*) how Nietzsche influenced him.[2] He relates a story (that Bien thinks may have been invented by Kazantzakis for the purpose of literary effect) of how a woman in

Paris approached him with a picture of Nietzsche in her hands. She pointed out the striking resemblance Kazantzakis had to Nietzsche. It was this encounter, which Kazantzakis says was one of the most decisive in his life, that led him to read Nietzsche's works. The point to be made here, however, is that reading Nietzsche had a *personal* effect on Kazantzakis because the latter started to internalize "the rabid rage" for destruction, sarcasm, and cynicism found in Nietzsche. In addition, Kazantzakis admired Nietzsche's refusal to say "I am fine here, I shall go no further." Rather, no matter how joyful or bitter one is, there is a need to proceed into the future without fear. That is, none of the standard consolations for life's tragedies are acceptable: gods, facile moralities, half-truths, and so on. Like Nietzsche, Kazantzakis felt no desire to succumb to a "crafty" (closed) religion where rewards and punishments were transplanted to a future life in order to comfort cowards, the enslaved, and the aggrieved. Traditional (closed) religion seemed to Kazantzakis to be an enclosure where thousands of panic-stricken sheep bleated away night and day, and in *Report to Greco* he thanks Nietzsche for opening up his eyes to this fact.

Bien thinks it crucial, however, to note that when Kazantzakis looks back on his early stay in Paris (around 1908) and on his doctoral dissertation on Nietzsche (1909), he seems to do so a bit anachronistically. (Much of what he has to say about Nietzsche in *Report to Greco* was actually written in 1926.) Kazantzakis had read and scorned Nietzsche before he went to Paris, such that what he discovered there was not Nietzsche but how to appreciate Nietzsche for the first time. What he learned was that Nietzsche was an effect of the decadence and flabbiness of modern Western civilization, not its cause. Nietzsche "kills" a view of God that should have been killed some time before, and he rejects any sort of supernatural, divine, preordained plan for humanity.[3]

Nietzsche's "murder" of the traditional God has implications for anthropology, because if God is the supreme model for the solitary, self-sufficient, isolated self, and if in the modern period the sovereign, isolated human self was made in God's image, then the death of God entails the death of the substantial self. If there is no single, far-off, divine reality to which we are subservient, then human beings are free, on Nietzschean-Kazantzakian grounds, to struggle on their own, without the hope of divine reward or punishment, or even of the assurance that there will be an enduring self in "one's own" life that will enjoy the struggle.[4]

Important Differences

It is also Kazantzakis himself in *Report to Greco* (and *England*) who alerts us to the important differences between his views and Nietzsche's. Throughout the chapter in *Report to Greco* on Nietzsche, Kazantzakis has his thoughts on Nietzsche interpenetrate with his own concern for transubstantiation, indeed with his "open" treatment of Christianity.[5] God's countenance in the modern (or postmodern) world can be seen in frenetic Paris, with its streets, parks, libraries, museums, theaters, and Gothic churches (which are also ironically found in Nietzsche's natal village). Kazantzakis tells us that his task is to transubstantiate the hate that he derived from reading Nietzsche into love. Likewise, Nietzsche's Dionysian intoxication had to be transmuted into mystic ecstasy. That is, Nietzsche may have been premature in denigrating Wagner because the latter took up Christian themes in *Parsifal*, themes also taken up (but dealt with in a Bergsonian way) by Kazantzakis in *The Last Temptation of Christ, Spain, Saint Francis, The Greek Passion*, and elsewhere.

Twice Kazantzakis emphasizes the fact that the "wound" he received by reading Nietzsche, a wound that penetrated deeply, was a fascination of his youth. While in Paris, however, his "heart's calmness always returned" when he went to hear Bergson's "magical voice." Bergson's "mystic salves" did not give permanent relief because as long as he remained young Nietzsche's "sores" periodically opened again and bled. But Kazantzakis cannot resist the temptation of comparing these sores to those of St. Francis who, late in life, received the stigmata of Christ, or to those afflictions brought down by apocalyptic angels. These are comparisons that Nietzsche would have found anathema.

Kazantzakis knows this, but his desire was not so much to become a follower of Nietzsche as to use Nietzsche as part of a grander (Bergsonian) whole. On Kazantzakis's interpretation, Nietzsche himself could not be easily Christianized because Nietzsche really did (despite current efforts by deconstructionists to declaw Nietzsche) believe in the dictum "*Rastí Roustí*—Might is Right."[6] In fact, Kazantzakis, writing during World War II, thinks that Nietzsche would have approved of the then current ideas about longing to expand and dominate, and that the war was an understandable result of the seeds he had sown.

It is obviously not the purpose of this appendix to do original research on Nietzsche, but to explore in more detail than I have thus far the precise nature of Kazantzakis's debt to Nietzsche. Nor was Kazantzakis himself particularly interested in doing original research on Nietzsche, but rather in taking Nietzsche's Dionysian passion and employing it in a way analogous to the efforts of the architects of the great Gothic cathedrals in Paris: to shoot a sharp, daring arrow into the sky like a lightning rod so as to make contact with God and to pull the divine electricity back to earth. Nietzsche's passion influenced Kazantzakis, but not his view of super*man*, whom Kazantzakis explicitly rejects as a deceptive mirage.[7]

Bien's way to put the point is to suggest that Nietzsche's chief usefulness to Kazantzakis was as a destroyer of the old, whereas Bergson was useful to him as a provider of the basic structure to his positive worldview. That is, there are Kazantzakian limits to any Nietzschean homeopathy wherein the cure for nihilism is seen to lie in a drug that produces the same symptoms as the disease itself. The most basic natural law of the universe, for Kazantzakis, as we have seen, is not the drive to become an *Übermensch*, but the transubstantiation of matter into spirit. Bien quotes Kazantzakis as follows: "I loved [Nietzsche] for the questions he asked . . . not however for his answers, which were not good."[8]

It seems that his "answers" were not good, from Kazantzakis's point of view, because of his anthropocentrism, indeed because of his egoism. Whereas Kazantzakis insists in *Spiritual Exercises* that the spiritual exercitant should quickly move beyond egoism to a concern for all humanity, to a concern for all sentient life, even to a concern for the cosmos, there is not much evidence in Nietzsche that he had a great deal of concern even for suffering humanity (to the contrary!). In fact, his egoism is legendary. I will cite one example. In Nietzsche's second or positivistic period, where he entertained the possibility that science would resolve the issues that religion had previously resolved, and give meaning to life just as religion had previously done so, he considered himself to be practicing a philological-philosophical science. With a vanity characteristic of Nietzsche that is entirely absent in Kazantzakis, the former refers to his own work as leading to "the greatest triumph" of science,[9] an estimation that is as bothersome to those who are familiar with the history of science as it is to theocentrists.

Further, it was Bergson rather than Nietzsche who enabled Kazantzakis to reconcile the rift Kazantzakis saw as a young man between science and religion, a rift brought about by being exposed to the theory of evolution for the first time, as detailed by Bien. Consider that there are four possible combinations of the following two variables: belief in God (G) and belief in theory of evolution (E). These four options are: (1) G, not-E; (2) not-G, E; (3) not-G, not-E; and (4) G, E. As far as I know, no one has ever defended option (3). Option (1) is the traditional theistic view that Kazantzakis rejects, but it is crucial to notice that he also rejects Nietzsche's view, option (2). That is, it is no mere coincidence that Kazantzakis adopts the same view as that of Bergson, option (4).

Deconstructionist Theology

The relationship between Kazantzakis and Nietzsche on the issue of God is perhaps complicated in light of some recent developments in Nietzsche scholarship, specifically the appropriation of Nietzsche for the purposes of deconstructionist literary criticism, cultural critique, and theology. In fact, one of the most important deconstructionist theologians refers to deconstructionism as the hermeneutic of Nietzsche's death of God. The nihilism indicated (caused?) by Nietzsche's "killing" God perhaps makes it possible to engage in a postmodern, Dionysian, "divine" way of thinking;[10] and perhaps, it might be held, it is this sort of thinking that Kazantzakis had in mind.

There are good reasons, however, not to adopt the deconstructionist strategy, neither on its own merits nor as an attempt to have us "better" understand Kazantzakis (the phrase "better than" makes no sense in a deconstructionist context, as far as I can tell). As was noted in the introduction, there is a tremendous difference between the trajectory of deconstructionist postmodernism—which finishes the arc from early modern cosmic dualism, to the death of a supernatural God who functioned merely as a fifth wheel, to Nietzschean/deconstructionist nihilism—and that of constructive or reconstructive postmodernism, which rethinks the cosmological dualism of the early modern period, a dualism that fuels the decline of theism and the rise of nihilism noticed/caused by Nietzsche. As I have argued throughout this book, Kazantzakis (but not Nietzsche!) wants a new Middle Ages and a better view of God than that found in the modern period.[11]

Kazantzakis is certainly interested in incorporating Dionysian passion into the spiritual life; his mythopoesis of Bergson's *élan vital* is evidence of this. But Kazantzakis is not like Nietzsche in defending the view not only that we cannot ever be completely sure that we know the truth, but that there is *no truth* to be known, a denial that has severe theological ramifications. As Griffin puts it:

> One of the differences between the constructive and deconstructive forms of postmodern philosophy with respect to relativism is that the former speaks of God. This speaking betokens no return . . . to the traditional deity of premodern and early modern philosophy and theology. But God as something like a soul of the universe, as that which makes the universe an experiencing individual, is affirmed. . . . Deconstructive postmodernism has been heavily influenced by what Arthur Danto calls "Nietzsche's Perspectivism." If God (in every sense) is dead, so that we believe that there is no all-inclusive perspective but only a multiplicity of finite perspectives, then it is difficult to see how the truth about anything could exist, because it could have no locus. Whitehead sums up the position of constructive postmodern philosophy in saying that "the truth itself is nothing else than how the [things] of the world obtain adequate representation in the divine nature."[12]

What is worse, if Nietzsche's perspectivism is "true," then not only could we not know the truth with any degree of assurance, we could not even know that certain theories or moral judgments or theological beliefs are false. Nietzsche's death of God means absolute relativism and a denial of Bergsonian/ Kazantzakian commitment to the progressive spiritualization of (or transubstantiation of) matter.

If Nietzsche and deconstructive postmodernists (e.g., Derrida) are "right," then meaningful criticism of one position from another perspective is not possible; the second position is merely different from the first. One problem here is that *in practice* Nietzsche and deconstructive postmodernists like Mark Taylor or Carl Raschke *do* criticize the perspectives of others; indeed, they are not afraid to engage in polemical invective, which gets especially vicious in Nietzsche's case. And, as we have seen Kazantzakis himself notice, Nietzschean and deconstructive postmodernist perspectivism ruins the distinction between good and evil such that a might makes right approach is a logical result.[13]

There is much to be said for the older interpretation of Nietzsche to the effect that "beyond question the major premise of Nietzsche's philosophy is atheism."[14] And even if Nietzsche's atheism is more of a diagnosis of modern civilization than a metaphysical claim about (the lack of) ultimate reality, this parsimony on Nietzsche's part nonetheless fits hand in glove with his view that the attempt to try to respond to life's problems by appeal to God (no qualifiers here—apparently Nietzsche meant *any* sort of God) constitutes a "gross answer" and a refusal to think as a human being.[15] Traditional theism did, in fact, constitute a gross answer, and Kazantzakis was wise to be influenced by Nietzsche in this regard. But the efforts of deconstructionist postmodernist theologians to Christianize Nietzsche or to make him look theocentric are both implausible at face value, given all of the nasty things Nietzsche has to say about God and about belief in God, and intellectually thin when even the most promising passages—from a deconstructionist perspective—are considered. It is true that there are some passages where Nietzsche does not deny that he believes in God, and some passages where he speaks vaguely of Dionysian passion as "divine," but there are, as far as I am aware, none where he flatly contradicts the numerous atheistic passages in his writings and none where he positively commits to theism.[16] Consider the following passage, where Nietzsche, once again, makes no effort to qualify his position. Belief in God or in "another world" is, quite simply, an error, a failure of the intellect, even if such belief is part of a revised, Bergsonian/Kazantzakian open, metaphysical theism:

> *Of the origin of religion.*—The metaphysical need is not the origin of religions, as Schopenhauer supposed, but merely a late offshoot. Under the rule of religious ideas, one has become accustomed to the notion of "another world (behind, below, above)"—and when religious ideas are destroyed one is troubled by an uncomfortable emptiness and deprivation. From this feeling grows once again "another world," but now merely a metaphysical one that is no longer religious. But what first led to the positing of "another world" in primeval times was not some impulse or need but an error in the interpretation of certain natural events, a failure of the intellect.[17]

Nietzsche did not think through carefully enough the alternatives. To believe in God is not *necessarily* to rob this world of meaning, as Bergson and Kazantzakis realized. To succumb to Nietzsche's perspectivism is to claim, contra Kazantzakis, that there is no order, not even a Bergsonian/Kazantzakian dynamic order, to which our thoughts or writings correspond. For Nietzsche, "There are no facts (*Tatsachen*), only interpretations," such that there really would be no world if we subtracted the perspectival.[18] It is one thing to say that we cannot come into contact with a thing save through a perspective (Kazantzakis's initial Kantianism in *Spiritual Exercises* is compatible with this view), it is quite another to make the Nietzschean and deconstructionist claim that we can not say anything meaningful about whatever it is on which there are perspectives.[19] Quite ironically, Kazantzakis used Nietzsche to help him discover the truth despite the fact that for Nietzsche (and deconstructionists) there is no truth to discover.[20]

The Marriage of Philosophy and Art

Despite all of the above intellectual differences between Nietzsche and Kazantzakis concerning God, humanity, truth, progress, and the belief in *reality* as dynamic process, it still must be admitted that Kazantzakis paid a significant debt to Nietzsche because what he borrowed from him was ultimately not intellectual. The debt was primarily personal, and it involved a style or a tone whereby philosophy and art could be married. (But we should not forget that Bergson's Nobel Prize was in *literature*, and that Kazantzakis was enamored of Bergson's "magical voice.") Bien frames the Nietzschean influence appropriately; he says the following regarding the Nietzschean marriage between art and philosophy that influenced Kazantzakis:

> Some would say that this was to the detriment of both partners in the marriage. Kazantzakis could always invoke his prophetic or philosophic side to excuse defects in artistic craftsmanship; conversely, he could always invoke the artistic values of warmth, vividness and imagination to excuse repetition, inconsistency and derivativeness in his thought. Others, however, would claim that the marriage of philosophy and art was Kazantzakis' distinctive quality, his virtue. In either case, it is clear that he saw himself carrying on Nietzsche's example in this regard.[21]

Charles Hartshorne has recently complained that process or neoclassical theism has not had a writer to do poetic justice to its theoretical view of God as Dante did to traditional theism. Kazantzakis's mythopoesis of process thought is the best example to date of a "process Dante," of a marriage of art and process philosophy or theology. It is no accident that Kazantzakis himself loved and translated Dante, and this despite the fact that he did not love the type of theism to which Dante's art was devoted. In the final analysis, Kazantzakis's positive ideas about God are primarily Bergsonian. But both Bergson and Nietzsche made it easier for him to give these ideas his unique artistic radiance.

NOTES

Introduction

1. Regarding the features of constructive postmodern theism discussed below see the introductions to David Ray Griffin, ed., *Founders of Constructive Postmodern Philosophy* (Albany: State University of New York Press, 1993), and *Varieties of Postmodern Theology* (Albany: State University of New York Press, 1989). Also see Griffin's own *God and Religion in the Postmodern World* (Albany: State University of New York Press, 1989), and his two important works on the theodicy problem: *God, Power, and Evil* (Philadelphia: Westminster, 1976), and *Evil Revisited* (Albany: State University of New York Press, 1991).

1. The Bergsonian Background

1. Henri Bergson, *An Introduction to Metaphysics*, tr. by T. E. Hulme (Indianapolis: Bobbs-Merrill, 1955). Originally published as "Introduction à la métaphysique," *Revue de Métaphysique et de Morale* (1903).

2. Ibid., pp. 9–13.

3. Ibid., pp. 14–15.

4. Ibid., pp. 17–20.

5. Ibid., pp. 21–26.

6. Ibid., pp. 27–38.

7. Ibid., pp. 39–62.

8. See Henri Bergson, *The Two Sources of Morality and Religion*, tr. by R. A. Audra and Cloudesley Brereton (Notre Dame, Ind.: University of Notre Dame Press, 1977). Originally published as *Les deux sources de la morale et de la religion* (Paris: 1932).

9. Ibid., pp. 9–33.

10. Ibid., pp. 34–43.

11. Ibid., pp. 44–57.

12. Ibid., pp. 58–84.

13. Ibid., pp. 96–124.

14. Ibid., pp. 128–51.

15. Ibid., pp. 153–59.

16. Ibid., pp. 176–200.

17. Ibid., p. 212.

18. Ibid., pp. 209–17.

19. Ibid., pp. 218–34.

20. Ibid., pp. 237–43.

21. Ibid., pp. 244–55.

22. Ibid., pp. 256–65.

23. Ibid., pp. 298–317.

24. Henri Bergson, *Laughter*, tr. by Cloudesley Brereton and Fred Rothwell (New York: Macmillan, 1917). Originally published as *Le Rire* (Paris: 1900).

25. Ibid., pp. 10, 25, 39.

26. Ibid., p. 130.

27. Ibid., pp. 46, 68, 113, 147.

28. See Peter Bien, *Kazantzakis: Politics of the Spirit* (Princeton, N.J.: Princeton University Press, 1989), pp. 23–24.

29. See William James, *The Varieties of Religious Experience* (Cambridge, Mass.: Harvard University Press, 1985); originally published in 1902. Also see Henri Bergson, "On the Pragmatism of William James," in *The Creative Mind*, tr. by Mabelle Andison (New York: Philosophical Library, 1946). Originally published as *La Pensée et la mouvant* (Paris: 1934).

30. See A. R. Lacey, *Bergson* (New York: Routledge, 1989), pp. 206–7, 210. Also see Leszek Kolakowski, *Bergson* (Oxford: Oxford University Press, 1985).

31. Peter Bien, *Kazantzakis: Politics of the Spirit*, p. 50.

32. *Freedom or Death*, tr. by Jonathan Griffin (New York: Simon & Schuster, 1955), pp. 9, 43.

33. Ibid., pp. 58, 117, 123, 150–51, 209–11.

34. Ibid., pp. 156–57, 282.

35. Ibid., pp. 256, 285, 344, 398.

36. *Journeying*, tr. by Themi Vasils and Theodora Vasils (San Francisco: Creative Arts, 1984), pp. 4–6.

37. Ibid., pp. 15, 19, 22–23, 50–51, 55–57, 59.

38. Ibid., pp. 66–67, 78–79.

39. Ibid., p. 92.

40. Ibid., pp. 87–88, 95, 97, 99.

41. Ibid., pp. 138–39.

42. Ibid., pp. 100, 115, 123, 133–135, 140.

43. Ibid., p. 146.

44. Ibid., pp. 148, 157–58, 168.

45. Ibid., pp. 169, 173, 178–79, 180–81.

46. Ibid., p. 186.

47. *Journey to the Morea*, tr. by F. A. Reed (New York: Simon & Schuster, 1965), pp. 22–23.

48. Ibid., pp. 11–12, 14, 24.

49. Ibid., pp. 36, 64, 67, 71–72, 85, 89, 111, 141.

50. Ibid., pp. 118–22, 125, 127, 138–39, 154–55.

51. Ibid., pp. 167–68, 170–72.

52. See Darren Middleton, "Dove of Peace or Bird of Prey: Nikos Kazantzakis on the Activity of the Holy Spirit," *Theology Themes* (1993): 15–18; and "Nikos Kazantzakis and Process Theology," *Journal of Modern Greek Studies* 12 (1994): 57–74. Also see John Cobb, *God and the World* (Philadelphia: Westminster, 1979), pp. 52–66.

53. *Report to Greco*, tr. by Peter Bien (New York: Simon & Schuster, 1965), pp. 291–92. Cobb's treatment of this passage was under the influence of David Ray Griffin.

2. Transubstantiation

1. A recent Catholic defender of "Concrete Presence" is Kenneth Schmitz in *Communio* (Fall 1987): 300–15. On the attempt to see transubstantiation as an

intelligible process, see a Catholic thinker, Robert Mellert, *What Is Process Theology?* (New York: Paulist Press, 1975), pp. 106–7, and a Protestant, John Cobb, "The Presence of the Past and the Eucharist," *Process Studies* 13 (1983): 218–31. Also see D. C. Cassidy, "Is Transubstantiation without Substance?" *Religious Studies* 30 (1994): 193–99.

2. See chapter 5 in the present book on Kazantzakis's dipolar theism.

3. Theodora Vasils's introduction to *Serpent and Lily*, tr. by Theodora Vasils (Berkeley: University of California Press, 1980), pp. 9–10.

4. *Saint Francis*, tr. by Peter Bien (New York: Simon & Schuster, 1962), p. 11. See the Greek edition, *O ftohoulis tou Theou* (Athens: Diphros, 1956), p. 9.

5. It should be noted that the Christian Eucharist is an outgrowth of Dionysian intoxication, whereby drinking wine brought not only intoxication but also divine inhabitation.

6. *Zorba the Greek*, tr. by Carl Wildman (New York: Simon & Schuster, 1952), p. 278. See the Greek edition, *Vios kai politeia tou Aleksi Zorba* (Athens: Trikorphon, 1970), p. 328. In this quotation there is an obvious tension between Kazantzakis's belief that there can, in fact, be transubstantiation and his claim that there is ultimately only one substance in the universe.

7. See the introduction to *The Odyssey: A Modern Sequel*, tr. by Kimon Friar (New York: Simon & Schuster, 1958), p. xxiii.

8. See *The Fratricides*, tr. by Athena Gianakas Dallas (New York: Simon & Schuster, 1964), pp. 38, 46, 80–81, 83–84.

9. On the life-affirming powers of asceticism see my "Asceticism as Athletic Training in Plotinus," *Aufsteig und Niedergang der Römischen Welt* 36.1 (Berlin: DeGruyter, 1987), pp. 701–12.

10. See *The Greek Passion*, tr. by Jonathan Griffin (New York: Simon & Schuster, 1953), pp. 69, 378. Also see the Greek edition, *O Hristos ksanastavronetai* (Athens: Diphros, 1955), pp. 79, 409.

11. *The Last Temptation of Christ*, tr. by Peter Bien (New York: Simon & Schuster, 1960), pp. 332, 416–17. See the Greek edition, *O teleftaios peirasmos* (Athens: Diphros, 1955), pp. 338–39, 425.

12. See *Freedom or Death*, pp. 398–99. Also the Greek edition, *O Kapetan Mihalis* (Athens: Diphros, 1955), pp. 451–52.

13. See *Serpent and Lily*, pp. 41, 62, as well as Vasils' remarks on p. 8.

14. *Buddha*, tr. by Kimon Friar and Athena Dallas–Damis (San Diego: Avant Books, 1983), p. 2.

15. *The Odyssey*, X.1300–10.

16. Ibid., XII.1264–65.

17. *Zorba*, pp. 66–67; *Aleksi Zorba*, p. 90.

18. *Zorba*, p. 113; *Aleksi Zorba*, p. 144.

19. *Zorba*, p. 115; *Aleksi Zorba*, p. 146.

20. *Zorba*, p. 232; *Aleksi Zorba*, p. 276.

21. *Zorba*, p. 233; *Aleksi Zorba*, p. 278.

22. *Zorba*, p. 289; *Aleksi Zorba*, p. 341.

23. See "Sinai" in *Journeying*, p. 107.

24. *The Last Temptation of Christ*, p. 191; *O teleftaios peirasmos*, p. 194.

25. See Helen Kazantzakis, *Nikos Kazantzakis: A Biography Based on His Letters*, tr. by Amy Mims (New York: Simon & Schuster, 1968), pp. 374–75. On Kazantzakis and eating, see the following chapter of the present book.

26. See James Lea, *Kazantzakis: The Politics of Salvation* (Tuscaloosa: University of Alabama Press, 1979), pp. 33–34.

27. *Report to Greco*, p. 480. See the Greek edition, *Anafora ston Greko* (Athens: 1965), p. 578.

28. *Report to Greco*, p. 477; *Anafora ston Greko*, p. 574.

29. *Report to Greco*, p. 483; *Anafora ston Greko*, p. 581.

30. *The Odyssey*, IV.260–62.

31. See Helen Kazantzakis, *Nikos Kazantzakis*, p. 109.

32. Nikos Kazantzakis, *The Rock Garden*, tr. from the French by Richard Howard (New York: Simon & Schuster, 1963), p. 185.

33. See Peter Bien, *Nikos Kazantzakis* (New York: Columbia University Press, 1972), p. 36. Also see Kimon Friar's introduction to *The Saviors of God: Spiritual Exercises* (New York: Simon & Schuster, 1960), pp. 17, 21: "Like the God who created him, he longed to transmute the Word directly into flesh, that flesh might in time be transubstantiated into something more spiritual, more refined than either words or flesh. His was the vain search and dilemma of the true mystic, and all his works must be considered to be the vain betrayers of his vision. . . . [A] definition which was to become unshakably the cornerstone and key of all his work and thought; if it could be expressed in one sentence, it would be: *to transubstantiate matter and to turn it into spirit. The Saviors of God* is the distilled expression of this purpose, the Word which he naively thought would transform the materialistic basis of communism into spirituality."

34. *Kouros* in *Three Plays*, tr. by Athena Gianakas Dallas (New York: Simon & Schuster, 1965), pp. 246, 249, 277.

35. *Report to Greco*, p. 486; *Anafora ston Greko*, pp. 585–86. Also see Theodora Vasils in *Serpent and Lily*, p. 12.

36. *Spain*, tr. by Amy Mims (New York: Simon & Schuster, 1963), pp. 138, 160–61.

37. *Symposium*, tr. by Theodora Vasils and Themi Vasils (New York: Minerva Press, 1974), p. 32.

38. Ibid., pp. 82–83.

39. Ibid., p. 54. W. B. Stanford, *The Ulysses Theme* (Oxford: Basil Blackwell, 1963), p. 233, rightly points out the cycle of transubstantiation in *The Odyssey*: Odysseus transubstantiates flesh into spirit only to return to dust at death.

40. See Helen Kazantzakis, *Nikos Kazantzakis*, p. 291. It should be noted, however, that human beings cannot eat dirt so as to transubstantiate it, as in the case of the starving boy in *The Fratricides*, p. 47.

41. *The Odyssey*, IX.472–73.

42. Ibid., Prologue, 28–30.

43. *Spiritual Exercises*, p. 100. See the Greek edition, *Asketike: Salvatores Dei* (Athens: Sympan, 1951), p. 88.

44. *Spiritual Exercises*, p. 108; *Asketike*, p. 95.

45. Quoted in Kimon Friar's introduction to *Spiritual Exercises*, pp. 37–38. Also see B. T. McDonough, *Nietzsche and Kazantzakis* (Washington, D.C.: University Press of America, 1978). On Bergson see *The Rock Garden*, p. 65: "That is why you have chosen as supreme symbols the rising sun, the chrysanthemum and the carp. The sun is your symbol of the three cardinal virtues: wisdom, kindness and bravery; the chrysanthemum resists the severest frost and blooms even in the snow; and the carp swims upstream and conquers the terrible forces which seek to drive it down—as one of our masters of Western thought would say, the emblem of the ascending *élan vital* which rises against the current of matter." Friar, however, in the introduction to *The Odyssey*, p. xxi, puts the point too strongly when he says that God is identical with humanity.

46. *Report to Greco*, pp. 24–25; *Anafora ston Greko*, pp. 27–28.

47. *Report to Greco*, p. 163.

48. Ibid., p. 436. Also *Anafora ston Greko*, p. 525.

49. See Helen Kazantzakis, *Nikos Kazantzakis*, p. 484. Kazantzakis refers to *Freedom or Death* in particular as a book that deals with this transformation of struggle into Spirit. And in *Report to Greco*, pp. 499–500, Kazantzakis compares the destiny of Greece to El Greco's depiction of the marriage feast of Cana, whereby El Greco's humble food was turned into the greatest work of art.

50. Quoted in *The Suffering God: Letters to Galatea and to Papastephanou*, tr. by Philip Ramp and Katerina Anghelaki Rooke (New Rochelle, N.Y.: Caratzas, 1979), p. 76.

51. Ibid., p. 105.

52. *The Odyssey*, VI.810.

53. See Helen Kazantzakis, *Nikos Kazantzakis*, p. 187.

54. Quoted in the introduction to *The Odyssey*, p. xvi.

55. See *Japan-China*, tr. by George Pappageotes (Berkeley, Calif.: Creative Arts, 1982), p. 221.

56. *Journeying*, pp. 20–21.

57. *The Odyssey*, XV.587.

58. Ibid., XV.1000, 1122–23.

59. *The Rock Garden*, p. 97.

60. Quoted in W. B. Stanford, *Ulysses Theme*, p. 227.

61. *Report to Greco*, p. 476; *Anafora ston Greko*, p. 573.

62. *Symposium*, p. 22.

63. *Saint Francis*, p. 323; *O ftohoulis tou Theou*, p. 316. Also on St. Francis, see Morton Levitt, *The Cretan Glance* (Columbus: Ohio State University Press, 1980), pp. 152–53.

64. *Saint Francis*, p. 21; *O ftohoulis tou Theou*, p. 19.

65. *Saint Francis*, p. 344; *O ftohoulis tou Theou*, p. 337.

66. *Symposium*, p. 83.

67. *England* (New York: Simon & Schuster, 1965), pp. 13, 254. Translated from the travel journal in Greek, *Anglia*.

68. See Lea, *Kazantzakis*, pp. 28, 125–26.

69. See Helen Kazantzakis, *Nikos Kazantzakis*, pp. 151, 261, 519. Also see *Zorba the Greek*, p. 133; *Aleksi Zorba*, p. 167.

70. See Helen Kazantzakis, *Nikos Kazantzakis*, p. 257.

71. *The Odyssey*, II.85–90; IV.653–57.

72. Ibid., VII.1080–82.

73. Ibid., XIV.1267–69.

74. See *Sodom and Gomorrah*, in *Two Plays*, tr. by Kimon Friar (Minneapolis, Minn.: Nostos, 1982), p. 7.

75. *Report to Greco*, p. 289; *Anafora ston Greko*, p. 347.

76. *Report to Greco*, p. 291; *Anafora ston Greko*, p. 349.

77. See Helen Kazantzakis, *Nikos Kazantzakis*, pp. 140–41.

78. Ibid., p. 189.

79. Ibid., p. 433.

80. Ibid., pp. 403, 507. Note the words "around him" in this quotation. Also see the quotation at note 75, above, where it is clear that Kazantzakis thinks it possible that one may merge with God.

81. *The Suffering God*, p. 19.

82. Ibid., p. 30.

83. See, e.g., *The Odyssey*, IX.449–50.

84. Ibid., X.840.

85. Ibid., XII.276.

86. Ibid., XXI.1293.

87. *Spiritual Exercises*, p. 129; *Asketike*, p. 110.

88. *Spiritual Exercises*, p. 106; *Asketike*, p. 93.

89. See chapter 5 on Kazantzakis's dipolar theism.

90. *Spiritual Exercises*, p. 122; *Asketike*, p. 108.

3. Eating and Spiritual Exercises

1. This is similar to the ancient Greek notion of *sōphrosunē* or moderation, which is also embodied in the Delphic dictum "Nothing in excess" or in Aristotle's "golden mean." A defender of this ancient Greek conception of temperance would probably see penance as extreme.

2. See Ignatius of Loyola, *The Spiritual Exercises of St. Ignatius*, tr. with a contemporary reading by David Fleming (St. Louis, Mo.: Institute of Jesuit Sources, 1978), p. 57.

3. Ibid., p. 59.

4. Ignatius of Loyola, *The Spiritual Exercises of St. Ignatius of Loyola*, tr. with a commentary by W. H. Longridge (London: Mowbray, 1950), p. 74.

5. Ibid., p. 145, where the commentator suggests that *manjares* in this instance probably refers to meats or fish.

6. See Fleming, *Spiritual Exercises*, p. 121.

7. See Longridge, *Spiritual Exercises*, p. 147.

8. See William Peters, *The Spiritual Exercises of St. Ignatius: Exposition and Interpretation* (Jersey City, N.J.: Program to Adapt the Spiritual Exercises, 1968), p. 140. Peters is on weaker ground, however, when he talks about eating as a form of penance. He says that St. Ignatius is not offering these rules as a form of penance, yet the rules give clear expression to the marriage between contemplation and the practicing of penance, pp. 140–41.

9. A very good treatment of this notion can be found in Peter Bien, *Nikos Kazantzakis*; to some extent I am borrowing from Bien.

10. Quoted by Kimon Friar, "Introduction," in Nikos Kazantzakis, *The Odyssey*, p. xvi. Also found in Peter Bien, *Kazantzakis: Politics of the Spirit*, pp. 45–46.

11. Friar, "Introduction," p. xxv.

12. Once again, I am more interested in the different *facets* of Kazantzakis's thought than in the chronological *phases* he went through. It should be noted, however, that all three of these works are from late in his career.

13. *Saint Francis*, pp. 19, 40.

14. Ibid., pp. 107, 160.

15. Ibid., p. 173.

16. Ibid., p. 178; *O ftohoulis tou Theou*, p. 173.

17. *Saint Francis*, pp. 179, 268.

18. Ibid., pp. 180–81.

19. Ibid., p. 67.

20. Ibid.

21. Ibid., pp. 89, 297.

22. Ibid., p. 304.

23. Ibid., p. 282.

24. Ibid., p. 344; *O ftohoulis tou Theou*, p. 337.

25. *Zorba the Greek*, p. 61.

26. Ibid., p. 34.

27. Ibid., p. 66.

28. Ibid., pp. 66–67; *Aleksi Zorba*, p. 90.

29. *Zorba the Greek*, pp. 74, 213.

30. Ibid., p. 113.

31. Ibid., p. 124.

32. Ibid., pp. 133, 232.

33. *The Last Temptation of Christ*, p. 225.

34. Ibid., pp. 69–70; *O teleftaios peirasmos*, p. 72.

35. *Zorba the Greek*, p. 186; *Aleksi Zorba*, p. 225.

4. The New Middle Ages

1. See Helen Kazantzakis, *Nikos Kazantzakis*, p. 343.

2. Ibid., p. 355.

3. Once again, see Friar's "Introduction" to *The Odyssey*, p. xvi; and Bien, *Kazantzakis: Politics of the Spirit*, p. 45.

4. Helen Kazantzakis, *Nikos Kazantzakis*, p. 356.

5. Ibid., p. 384.

6. Ibid., p. 207. Berdyaev's "The New Middle Ages" can be found in *The End of Our Time*, tr. by Donald Atwater (New York: Sheed and Ward, 1933).

7. Ibid., p. 69.

8. Ibid., p. 74.

9. Ibid., p. 80.

10. Ibid., p. 93.

11. Ibid., p. 102.

12. Ibid., p. 105.

13. See "The Sickness of the Age" in *Serpent and Lily*.

14. Ibid., p. 89.

15. Ibid., p. 92.

16. Ibid., pp. 98–99.

17. Ibid., pp. 94, 97.

18. *Spain*, p. 18.

19. Ibid., pp. 56–64.

20. Ibid., pp. 77, 133.

21. Ibid., p. 176.

22. See *The Collected Works of St. Teresa of Avila*, vol. 2, tr. by Kieran Kavanaugh and Otilio Rodriguez (Washington, D.C.: Institute for Carmelite Studies Publications, 1980). Also see my *St. John of the Cross* (Albany: State University of New York Press, 1992). Finally, on the butterfly metaphor see Del Presley, "Buddha and the Butterfly: Unifying Motifs in Kazantzakis's *Zorba*," *Notes on Contemporary Literature* 2 (1972): 2–4.

23. *The Collected Works of St. Teresa of Avila*, 2:341–42.

24. Ibid., pp. 354, 378, 391, 421.

25. Ibid., pp. 344–45.

26. Ibid., p. 350.

27. Ibid., p. 392.

28. Lea, *Kazantzakis*, pp. 66–72.

29. Ibid., pp. 82, 108, 117.

30. *Report to Greco*, p. 236; *Anafora ston Greko*, p. 284.

31. Levitt, *Cretan Glance*, p. 115.

32. Ibid., pp. 118–22.

33. *Journey to the Morea*, p. 14.

34. Ibid., p. 59.

35. *Spiritual Exercises*, p. 103; *Asketike*, p. 90: "O theos mou den einai pantodynamos."

36. *Journey to the Morea*, pp. 167–72.

37. An American philosopher who agrees with Kazantzakis's belief that modern philosophy is largely defective because it leaves spiritual concerns in a diseased state is the prolific Charles Hartshorne. See, for example, his *Omnipotence and Other Theological Mistakes* (Albany: State University of New York Press, 1984). Also see the film *My Dinner with André* for a moving defense of a new, countercultural monasticism.

38. Alasdair MacIntyre, *After Virtue* (Notre Dame, Ind.: University of Notre Dame Press, 1981).

39. Ibid., p. 238.

40. Ibid., pp. 239–40.

41. Ibid., p. 243.

42. *Report to Greco*, p. 32.

43. *The Last Temptation of Christ*, p. 54.

44. Ibid., p. 70.

45. Ibid., p. 145.

46. Ibid., pp. 138, 258.

47. Ibid., p. 248.

48. *Saint Francis*, pp. 14, 24, 47, 74, 100.

49. Ibid., p. 36.

50. Ibid., pp. 178–79.

51. Ibid., p. 300.

5. Theism: Traditional and Dipolar

1. Kimon Friar, "Introduction," to *The Saviors of God: Spiritual Exercises*, p. 20, also pp. 37–38. The title to Kazantzakis's original edition of 1927 was *Salvatores Dei*, and the subtitle *Asketike*. The revised edition of 1945 reversed this order. Although Friar's translation relies on the 1945 edition, he prefers the original ordering of title and subtitle.

2. Levitt, *Cretan Glance*, pp. 12–13. Also see Rooke, "Introduction" to *The Suffering God*, a collection of Kazantzakis's letters, p. 17. However, Rooke notices that Kazantzakis's treatment of God's essence has "all sorts of opposite and contrary elements." These are the elements I will try to reconcile in this chapter as well as in the book as a whole.

3. I will concentrate on two of Hartshorne's many works: *Philosophers Speak of God* (Chicago: University of Chicago Press, 1953), and *Insights and Oversights of Great Thinkers* (Albany: State University of New York Press, 1983). Whitehead's dipolar theism can be found at the end of his classic work, *Process and Reality*, corrected edition, ed. by David Ray Griffin and Donald Sherburne (New York: Free Press, 1978). It may well be the case that Whitehead's primordial nature of God is closer to Kazantzakis's "Cry" or lure forward than anything said about God in Hartshorne, who insists that God's life is an everlasting series of events rather than an eternal and primordial Cry or Call to transubstantiate matter into spirit. But I assume that there is a family resemblance among Whitehead's, Hartshorne's, and Kazantzakis's dipolar theisms. Also, regarding the possible criticism that Kazantzakis' God is excessively male, as is the God of traditional theism, it should be noted that in "The Relationship between God and Man" in *Spiritual Exercises* he says that God is both man and woman: *andras kai yinaika*.

4. Hartshorne, *Philosophers Speak of God*, p. 3.

5. Ibid., pp. 14–15.

6. Ibid., p. 24.

7. "The Relationship between God and Man," in *Spiritual Exercises*, p. 103. *Asketike*, p. 90: "*O theos mou den einai pantodynamos.*" Also see Hartshorne's *Omnipotence and Other Theological Mistakes* (Albany: State University of New York Press, 1984).

8. *Spiritual Exercises*, p. 103; *Asketike*, p. 91: "*O theos mas den einai panagathos.*"

9. *Spiritual Exercises*, p. 104; *Asketike*, p. 91: "*O theos mou den einai pansofos.*"

10. Ibid., "The Preparation," pp. 48–49.

11. "Essence" is a translation of *ousia* here.

12. "Invisible" is a translation of *aorate* here.

13. "The Ego," p. 68; *Asketike*, p. 58.

14. "Mankind," p. 78.

15. Ibid., p. 80.

16. "The Earth," p. 84; *Asketike*, p. 73: "*kapoion allon.*"

17. "The Earth," p. 84; *Asketike*, p. 73: "pnoe." Also see Friar, in *Spiritual Exercises*, p. 142.

18. "The Earth," p. 84; *Asketike*, p. 74: "*aionioteta.*"

19. "The Vision," p. 89; *Asketike*, p. 78.

20. "The Vision," p. 91; *Asketike*, p. 80: "*Okso apo to kathe prama!*"

21. "The Vision," pp. 92–93.

22. Ibid., p. 92; *Asketike*, p. 81: "*E ousia tou theou mou einai o agonas.*"

23. "The Vision," pp. 92–93; *Asketike*, p. 81: "*Megale Pnoe.*"

24. "The Vision," pp. 92–93; *Asketike*, p. 81: "*hrono, topo ki aitioteta.*"

25. "The Vision," p. 95; *Asketike*, p. 84: "*o megas Ekstatikos.*"

26. "The Relationship between God and Man," pp. 99–101; *Asketike*, pp. 87–88: "*Athanato.*"

27. "The Relationship between Man and Man," p. 109; *Asketike*, p. 95: "*panta o idios.*"

28. "The Relationship between Man and Man," p. 113.

29. Ibid., p. 116; *Asketike*, p. 102: "*E ousia ton theon mas einai skoteine.*"

30. *Asketike*, p. 102: "*fisi.*"

31. "The Relationship between Man and Nature," p. 124. Also see "The Silence," p. 130; *Asketike*, p. 112. In *The Suffering God* Kazantzakis offers further evidence for his belief in a dipolar God. Examples of terms on the left side of the table include the following: God as the Invisible One; a God who partially escapes time and place; God as "Someone Else"; the "Great Ecstatic"; God as "indestructible"; human beings as *reflections* of God; human beings polluting God, but God is nonetheless beyond our "ephemeral worldly essence."

32. Leonard Eslick, "Plato as Dipolar Theist," *Process Studies* 12 (1982): 243–51. Also see his "The Dyadic Character of Being," *Modern Schoolman* 21 (1953–54): 11–18.

33. Notice the importance of power (*dynamis*) for both Plato and Kazantzakis; see above, notes 7 and 19.

34. Leonard Eslick, "Plato as Dipolar Theist," p. 244.

35. In addition to Eslick, see P. E. More, *The Religion of Plato* (Princeton, N.J.: Princeton University Press, 1921).

36. This new dynamic meaning of perfection refers to both *psyche* and *nous*.

37. Kazantzakis's God has what the ancient Greeks would call *eros*, not *agape*. See, for example, "The Relationship between Man and Man," pp. 110–11.

38. "The Vision," p. 89; *Asketike*, p. 78.

39. See, for example, "The Earth" and "The Vision," p. 91.

40. *Metaphysics* A.

6. Two Sides of Mysticism

1. See Rooke's "Introduction" to *The Suffering God*, p. 19.

2. See Helen Kazantzakis, *Nikos Kazantzakis*, p. 433.

3. Bien, *Kazantzakis: Politics of the Spirit*, p. 12.

4. Pandelis Prevelakis, *Nikos Kazantzakis and His Odyssey* (New York: Simon & Schuster, 1961), p. 181.

5. See Helen Kazantzakis, *Nikos Kazantzakis*, pp. 84, 189.

6. Bien, *Kazantzakis: Politics of the Spirit*, pp. 101, 198–99.

7. Regarding these two sorts of mysticism, see Charles Hartshorne, "Mysticism and Rationalistic Metaphysics," *Monist* 59 (1976): 463–69.

8. Quoted in Helen Kazantzakis, *Nikos Kazantzakis*, p. 257; also see pp. 63, 140–41.

9. Ibid., pp. 269, 294, 403.

10. See Rooke, "Introduction," pp. 26, 39, 101.

11. *The Fratricides*, pp. 8, 11, 79.

12. *Japan, China*, p. 221.

13. *Zorba the Greek*, pp. 51, 136, 208.

14. *Symposium*, p. 11.

15. *Report to Greco*, p. 18, also p. 17.

16. Ibid., p. 45.

17. Ibid., p. 49.

18. Ibid., pp. 231, 242, 302, 306.

19. "The Sickness of the Age," in *Serpent and Lily*, pp. 89, 94.

20. *Spain*, pp. 61–62; also p. 18.

21. Ibid., p. 77; also p. 63.

22. Ibid., pp. 138, 145, 160–61.

23. *The Rock Garden*, pp. 53, 229.

24. *The Greek Passion*, pp. 69, 378.

25. *The Odyssey*, XIV.8.

26. *Spiritual Exercises*, p. 91.

27. Ibid., p. 103.

28. Ibid., p. 119; also p. 105.

29. Bien, *Kazantzakis: Politics of the Spirit*, p. 95.

30. Ibid., p. 224; also p. 168.

31. Prevelakis, *Kazantzakis and His Odyssey*, p. 130.

32. See Richard Chilson, "The Christ of Nikos Kazantzakis," *Thought* 47 (1972): 72–73. Also see Adele Bloch's studies, "Kazantzakis and the Image of Christ," *Literature and Psychology* 15 (1965): 2–11; and "The Dual Masks of Nikos Kazantzakis," *Journal of Modern Literature* 2 (1971): 189–98.

33. See Lea, *Kazantzakis*, pp. 84, 106.

34. See Peter Bien, *Tempted by Happiness: Kazantzakis' Post-Christian Christ* (Wallingford, Pa.: Pendle–Hill, 1984), pp. 15–16.

35. Minas Savvas, "Kazantzakis and Marxism," *Journal of Modern Literature* 2 (1971): 291.

36. See Levitt, *Cretan Glance*, pp. 52–53, 79–80.

37. Bien, *Kazantzakis: Politics of the Spirit*, pp. 50, 104.

38. See Maurice Friedman, *To Deny Our Nothingness* (New York: Delacorte, 1967), pp. 69–70, 76.

39. George Pollby, "Kazantzakis' Struggle," *Commonweal* (April 23, 1971), p. 175.

40. Andreas Poulakidas, "Kazantzakis and Bergson: Metaphysic Aestheticians," *Journal of Modern Literature* 2 (1971): 275–78.

41. *Spiritual Exercises*, pp. 52–53.

42. Ibid., pp. 56, 84.

43. Ibid., pp. 95, 101–2, 109, 124, 130–31.

44. Ibid., p. 116.

45. Helen Kazantzakis, *Nikos Kazantzakis*, p. 507; also see pp. 60, 115, 126.

46. See Rooke, pp. 30–31, 33–34, 36–37, 106.

47. *The Fratricides*, p. 17.

48. *Japan, China*, p. 112.

49. *Symposium*, pp. 22, 74, 79.

50. *Report to Greco*, pp. 16, 150. Also see my *St. John of the Cross*.

51. *Report to Greco*, p. 290; also pp. 152, 240. Regarding Kazantzakis and Ignatius of Loyola, see Bien, *Kazantzakis: Politics of the Spirit*, p. 254. Finally, on Thomas Aquinas and silence, see Josef Pieper, *The Silence of Saint Thomas* (Chicago: Regnery, 1965).

52. *Report to Greco*, pp. 336–37, 385.

53. *The Greek Passion*, pp. 162–63, 372.

54. *The Rock Garden*, pp. 37, 52, 86, 188–89.

55. *Spain*, pp. 102–3; also p. 57.

56. *England*, p. 283.

57. See Jerry Gill, "Conflict and Resolution: Some Kazantzakian Themes," *Encounter* 36 (1974): 220–21. Also see Chilson, "The Christ," p. 75.

58. See, e.g., Andreas Poulakidas, "Kazantzakis' *Spiritual Exercises* and Buddhism," *Comparative Literature* 27 (1975): 213–15.

59. See Joseph Blenkinsopp, "My Entire Soul Is a Cry," *Commonweal* 93 (February 26, 1971), p. 518. Also see Levitt, *Cretan Glance*, p. 12.

60. See John Smith's "Introduction" to William James, *The Varieties of Religious Experience*, p. xlviii. Cf. Peter Hartocollis, "Mysticism and Violence," *International Journal of Psycho-Analysis* 55 (1974).

61. Stephen R. L. Clark, *A Parliament of Souls* (Oxford: Clarendon Press, 1990), p. 159.

62. On apotheosis see, e.g., *The Odyssey*, XIV.210–11.

63. See Bien, *Kazantzakis: Politics of the Spirit*, pp. 48, 53, 72, 75, 111–12, 133, 135, 137.

64. See the works by Poulakidas, Prevelakis, Vrettakos, and Frangopoulos listed in Bien's bibliography at the end of *Kazantzakis: Politics of the Spirit*. Bien, however, cites one quotation from Kazantzakis, pp. 139–40, where Asian mysticism is seen as superior to Western mysticism; but Kazantzakis, as I hope I have shown, is by no means consistent on this point, as Bien implies on pp. 141, 195. There is a dialectic in Kazantzakis between Bergson and Buddha, but the latter is subsumed under the former.

65. Bien, *Kazantzakis: Politics of the Spirit*, pp. 138, 142, 197, 268. In the following section on religious language I have relied heavily on the thought of Charles Hartshorne, particularly his *Creative Synthesis and Philosophic Method* (LaSalle, Ill.: Open Court, 1970). Also see David Ray Griffin, *God and Religion in the Postmodern World* (Albany: State University of New York Press, 1989).

66. See Vladimir Lossky, *The Mystical Theology of the Eastern Church* (London: James Clarke, 1957), p. 12. Also see Sergius Bulgakov, *The Orthodox Church* (New York: Morehouse, 1935).

67. See Timothy Ware, *The Orthodox Church* (Baltimore, Md.: Penguin, 1963), p. 73.

68. See John Meyendorff, *Byzantine Theology* (New York: Fordham University Press, 1983), pp. 66–72. Also see Ware, *Orthodox Church*, pp. 74–75.

69. See Ware, *Orthodox Church*, pp. 76–77. Ware relies here on Gregory Palamas.

70. Ibid., pp. 77–78. Also see Meyendorff, *Byzantine Theology*, pp. 76–78. On Eastern Orthodoxy and Kazantzakis, see Lewis Richards, "Christianity in the Novels of Kazantzakis," *Western Humanities Review* 21 (1967): 49–55; and on monasticism see "Nikos Kazantzakis and Chaucer," *Comparative Literature Studies* 6 (1969): 141–47.

7. Method and Purpose

1. *Symposium*, pp. 22, 74, 79.

2. Bien, "*Zorba the Greek*, Nietzsche, and the Perennial Greek Predicament," *The Antioch Review* 25 (1965): 147–63.

3. *Report to Greco*, p. 166; *Anafora ston Greko*, p. 199.

4. On Kazantzakis and Nietzsche, see Bien, "Kazantzakis' Nietzschianism," *Journal of Modern Literature* 2 (1971): 245–66; Reed Merrill, "*Zorba the Greek* and Nietzschean Nihilism," *Mosaic* 8 (1975): 99–113; and Andreas Poulakidas, "Kazantzakis' *Zorba the Greek* and Nietzsche's *Thus Spake Zarathustra*," *Philological Quarterly* 49 (1970): 234–44.

5. Quoted in Everett Ferguson, "God's Infinity and Man's Mutability: Perpetual Progress According to Gregory of Nyssa," *The Greek Orthodox Theological Review* 18 (1973): 73.

6. Maximos Aghiorgoussis, "Christian Existentialism of the Greek Fathers," *The Greek Orthodox Theological Review* 23 (1978): 15–41.

7. See John Behr, "Irenaeus AH3.23.5 and the Ascetic Ideal," *St. Vladimir's Theological Quarterly* 37 (1993): 305–13. Also see Matthew Chapman, "Notes on the Nature of God, the Cosmos, and Novus Homo," *The Greek Orthodox Theological Review* 21 (1976): 251–64.

8. Joseph Flay, "The Erotic Stoicism of Nikos Kazantzakis," *Journal of Modern Literature* 2 (1971): 293–302.

9. Stephen R. L. Clark, *The Mysteries of Religion* (Oxford: Basil Blackwell, 1986), p. 74.

10. Ibid., pp. 76–77.

11. Ibid., p. 79.

12. Ibid., pp. 222–23.

13. Clark, *Civil Peace and Sacred Order* (Oxford: Clarendon Press, 1989), pp. 24–25.

14. Ibid., pp. 114–15.

15. Ibid., p. 117.

16. See my *Christian Pacifism* (Philadelphia: Temple University Press, 1991).

17. Clark, *Civil Peace and Sacred Order*, pp. 33–35.

18. Clark, *The Mysteries of Religion*, pp. 78–79.

19. Ibid., p. 80.

20. Ibid., p. 81. Also see W. F. Otto, *The Homeric Gods* (Salem, N.H.: Ayer, 1978).

21. Clark, *The Mysteries of Religion*, p. 87.

22. Ibid., pp. 108–9, 112.

23. Clark, *From Athens to Jerusalem* (Oxford: Clarendon Press, 1984), pp. 192–93, 196, 209.

24. Ibid., pp. 212–13.

25. Clark, *Civil Peace and Sacred Order*, p. 178.

26. Clark, "How to Believe in Fairies," *Inquiry* 30 (1987): 352–54.

27. See Steven Katz, ed., *Mysticism and Philosophical Analysis* (Oxford: Oxford University Press, 1978), especially pp. 27–35; and Steven Katz, *Mysticism and Religious Traditions* (New York: Oxford University Press, 1983). Also see Nelson Pike, *Mystic Union: An Essay in the Phenomenology of Mysticism* (Ithaca, N.Y.: Cornell University Press, 1992).

28. See Walter Stace, *Mysticism and Philosophy* (Philadelphia: Lippincott, 1960). Also see Stace, *The Teachings of the Mystics* (New York: New American Library, 1960).

29. See Ninian Smart, "Interpretation and Mystical Experience," *Religious Studies* 1 (1965): 75–87.

30. See Pike, *Mystic Union*, pp. 81–82.

31. See *Buddha*, pp. 2, 4, 10, 16, 19, 48, 110.

32. Ibid., p. 22.

33. Ibid., pp. 39–40, 43.

34. Ibid., pp. 49, 51, 89, 101, 131, 140. Also see Tom Doulis, "Kazantzakis and the Meaning of Suffering," *Northwest Review* 6 (1963): 33–57, on God as compassionate in Kazantzakis because it is through suffering that we are saved.

35. *Buddha*, pp. 142, 152, 156–57, 160–62.

36. Ibid., pp, 165–67, 171.

37. *Toda Raba*, tr. by Amy Mims (New York: Simon & Schuster, 1964), pp. 18–19, 39, 43, 52–54, 61, 64. On heroes see Alexander Karanikas, "Kazantzakis and His Heroes," *Athene* 18 (1957): 4–9.

38. *Toda Raba*, pp. 90–91; also pp. 89, 119. On Kazantzakis's relationship to Marxism regarding *praxis*, see Stephen Weber, "Existentialism versus Marxism: A Kazantzakian Synthesis," *Journal of Social Philosophy* 9 (1978): 1–8.

39. *Toda Raba*, pp. 98, 103, 110–11, 116–18, 120.

40. Ibid., p. 124.

41. Ibid., pp. 133, 160, 180.

42. Ibid., pp. 207–8. (Kazantzakis is quoted here by Helen Kazantzakis in "An Afterword.")

43. Ibid., p. 212.

44. Ibid., p. 216.

45. *Russia*, tr. by Michael Antonakes and Thanasis Maskaleris (Berkeley, Calif.: Creative Arts, 1989), pp. xii, 5.

46. Ibid., p. 31.

47. Ibid., pp. 33, 41–42.

48. Ibid., p. 112. Also pp. 43–44, 46–47, 61, 92, 177–78, 195–96.

49. Ibid., pp. 114–15, 118, 120, 125, 127, 140, 143. On the relationship between Kazantzakis and Dostoevsky, see Andreas Poulakidas, "Dostoevsky, Kazantzakis' Unacknowledged Mentor," *Comparative Literature* 21 (1969): 307–18; and Friedrich Hoffman, "The Friends of God: Dostoevsky and Kazantzakis," in *The Imagination's New Beginning* (Notre Dame, Ind.: University of Notre Dame Press, 1967).

50. *Russia*, pp. 144, 146, 175–76.

51. Ibid., p. 187.

52. Ibid., pp. 210–11; also pp. 195–96, 206–7.

53. Ibid., pp. 212–13.

54. Ibid., p. 216; also pp. 214–15.

55. Ibid., p. 217; also p. 218.

56. Ibid., p. 235; also pp. 228, 230–31.

57. Ibid., p. 237.

58. Ibid., p. 249; also pp. 240–41, 246–48.

59. Ibid., p. 253.

60. Ibid., p. 254.

61. See N. Georgopoulos, "Kazantzakis, Bergson, Lenin, and the 'Russian Experiment'," *Journal of the Hellenic Diaspora* 5 (1979), pp. 33–44.

62. Friar, "Introduction," to *Two Plays*, p. 4; also pp. 3, 5–6.

63. "Sodom and Gomorrah," in *Two Plays*, pp. 8, 10, 14–15, 20.

64. Ibid., pp. 23, 27–28, 34, 38, 60, 68–69.

65. "Christopher Columbus," in *Three Plays*, pp. 12, 14, 25–26, 39.

66. Ibid., pp. 68–69; also pp. 27, 63, 66–67.

67. *Melissa*, in *Three Plays*, pp. 150–51.

68. *Kouros*, in *Three Plays*, pp. 236–37.

69. Ibid., pp. 246, 249, 257, 259, 265.

70. Ibid., pp. 270–71, 274–75, 280–83. Also on the myth of the Minotaur, see Kazantzakis's similar views in his novel *At the Palaces of Knossos*, tr. by Themi and Theodora Vasils (Athens: Ohio University Press, 1988). And on a youthful hero much like Theseus, see Kazantzakis's novel *Alexander the Great*, tr. by Theodora Vasils (Athens: Ohio University Press, 1982).

8. *Panexperientialism and Death*

1. *Journeying*, p. 92.

2. *Report to Greco*, p. 477.

3. *Symposium*, pp. 54, 82–83.

4. *The Odyssey*, Prologue.

5. *Spiritual Exercises*, pp. 80, 91.

6. *Zorba the Greek*, pp. 51, 136, 208.

7. See *The Odyssey*, XIV.8.

8. See Gregory Telepneff and Bishop Chrysostomos, "The Person, *Pathe*, Asceticism, and Spiritual Restoration in Saint Maximos," *The Greek Orthodox Theological Review* 34 (1989): 249–61.

9. See George Papademetriou, "The Human Body According to Saint Gregory of Palamas," *The Greek Orthodox Theological Review* 34 (1989): 1–9.

10. See Seyyed Hossein Nasr, "The Prayer of the Heart in Hesychasm and Sufism," *The Greek Orthodox Theological Review* 31 (1986): 195–203.

11. See John Chryssavgis, "Love and Sexuality in the Image of Divine Love," *The Greek Orthodox Theological Review* 36 (1991): 341–52.

12. See S. A. Mousalimas, "The Divine in Nature: Animism or Panentheism," *The Greek Orthodox Theological Review* 35 (1990): 367–75.

13. In this section I have borrowed loosely from the work of Charles Hartshorne. See his *Insights and Oversights of Great Thinkers* and his *Philosophers Speak of God*; finally see his *The Divine Relativity* (New Haven, Conn.: Yale University Press, 1948).

14. See Karl Popper, *Objective Knowledge* (Oxford: Clarendon Press, 1979).

15. Charles Hartshorne, *Man's Vision of God* (New York: Harper and Row, 1941), p. 89; also pp. xvi, 14.

16. Ibid., p. 294; also pp. 205, 232, 244. Also on the natural world as God's body see Blair Reynolds, *Toward a Process Pneumatology* (Selinsgrove, Pa.: Susquehanna University Press, 1990).

17. See *Buddha*, pp. 54, 58.

18. *Toda Raba*, p. 203; also pp. 88, 163, 172.

19. *Russia*, p. 3; also p. 1.

20. *The Fratricides*, p. 79.

21. *Russia*, p. 250.

22. *Sodom and Gomorrah*, in *Two Plays*, p. 61.

23. *Christopher Columbus*, in *Three Plays*, pp. 41–44.

24. *Journeying*, p. 149.

25. See *Kouros*, in *Three Plays*, pp. 224–25, 265.

26. Thomas Nagel, *Mortal Questions* (Cambridge: Cambridge University Press, 1991), p. 2. I have loosely borrowed from Nagel's thought in this section.

27. *Freedom or Death,* p. 325.

28. Nagel, *Mortal Questions,* p. 8.

29. Ibid., pp. 9–10.

30. Ibid., p. 10.

31. Ibid., p. 13.

32. Ibid., p. 20.

33. *Melissa,* in *Three Plays,* p. 153.

34. *Russia,* p. 209; also p. 266.

35. *Freedom or Death,* pp. 325, 398–99.

36. *Report to Greco,* pp. 291–92. Also see *Zorba the Greek,* pp. 310–11; *Spiritual Exercises,* p. 103; and *The Last Temptation of Christ,* p. 54.

37. See *Toda Raba,* p. 115; and *Spiritual Exercises,* p. 59.

38. See Darren Middleton and Peter Bien, "Spiritual *Levendía*: Kazantzakis's Theology of Struggle," in Middleton and Bien, eds., *God's Struggler* (Macon, Ga.: Mercer University Press, 1996): 1–22.

39. Jerry Gill is extremely helpful on this point. See his "Kazantzakis and Kierkegaard," in Middleton and Bien, eds., *God's Struggler,* p. 186. Gill is also very helpful at p. 180 in pointing out that Kazantzakis's process God is at odds with Luther's view of God as a mighty fortress who is omnipotent and is independent of the natural world.

40. *Report to Greco,* p. 469.

41. *The Greek Passion,* p. 372.

42. I have been positively influences here by Darren Middleton, "Vagabond or Companion?: Kazantzakis and Whitehead on God," in Middleton and Bien, eds., *God's Struggler.*

43. See Peter Bien, "Kazantzakis's Long Apprenticeship to Christian Themes," in Middleton and Bien, eds., *God's Struggler,* pp. 113, 116, 118, 122.

44. Frederick Sontag, "Anthropodicy and the Return of God," in Stephen David, ed., *Encountering Evil* (Atlanta, Ga.: John Knox Press, 1981).

45. See Lambros Kamperidis, "The Orthodox Sources of *The Saviors of God,*" in Middleton and Bien, eds., *God's Struggler,* p. 58.

Appendix: Nietzsche

1. Frederick Copleston, *Friedrich Nietzsche, Philosopher of Culture* (London: Burns, Oates, Washbourne, 1942), pp. 205–13.

2. *Report to Greco*, pp. 317–39. This material is largely the same as that found in *England*, pp. 186–99. Also see the index in Helen Kazantzakis, *Nikos Kazantzakis*, regarding some scattered references to Nietzsche.

3. See Bien's excellent "Kazantzakis' Nietzschianism," where Kazantzakis's dissertation, *Friedrich Nietzsche's Philosophy of Law and the State*, is summarized in detail; also see Bien's *Kazantzakis: Politics of the Spirit*, especially pp. 24–36.

4. See Griffin, "Postmodern Theology and A/theology," in Griffin, ed., *Varieties of Postmodern Theology*. Also see Alexander Nehamas, *Nietzsche: Life as Literature* (Cambridge, Mass.: Harvard University Press, 1985), p. 152. Finally, see B. T. McDonough's excellent study of the relationship between Nietzsche's *The Birth of Tragedy* and Kazantzakis's *Zorba the Greek*, but McDonough does not pay much attention the issue of God.

5. *Report to Greco*, pp. 317–39.

6. Ibid., pp. 330–31, 333.

7. Ibid., p. 339.

8. Bien, "Kazantzakis' Nietzschianism," p. 263; also pp. 249, 254, 261, 266.

9. See Friedrich Nietzsche, *Human, All Too Human*, tr. by Marion Faber (Lincoln: University of Nebraska Press, 1984), 16.

10. Mark Taylor, *Erring: A Postmodern A/theology* (Chicago: University of Chicago Press, 1984), pp. 6, 170. Taylor relies here on Nietzsche's *The Will to Power*, tr. by Walter Kaufmann (New York: Random House, 1968). Finally, see Carl Raschke, *Theological Thinking* (Atlanta, Ga.: Scholars Press, 1988).

11. See Griffin, "Postmodern Theology and A/theology," pp. 29–32.

12. Griffin, *God and Religion in the Postmodern World*, p. 29.

13. Griffin, "Postmodern Theology and A/theology," pp. 33–61.

14. George Morgan, *What Nietzsche Means* (Cambridge, Mass.: Harvard University Press, 1941), p. 36.

15. Friedrich Nietzsche, *Ecce Homo*, tr. by Walter Kaufmann (New York: Random House, 1969), "Why I Am So Clever," 1.

16. See, e.g., *The Antichrist*, tr. by Walter Kaufmann (New York: Viking, 1968), 47. Also see Walter Kaufmann, "The Death of God and the Revaluation," in Robert Solomon, ed., *Nietzsche* (Notre Dame, Ind.: University of Notre Dame Press, 1980).

17. Friedrich Nietzsche, *The Gay Science*, tr. by Walter Kaufmann (New York: Random House, 1974), 151. Also see related ideas in *The Will to Power*.

18. Friedrich Nietzsche, *Der Wille zur Macht*, in *Werke in drei Bänden*, ed. by Karl Schlechta (Munich: Carl Hanser, 1954–65), p. 903.

19. Ibid., pp. 729, 903.

20. See Arthur Danto, "Nietzsche's Perspectivism," in Robert Solomon, ed., *Nietzsche* (Notre Dame, Ind.: University of Notre Dame Press, 1980), pp. 37, 52.

21. Bien, "Kazantzakis' Nietzschianism," p. 250.

BIBLIOGRAPHY

Two very good bibliographies that are easily accessible are Peter Bien, *Kazantzakis: Politics of the Spirit* (Princeton, N.J.: Princeton University Press, 1989); and Donald Falconio, "Critics of Kazantzakis: Selected Checklist of Writings in English," *Journal of Modern Literature* 2 (1971): 314–26. Also see two even better bibliographies that are not so accessible, G. Katsimbalis, *Bibliografia N. Kazantzaki, 1906–1948* (Athens, 1958); and Peter Bien, "Nikos Kazantzakis: A Check List of Primary and Secondary Works Supplementing the Katsimbalis Bibliography," *Mandatoforos* (November 5, 1974): 7–53. Both of the Bien bibliographies and the Katsimbalis bibliography are essential for those who are interested in the chronology of Kazantzakis's writings. The dates of composition listed below regarding Kazantzakis's own writings largely rely on Bien's *Kazantzakis: Politics of the Spirit*.

Primary Sources

Alexander the Great. Tr. by Theodora Vasils. Athens: Ohio University Press, 1982. Date of composition: 1940–41.

At the Palaces of Knossos. Tr. by Themi Vasils and Theodora Vasils. Athens: Ohio University Press, 1988. Date of composition: 1940–41.

Buddha. Tr. by Kimon Friar and Athena Dallas–Damis. San Diego, Calif.: Avant Books, 1983. Date of composition: 1941–43.

England. New York: Simon & Schuster, 1965. Date of composition: 1940.

The Fratricides. Tr. by Athena Gianakas Dallas. New York: Simon & Schuster, 1964. Date of composition: 1949.

Freedom or Death. Tr. by Jonathan Griffin. New York: Simon & Schuster, 1955. Also *O Kapetan Mihalis.* Athens: Diphros, 1955. Date of composition: 1949–51.

The Greek Passion. Tr. by Jonathan Griffin. New York: Simon & Schuster, 1953. Also *O Hristos ksanastavronetai.* Athens: Diphros, 1955. Date of composition: 1948.

Japan-China. Tr. by George Pappageotes. Berkeley, Calif.: Creative Arts, 1982. Date of composition: 1935.

Journey to the Morea. Tr. by F. A. Reed. New York: Simon & Schuster, 1965. Date of composition: 1937.

Journeying. Tr. by Themi Vasils and Theodora Vasils. San Francisco: Creative Arts, 1984. Date of composition: 1926–.

The Last Temptation of Christ. Tr. by Peter Bien. New York: Simon & Schuster, 1960. Also *O teleftaios peirasmos.* Athens: Diphros, 1955. Date of composition: 1950–51.

The Odyssey: A Modern Sequel. Tr. by Kimon Friar. New York: Simon & Schuster, 1958. Date of composition: 1925–38.

Report to Greco. Tr. by Peter Bien. New York: Simon & Schuster, 1965. Also *Anafora ston Greko.* Athens: 1965. Date of composition: 1955–56.

The Rock Garden. Tr. from the French by Richard Howard. New York: Simon & Schuster, 1963. Date of composition: 1936.

Russia. Tr. by Michael Antonakes and Thanasis Maskaleris. Berkeley, Calif.: Creative Arts, 1989. Date of composition: 1925, 1927.

Saint Francis. Tr. by Peter Bien. New York: Simon & Schuster, 1962. Also *O Ftohoulis tou Theou.* Athens: Diphros, 1956. Date of composition: 1953.

The Saviors of God: Spiritual Exercises. New York: Simon & Schuster, 1960. Also *Asketike: Salvatores Dei.* Athens: Sympan, 1951. Date of composition: 1923.

Serpent and Lily. Tr. by Theodora Vasils. Berkeley: University of California Press, 1980. Date of composition: 1906.

Spain. Tr. by Amy Mims. New York: Simon & Schuster, 1963. Date of composition: 1926–36.

The Suffering God: Selected Letters to Galatea and Papastephanou. Tr. by Philip Ramp and Katerina Anghelaki Rooke. New Rochelle, N.Y.: Caratzas, 1979. Date of composition: 1921–23.

Symposium. Tr. by Theodora Vasils and Themi Vasils. New York: Minerva Press, 1974. Date of composition: 1924.

Three Plays. Tr. by Athena Gianakas Dallas. New York: Simon & Schuster, 1965. Date of composition: 1937, 1949, 1949.

Toda Raba. Tr. by Amy Mims. New York: Simon & Schuster, 1964. Date of composition: 1929.

Two Plays. Tr. by Kimon Friar. Minneapolis, Minn.: Nostos Books, 1982. Date of composition: 1909, 1948.

Zorba the Greek. Tr. by Carl Wildman. New York: Simon & Schuster, 1952. Also *Vios kai politeia tou Aleksi Zorba*. Athens: Trikorphon, 1970. Date of composition: 1941–43.

Secondary Sources

Aghiorgoussis, Maximos. "Christian Existentialism of the Greek Fathers." *The Greek Orthodox Theological Review* 23 (1978): 15–41.

Behr, John. "Irenaeus AH3.23.5 and the Ascetic Ideal." *St. Vladimir's Theological Quarterly* 37 (1993): 305–13.

Berdyaev, Nicholas. "The New Middle Ages." In *The End of Our Time*. Tr. by Donald Atwater. New York: Sheed and Ward, 1933.

Bergson, Henri. *Laughter*. Tr. by Cloudesley Brereton and Fred Rothwell. New York: Macmillan, 1917. Originally published as *Le Rire* (Paris: 1900).

———. *An Introduction to Metaphysics*. Tr. by T. E. Hulme. Indianapolis, Ind.: Bobbs-Merrill, 1955. Originally published as "Introduction à la métaphysique." *Revue de Métaphysique et de Morale* (1903).

———. *The Two Sources of Morality and Religion*. Tr. by R. A. Audra and Cloudesley Brereton. Notre Dame, Ind.: University of Notre Dame Press, 1977. Originally published as *Les deux sources de la morale et de la religion* (Paris: 1932).

———. "On the Pragmatism of William James." In *The Creative Mind*. Tr. by Mabelle Andison. New York: Philosophical Library, 1946. Originally published as *La pensée et la mouvant* (Paris: 1934).

Bidal-Baudier, Marie-Louise. *Nikos Kazantzaki* (Paris: Plon, 1974).

Bien, Peter. "*Zorba the Greek*, Nietzsche, and the Perennial Greek Predicament." *The Antioch Review* 25 (1965): 147–63.

———. "Kazantzakis' Nietzschianism." *Journal of Modern Literature* 2 (1971): 245–66.

———. *Nikos Kazantzakis*. New York: Columbia University Press, 1972.

———. *Tempted by Happiness: Kazantzakis' Post-Christian Christ*. Wallingford, Pa.: Pendle-Hill, 1984.

———. *Kazantzakis: Politics of the Spirit*. Princeton, N.J.: Princeton University Press, 1989.

———. "Kazantzakis's Long Apprenticeship to Christian Themes." In *God's Struggler*, ed. by Middleton and Bien. Macon, Ga.: Mercer University Press, 1996.

Blenkinsopp, Joseph. "My Entire Soul Is a Cry." *Commonweal* 93 (February 26, 1971): 514–18.

Bloch, Adèle. "Kazantzakis and the Image of Christ." *Literature and Psychology* 15 (1965): 2–11.

———. "The Dual Masks of Nikos Kazantzakis." *Journal of Modern Literature* 2 (1971): 189–98.

Bulgakov, Sergius. *The Orthodox Church*. New York: Morehouse, 1935.

Calian, Carnegie Samuel. "Kazantzakis: Prophet of Non-Hope." *Theology Today* 28 (1971): 37–49.

Cassidy, D. C. "Is Transubstantiation without Substance?" *Religious Studies* 30 (1994): 193–99.

Chapman, Matthew. "Notes on the Nature of God, the Cosmos, and Novus Homo." *The Greek Orthodox Theological Review* 21 (1976): 251–64.

Chilson, Richard. "The Christ of Nikos Kazantzakis." *Thought* 47 (1972): 69–89.

Chryssavgis, John. "Love and Sexuality in the Image of Divine Love." *The Greek Orthodox Theological Review* 36 (1991): 341–52.

Clark, Stephen R. L. *From Athens to Jerusalem*. Oxford: Clarendon Press, 1984.

———. *The Mysteries of Religion*. Oxford: Basil Blackwell, 1986.

———. "How to Believe in Fairies." *Inquiry* 30 (1987): 337–55.

———. *Civil Peace and Sacred Order*. Oxford: Clarendon Press, 1989.

———. *A Parliament of Souls*. Oxford: Clarendon Press, 1990.

Cobb, John. *God and the World*. Philadelphia: Westminster, 1979.

———. "The Presence of the Past and the Eucharist." *Process Studies* 13 (1983): 218–31.

Copleston, Frederick. *Friedrich Nietzsche: Philosopher of Culture*. London: Burns, Oates, Washbourne, 1942.

Danto, Arthur. "Nietzsche's Perspectivism." In *Nietzsche: A Collection of Critical Essays*, ed. by Robert Solomon. Notre Dame, Ind.: University of Notre Dame Press, 1980.

Dombrowski, Daniel. "Asceticism as Athletic Training in Plotinus." *Aufsteig und Niedergang der Römischen Welt* 36.1. Berlin: DeGruyter, 1987.

———. *Christian Pacifism*. Philadelphia: Temple University Press, 1991.

———. *St. John of the Cross*. Albany: State University of New York Press, 1992.

———. *Analytic Theism, Hartshorne, and the Concept of God*. Albany: State University of New York Press, 1996.

Doulis, Tom. "Kazantzakis and the Meaning of Suffering." *Northwest Review* 6 (1963): 33–57.

Eslick, Leonard. "The Dyadic Character of Being." *Modern Schoolman* 21 (1953–54): 11–18.

———. "Plato as Dipolar Theist." *Process Studies* 12 (1982): 243–51.

Ferguson, Everett. "God's Infinity and Man's Mutability." *The Greek Orthodox Theological Review* 18 (1973): 59–78.

Flay, Joseph. "The Erotic Stoicism of Nikos Kazantzakis." *Journal of Modern Literature* 2 (1971): 293–302.

Friar, Kimon. "Introduction" to Nikos Kazantzakis, *The Odyssey*. New York: Simon & Schuster, 1958.

———. "Introduction" to Nikos Kazantzakis, *The Saviors of God: Spiritual Exercises*. New York: Simon & Schuster, 1960.

———. "Introduction" to Nikos Kazantzakis, *Two Plays*. Minneapolis, Minn.: Nostos Books, 1982.

Friedman, Maurice. *To Deny Our Nothingness*. New York: Delacorte, 1967.

Georgopoulos, N. "Kazantzakis, Bergson, Lenin, and the 'Russian Experiment'." *Journal of the Hellenic Diaspora* 5 (1979): 33–44.

Gill, Jerry. "Conflict and Resolution: Some Kazantzakian Themes." *Encounter* 36 (1974): 204–21.

———. "Kazantzakis and Kierkegaard." In *God's Struggler*, ed. by Middleton and Bien. Macon, Ga.: Mercer University Press, 1996.

Griffin, David Ray. *God, Power, and Evil*. Philadelphia: Westminster, 1976.

———. *God and Religion in the Postmodern World*. Albany: State University of New York Press, 1989.

———, ed. *Varieties of Postmodern Theology*. Albany: State University of New York Press, 1989.

———. *Evil Revisited*. Albany: State University of New York Press, 1991.

———, ed. *Founders of Constructive Postmodern Philosophy*. Albany: State University of New York Press, 1993.

Hartocollis, Peter. "Mysticism and Violence." *International Journal of Psycho-Analysis* 55 (1974): 205–13.

Hartshorne, Charles. *Man's Vision of God*. New York: Harper and Row, 1941.

———. *The Divine Relativity*. New Haven, Conn.: Yale University Press, 1948.

———. *Philosophers Speak of God*. Chicago: University of Chicago Press, 1953.

———. *Creative Synthesis and Philosophic Method*. LaSalle, Ill.: Open Court, 1970.

———. "Mysticism and Rationalistic Metaphysics." *Monist* 59 (1976): 463–69.

————. *Insights and Oversights of Great Thinkers.* Albany: State University of New York Press, 1983.

————. *Omnipotence and Other Theological Mistakes.* Albany: State University of New York Press, 1984.

————. "Some Theological Mistakes and Their Effects on Modern Literature." *Journal of Speculative Philosophy* 1 (1987): 55–72.

Hoffman, Friedrich. "The Friends of God: Dostoevsky and Kazantzakis." In *The Imagination's New Beginning.* Notre Dame, Ind.: University of Notre Dame Press, 1967.

Ignatius of Loyola, *The Spiritual Exercises of St. Ignatius of Loyola.* Tr. by W. H. Longridge. London: Mobray, 1950.

————. *The Spiritual Exercises of St. Ignatius.* Tr. by David Fleming. St. Louis, Mo.: Institute of Jesuit Sources, 1978.

James, William. *The Varieties of Religious Experience.* Cambridge, Mass.: Harvard University Press, 1985. Originally published in 1902.

John of the Cross. *The Collected Works of St. John of the Cross.* Tr. by Kieran Kavanaugh and Otilio Rodriguez. Washington, D.C.: Institute of Carmelite Studies, 1973.

Kamperidis, Lambros. "The Orthodox Sources of *The Saviors of God.*" In *God's Struggler,* ed. by Middleton and Bien. Macon, Ga.: Mercer University Press, 1996.

Karanikas, Alexander. "Kazantzakis and His Heroes." *Athene* 18 (1957): 4–9.

Katz, Steven, ed. *Mysticism and Philosophical Analysis.* Oxford: Oxford University Press, 1978.

————. *Mysticism and Religious Traditions.* New York: Oxford University Press, 1983.

Kaufmann, Walter. "The Death of God and the Revaluation." In *Nietzsche: A Collection of Critical Essays,* ed. by Robert Solomon. Notre Dame, Ind.: University of Notre Dame Press, 1980.

Kazantzakis, Helen. *Nikos Kazantzakis: A Biography Based on His Letters.* Tr. by Amy Mims. New York: Simon & Schuster, 1968.

Kolakowski, Leszek. *Bergson.* Oxford: Oxford University Press, 1985.

Lacey, A. R. *Bergson.* New York: Routledge, 1989.

Lea, James. *Kazantzakis: The Politics of Salvation.* Tuscaloosa: University of Alabama Press, 1979.

Levitt, Morton. *The Cretan Glance.* Columbus: Ohio State University Press, 1980.

Lossky, Vladimir. *The Mystical Theology of the Eastern Church.* London: James Clarke, 1957.

MacIntyre, Alasdair. *After Virtue.* Notre Dame, Ind.: University of Notre Dame Press, 1981.

McDonough, B. T. *Nietzsche and Kazantzakis*. Washington, D.C.: University Press of America, 1978.

Mellert, Robert. *What Is Process Theology?* New York: Paulist Press, 1975.

Merrill, Reed. "Zorba the Greek and Nietzschean Nihilism." *Mosaic* 8 (1975): 99–113.

Meyendorff, John. *Byzantine Theology*. New York: Fordham University Press, 1983.

Middleton, Darren. "Dove of Peace or Bird of Prey: Nikos Kazantzakis on the Activity of the Holy Spirit." *Theology Themes* (1993): 15–18.

———. "Nikos Kazantzakis and Process Theology." *Journal of Modern Greek Studies* 12 (1994): 57–74.

———. "Vagabond or Companion? Kazantzakis and Whitehead on God." In *God's Struggler*, ed. by Middleton and Bien. Macon, Ga.: Mercer University Press, 1996.

———. "Process Poesis." Ph.D. dissertation. University of Glasgow, 1996.

———. "Apophatic Boldness." Forthcoming in *The Midwest Quarterly*.

Middleton, Darren and Peter Bien, eds. *God's Struggler*. Macon, Ga.: Mercer University Press, 1996.

More, P. E. *The Religion of Plato*. Princeton, N.J.: Princeton University Press, 1921.

Morgan, George. *What Nietzsche Means*. Cambridge, Mass.: Harvard University Press, 1941.

Mousalimas, S. A. "The Divine in Nature: Animism or Panentheism." *The Greek Orthodox Theological Review* 35 (1990): 367–75.

Nagel, Thomas. *Mortal Questions*. Cambridge: Cambridge University Press, 1991.

Nasr, Seyyed Hossein. "The Prayer of the Heart in Hesychasm and Sufism." *The Greek Orthodox Theological Review* 31 (1986): 195–203.

Nehamas, Alexander. *Nietzsche: Life As Literature*. Cambridge, Mass.: Harvard University Press, 1985.

Nietzsche, Friedrich. *The Will to Power*. Tr. by Walter Kaufmann. New York: Random House, 1968. Also *Der Wille zur Macht* in *Werke in drei Bänden*, ed. by Karl Schlecta. Munich: Carl Hanser, 1954–65.

———. *The Antichrist*. Tr. by Walter Kaufmann. New York: Viking, 1968.

———. *Ecce Homo*. Tr. by Walter Kaufmann. New York: Random House, 1969.

———. *The Gay Science*. Tr. by Walter Kaufmann. New York: Random House, 1974.

———. *Human, All Too Human*. Tr. by Marion Faber. Lincoln: University of Nebraska Press, 1984.

Osborn, Ronald. "A Modern Man's Search for Salvation." *Encounter* 35 (1974).

Otto, W. F. *The Homeric Gods*. Salem, N.H.: Ayer, 1978.

Papademetriou, George. "The Human Body According to Saint Gregory of Palamas." *The Greek Orthodox Theological Review* 34 (1989): 1–9.

Peters, William. *The Spiritual Exercises of St. Ignatius.* Jersey City, N.J.: Program to Adapt the Spiritual Exercises, 1968.

Petrolle, Jean. "Nikos Kazantzakis and *The Last Temptation.*" *Journal of Modern Greek Studies* 11 (1993).

Pieper, Josef. *The Silence of Saint Thomas.* Chicago: Regnery, 1965.

Pike, Nelson. *Mystic Union: An Essay in the Phenomenology of Mysticism.* Ithaca, N.Y.: Cornell University Press, 1992.

Pollby, George. "Kazantzakis's Struggle." *Commonweal* (April 23, 1971): 155, 175.

Popper, Karl. *Objective Knowledge.* Oxford: Clarendon Press, 1979.

Poulakidas, Andreas. "Dostoevsky, Kazantzakis's Unacknowledged Mentor." *Comparative Literature* 21 (1969): 307–18.

———. "Kazantzakis's Zorba the Greek and Nietzsche's Thus Spake Zarathustra." *Philological Quarterly* 49 (1973): 234–44.

———. "Kazantzakis and Bergson: Metaphysic Aestheticians." *Journal of Modern Literature* 2 (1971): 267–83.

———. "Kazantzakis's Spiritual Exercises and Buddhism." *Comparative Literature* 27 (1975): 208–17.

Presley, Del. "Buddha and the Butterfly: Unifying Motifs in Kazantzakis's *Zorba.*" *Notes on Contemporary Literature* 2 (1972): 2–4.

Prevelakis, Pandelis. *Nikos Kazantzakis and his Odyssey.* Tr. by Philip Sherrard. New York: Simon & Schuster, 1961.

Racheotes, Nicholas. "Theogony and Theocide: Nikos Kazantzakis and the Mortal Struggle for Salvation." *East European Quarterly* 17 (1991).

Ramon, Brother. *Franciscan Spirituality.* London: SPCK, 1994.

Raschke, Carl. *Theological Thinking.* Atlanta, Ga.: Scholars Press, 1988.

Richards, Lewis. "Christianity in the Novels of Kazantzakis." *Western Humanities Review* 21 (1967): 49–55.

———. "Nikos Kazantzakis and Chaucer." *Comparative Literature Studies* 6 (1969): 141–47.

Rooke, Katerina Anghelaki. "Introduction" to Nikos Kazantzakis, *The Suffering God: Letters to Galatea and to Papastephanou.* New Rochelle, N.Y.: Caratzas, 1979.

Savvas, Minas. "Kazantzakis and Marxism." *Journal of Modern Literature* 2 (1971): 284–92.

Schmitz, Kenneth. "Concrete Presence." *Communio* (1987): 300–15.

Smart, Ninian. "Interpretation and Mystical Experience." *Religious Studies 1* (1965): 75–87.

Smith, John. "Introduction" to William James, *The Varieties of Religious Experience*. Cambridge, Mass.: Harvard University Press, 1985.

Sontag, Frederick. "Anthropodicy and the Return of God." In *Encountering Evil*, ed. by Stephen Davis. Atlanta, Ga.: John Knox Press, 1981.

Stace, Walter. *Mysticism and Philosophy*. Philadelphia: Lippincott, 1960.

———. *The Teachings of the Mystics*. New York: New American Library, 1960.

Stanford, W. B. *The Ulysses Theme*. Oxford: Basil Blackwell, 1963.

Taylor, Mark. *Erring: A Postmodern A/theology*. Chicago: University of Chicago Press, 1984.

Telepneff, Gregory and Bishop Chrysostomos. "The Person, *Pathe*, Asceticism, and Spiritual Restoration in Saint Maximos." *The Greek Orthodox Theological Review* 34 (1989): 249–61.

Teresa of Avila. *The Collected Works of St. Teresa of Avila*. Tr. by Kieran Kavanaugh and Otilio Rodriguez. Washington, D.C.: Institute of Carmelite Studies, 1980.

Vasils, Theodora. "Introduction" to Nikos Kazantzakis, *Serpent and Lily*. Berkeley: University of California Press, 1980.

Ware, Timothy. *The Orthodox Church*. Baltimore, Md.: Penguin, 1963.

Weber, Stephen. "Existentialism versus Marxism: A Kazantzakian Synthesis." *Journal of Social Philosophy* 9 (1978): 1–8.

Whitehead, Alfred North. *Science and the Modern World*. New York: Macmillan, 1957. Originally published in 1925.

———. *Religion in the Making*. New York: Macmillan, 1926.

———. *Process and Reality*, ed. by David Griffin and Donald Sherburne. New York: Free Press, 1978. Originally published in 1929.

———. *Adventures of Ideas*. New York: Free Press, 1967. Originally published in 1933.

Will, Frederick. "Kazantzakis' Making of God." *Iowa Review* 3 (1972): 109–24.

INDEX OF NAMES

189

NOTE ON

SUPPORTING CENTER

This series is published under the auspices of the Center for Process Studies, a research organization affiliated with the Claremont School of Theology and Claremont University Center and Graduate School. It was founded in 1973 by John B. Cobb, Jr., Founding Director, and David Ray Griffin, Executive Director; Mary Elizabeth Moore and Marjorie Suchocki are now also Co-Directors. It encourages research and reflection on the process of philosophy of Alfred North Whitehead, Charles Hartshorne, and related thinkers, and on the application and testing of this viewpoint in all areas of thought and practice. The center sponsors conferences, welcomes visiting scholars to use its library, and publishes a scholarly journal, *Process Studies*, and a newsletter, *Process Perspectives*. Located at 1325 North College, Claremont, California 91711, it gratefully accepts (tax-deductible) contributions to support its work.